D1526631

The
Jimmy Streater Story

By Chris Cawood

Book Number: _____/2000

Author Autograph

Jimmy Streater
Phil. 4:13

Other Books By Chris Cawood

The Spring of '68
(1998)

Carp
(1997)

1998: The Year of the Beast
(1996)

How to Live to 100 (and enjoy it!)
(1996)

Tennessee's Coal Creek War
(1995)

Legacy of the Swamp Rat
(Tennessee Quarterbacks who just said NO to Alabama!)
(1994)

This book or any of the above books may be ordered by sending $12 check or money order to: Magnolia Hill Press, P.O. Box 124, Kingston, Tn. 37763. Amount includes book rate postage and autograph by the author. A 50% discount is available on orders of 10 or more by calling: 1-800-946-1967.

The Jimmy Streater Story

By Chris Cawood

Magnolia Hill Press
Kingston, Tennessee

DyerGram by Bill Dyer reprinted by permission of the Knoxville *News-Sentinel*, Knoxville, Tennessee.

Cover photo by Chris Cawood. Cover design by Chris Cawood and Hartgraphics of Knoxville, Tennessee.

Printed in the United States.

Library of Congress Number: 99-70518

ISBN: 0-9642231-3-9

First Edition-First Printing-1999

Dedication

*This book is dedicated to the **1998 TENNESSEE VOLUNTEERS—NATIONAL CHAMPIONS**—who played twenty years after Jimmy Streater.*

Introduction

This is the book that I didn't want to write. I thought I never would. I didn't really see how I could.

I am a 1970 graduate of the University of Tennessee College of Law. When I was in undergraduate school and law school from 1965 through 1970, I was also a great fan of the football teams—and still am.

In those years of 1965 through 1970, I watched such quarterbacks as Dewey (the Swamp Rat) Warren, Charlie Fulton, Bubba Wyche, and Bobby Scott. I saw the artificial turf come to Shields-Watkins field, the walking horses prance down the sidelines, and the cannon fire near the corner of the north end zone.

Football players were bigger than life. I had been a high school athlete in basketball but always enjoyed football more as a spectator rather than as a participant (I have survived into my 50s with good knees). I was excited to be in a class at UT with Steve Kiner and Jack (Hacksaw) Reynolds.

i

In 1965 I listened to the Tennessee—UCLA game being played in Memphis as the Swamp Rat and teammates brought the Vols back to national prominence. Players such as Richmond Flowers, Walter Chadwick, Charlie Fulton, Austin Denney, Johnny Mills, Ron Widby, and Bob Johnson made me feel confident with Alabama coming to town in 1966 even though they had Kenny Stabler at quarterback, Ray Perkins at end, and Dennis Homan in the backfield. My heart sank when Gary Wright's field goal attempt sailed slightly wide right and Bama escaped with an eleven to ten victory. I felt Edgar Allan Poe's words applied to Alabama—"Take the beak from out my heart, and take thy form from off my door!"

In 1968 I watched the 17 to 17 tie with Georgia and then witnessed Bubba Wyche and the other Volunteers beat Alabama ten to nine to make it two in a row over the Tide.

Success over Alabama continued in 1970 even though Coach Doug Dickey had left for Florida after the 1969 season. I rejoiced with other Vol fans when Tennessee shut out the Tide 24 to 0 behind the passing of Bobby Scott, the receiving of Joe Thompson, the running of Curt Watson, and the intercepting by Buddy Bennett's Bandits—Tim Priest, Bobby Majors, and Conrad Graham, along with linebackers Jamie Rotella and Jackie Walker. It was the last time that the Vols have shut out the Tide. The rivalry with Alabama was then tied at twenty-three wins for each side, and they have not been even in victories since.

With Bill Battle taking over in 1970 and Doug Dickey bringing the Florida Gators back to Neyland Stadium, the Florida game became almost as big as Alabama. Tennessee won 38 to 7.

Quarterbacks have always been special at Tennessee. Ever since the T formation was reinstated in 1964, the quarterback has been the total yardage leader—except for 1971 when Curt Watson won that honor.

Condredge Holloway was Tennessee's first black quarterback to start. He played spectacularly in 1972, 1973, and 1974.

From 1965 to the present, the names rang true—

Warren, Wyche, Scott, Holloway, Wallace, Streater, Cockrell, Robinson, Dickey, Francis, Kelly, Shuler, Manning, and Martin.

It was with the remembrance of those long ago quarterbacks and reverence for the Tennessee—Alabama series that I set out in 1994 to write the book about the quarterbacks who had played on Tennessee teams that had beaten or tied Alabama. *Legacy of the Swamp Rat (Tennessee quarterbacks who just said No to Alabama)* was the title.

I went back and visited with those quarterbacks and relived those eight victories and two ties that occurred between 1965 and 1993. There were only eight quarterbacks on that short list—Dewey Warren, Charlie Fulton, Bubba Wyche, Bobby Scott, Alan Cockrell, Tony Robinson, Daryl Dickey, and Heath Shuler.

Some great quarterbacks like Holloway, Jimmy Streater, Randy Wallace, Jeff Francis, and Andy Kelly never were able to celebrate a victory over the Tide as players.

It was in 1994 at a spring practice session at the University of Kentucky where I was watching Daryl Dickey as an assistant coach that I met a North Carolina high school coach by the name of Boyce Deitz. Coach Deitz and some of his staff were there observing. He had been extraordinarily blessed during his long coaching tenure to have been associated with two All-American high school quarterbacks. Coach Deitz was an assistant at Sylva-Webster High School when Jimmy Streater played and was head coach at Swain County High School when Heath Shuler starred.

Coach Deitz invited me to visit him at school in Bryson City and talk about Heath Shuler. I did, a little bit later the same year. When we had finished talking about the Shuler exploits, Coach Deitz asked me, "Did you know Jimmy Streater is in the hospital over in Sylva? He's had a heart attack or stroke."

My mind wandered back. Jimmy Streater wasn't going to play a role in my book, but I remembered him as most Vol fans would—the willowy quarterback who ran and passed for Tennessee from 1977 through 1979. I knew a little about his recent history, about his brother, Steve, and the wreck, about some of Jimmy's medical problems. I didn't know the whole story though, and I wouldn't for a few years. But I knew enough that I thought I should stop by the hospital in Sylva and say "Hello."

Sylva was just thirty miles away, but Jimmy wasn't there when I arrived. After a few calls to relatives, I learned he was in a nursing home in Canton—another thirty miles down the road.

At Canton I wasn't prepared for what I found. It wasn't the youthful quarterback that I remembered but an almost old looking man in a wheel chair—a leg paralyzed by the stroke. "Are you Jimmy Streater?" I asked.

"Yes, who are you?" he asked.

"Just a Volunteer fan," I said.

Then his face brightened, his eyes sparkled, and he reached out a hand in greeting.

Many visits later Jimmy asked me to write his story. I put him off for three years. Did he have a book-length story in him? And what about the ending? What kind of ending could I give to a book about a former football star who has been living in a nursing home since he was thirty-six?

Well, this is the book I didn't want to write, but it is the story I became so engrossed in that I couldn't turn it loose. Jimmy's story runs deeper than football. It is a story of successes and failures, of ups and downs, of exhilaration and depression, of good choices and bad, and of freedom and slavery. It is an American story—about an All-American man.

The roots of Jimmy Streater's heritage run deep in the valleys that abut the Smoky Mountains in Western North Carolina. The story starts a long time ago.

Chris Cawood
Kingston, Tennessee
August, 1999

Part one:

Family History
and
Youth

1854 – 1976

1854

The cold air funneling down from the mountains to the west caused a fog to rise up from the Tuckaseegee River. The early November morning was cool, but the leaves turning gold and crimson on the hills masked the sadness of the day with their beauty. Two huddled groups stood fifty feet apart in misty shrouds of gray.

Whispering in one of the bunches were the sons and sons-in-law of David Rogers who had died the middle of September leaving a wife, three sons, and six daughters. It was time to take the inventory of the wealthy farmer's estate and decide on shares, if they could.

David Rogers had a rich heritage. He was born a year after the Constitution of the United States was ratified. His father, Hugh Rogers, fought in the battle of King's Mountain in the Revolutionary War and his mother, Nancy Thornton Rogers, had served water to Colonel John Sevier at the foot of the mountain and there met her future husband. Nancy's mother was a half-niece to George Washington.

The Hugh and David Rogers families had lived in North Carolina and then East Tennessee before David and his family settled in what is now Jackson County, North Carolina. David's farm was at Cullowhee, just a few miles from the county seat at Webster. When the county was formed in 1853 from parts of Haywood and Macon Counties, it was named Jackson in honor of Andrew Jackson, the former president who had died in 1845. And when the county seat was decided upon, it was named Webster for Daniel Webster who died in 1852.

1

It would be the sons and sons-in-law who would decide the value and disposition of David Rogers' estate since his daughters, as women, had no rights in such matters and would not soil themselves with such.

The other group standing fifty feet away was composed of the slaves of David Rogers. They looked at the Rogers heirs and wondered what their fate would be, as they had no rights or say-so in the decision. They were property standing there to be divided by the sons and sons-in-law of their master.

Eliza was 14, Silas, 30, Isham, 25, George, 21, Joe, 60, Allen, 58, Mandy, 50, Harriet, 49, and her two young children, Lewis, 3, and Louisa, 1. They were only given first names. The townspeople knew they belonged to David Rogers.

Harriet reached out and pulled her older son, George, to her. Tears puddled at the corners of her eyes when she glanced at the new owners. She clutched Louisa to her breast and whispered to George.

"We've got to stay together. We gotta look after each other. I've lived in Virginny before I was sold to Master Rogers. I don't want to go away from here."

George nodded. "They're good folks. Surely, they'll keep us together. Master David did."

"I hear some of them live in Georgia and South Carolina. I don't want to go there and not see my children," Harriet said.

"Don't worry, Ma. Young Master David said he wanted us. He'll see to it."

"Young Master David" was the youngest child of the now-deceased David Rogers. He was only three years older than slave George. They had worked side by side. Of all the children, he was the most jovial and had rescued a slave or two from serious retribution in the past. George knew young David had a good heart.

Hugh was the oldest son of the dead master. After he looked over the slaves, he announced to his brothers and brothers-in-law, "After our mother gets her dower, we'll divide the land and other property," he paused and nodded toward the group of slaves, "into nine shares. Mother wants Eliza for her house servant. So, that leaves nine for us to divide. There're nine of us." He paused again and looked down at Harriet's two young children and then over to the older men slaves. "Of course, they're not of equal value. So, everybody think about what they're worth and we'll bid on them and the division of the land. That's the only fair way to do it. You agree?"

The other heirs looked around and nodded their approval.

Just then a calf bolted around the barn, between the two groups, and ran toward the river.

"George, catch that calf!" David yelled.

George left his mother and sprinted after the calf while the owners watched. Within fifty yards, George had overcome the calf and wrestled it to the ground. He picked it up in his arms and began to carry it back toward the barn. His arm, chest, and back muscles bulged under the load.

David Rogers elbowed his brother, Hugh, "I'm bidding on George. He's the fastest, strongest, and smartest of the bunch."

"You're going to have to dig deep into that tight purse of yours, Little Brother, to get George."

"Okay, you each take turns stepping up on that stump. Turn around once and hold your arms above your head," Hugh said. "Some of us don't know you as well as the others. We've got to see what you look like."

The slaves did as they were told, each in turn stepping onto the stump and making a full turn. When they stood down some of the sons-in-law came over and had them to open their mouths so they could see their teeth and gums.

WHEN THE DAVID ROGERS heirs filed the inventory in the clerk's office at Webster on November 25, 1854, they listed the following values for the property of David

Rogers: David Rogers' widow, Polly, received as dower the tract of land with the house and barn, "one Negro Girl, Eliza, one Gray Filly, 4 milch cows, 10 head of sheep, all the hogs & poultry & 200 buchels of corn to be her own property and for her exclusive use during the term of her natural life."

Next, the inventory listed a second tract of land at $1400 value and another at $1200. Then the slaves were valued at: "Silas, $1000; Isham, $1037.50; George, $1050; Harriet and two young children, $825; Joe, $625; Allen, $575; and Mandy & Caney Fork land, $550."

Indeed, George was the most highly valued slave. The display of his physical prowess on the day of inventory had driven his value up to where he would be more costly than his mother, brother, and sister together.

When the David Rogers' estate was settled, the younger David Rogers was allotted the portion of land that was nearest his mother's house. He did dig deep into his purse and bought George, along with George's mother, Harriet, and her two young children, from the other heirs. The other two Rogers sons bought out some of the other heirs and were able to keep all the slaves of their father, David Rogers, on adjoining farms. It was the best the slave families could have hoped for. They were within walking distance of their near kin.

George, who was already a man familiar with cattle and horses, was encouraged by his new master to learn the trade of a tanner. He began to cure the hides and leather that he would then make into bridles, harnesses, and other leather goods needed around the sprawling farm.

David Rogers watched over the valley farm where he raised cattle, sheep, fruit, and vegetables along with fields of wheat. Slave ownership had been his father's idea—a substitute for failing to have enough sons to work the fields. He had six daughters and three sons. And now, the younger David had no children, or even a wife. He cared for his elderly mother and stood shoulder to shoulder with George working the fields.

He would buy no more slaves. The political situation in the nation made it a risky investment aside from his own doubts about it. The mountains shielded this area from much of what was happening in the country, but the rumors of secession and possibly war were reaching even into Jackson County.

For the next six years, George, his mother, Harriet, his brother, Lewis, and sister, Louisa, worked and lived peaceably with David Rogers and his mother, Polly.

George mastered the craft of a tanner and took in business from surrounding farms. David Rogers allowed George the extreme privilege of giving him a tenth of what he earned from his outside work for him to save or use to buy goods for his family.

"Just don't tell slaves on the other farms or let word slip to the owners that I'm giving you money," David cautioned George. "It would cause me trouble." Then he looked down at some of George's fine work. "But it shouldn't matter to anybody how I treat my slaves. You have a talent, George, a real talent."

ON THE ELEVENTH OF July, 1861, George saddled the best horse for his master David Rogers, led him to beneath the maple tree in front of his master's house, and waited for David Rogers to come out the door. The slaves had learned there was a war going on. The Southern states had split off from the North. Rumors were whispered around. A fort in South Carolina was fired upon after it had been taken over by the South. Now there was full-fledged fighting. North Carolina was one of the Confederate States of America.

David Rogers, now 31, was one of many in the area who had gone, or were preparing to go off, to fight the Yankees. Jackson County touched South Carolina on its southern side and its western flank rested against the mountain boundary with Tennessee. The county didn't have all that many slaves—250—compared to its white population of nearly six thousand. Indeed, it had a higher population of Cherokees—about a thousand—than slaves. But the majority of the county's population stood with the decision of the state to secede.

For George, his mother Harriet, and his young brother and sister, it would only mean more work. Master David would be gone. He was a hard worker.

Just then the door to the house opened and David Rogers walked down the steps with his aged mother, Polly, holding on to his elbow.

He looked at the bright and cloudless sky. "It's a good day to fight a war," he said and smiled at George. David had on a butternut jacket and matching trousers that had been recently tailored for the new soldier. He placed a large gray leather hat on his head as he descended the steps. A new pistol was holstered at his side. His shiny, black leather boots had attracted a faint coat of dust. He reached down and wiped them with a white handkerchief.

"I'm joining up with a regiment over in Asheville, George. We're going to whup those Yanks in a few weeks. I believe I'll be back before harvest."

His mother tugged at David's sleeve. "Don't go, Son. You're my youngest. I need you here."

David waved his arm toward George and then behind his mother to where Harriet stood. "I'm leaving you in good hands, Mother. George and Harriet can run this place as well as I can. They'll take care of you. Isn't that right, George?"

"Yes, Master David. You don't have to worry about your mother or the farm. We'll work it. My mother will see to all your mother's needs along with Eliza. You go on and fight those Yanks and get back here when you can."

"I had a dream that I would never see you alive again, Son," Polly said and began to cry.

"Mother, I'll be fine. We have good and brave men in the South and North Carolina who will put a quick conclusion to this matter. I'll be back before you know it. I have to go. I'm the only Rogers man who is young enough to go. We have to do our duty."

"Your duty is to take care of your old mother," Polly said. She turned and walked back up onto the porch with Harriet.

Beads of sweat formed on David Rogers' brow. He loosened his jacket.

"It's hot, Sir," George said and handed the bridle to his master. "This is a fine horse, Sir. There's no better in the county. Fit for a general. And I'm sure they'll make you a general when they see your fine horse, your new uniform, and learn about your bravery and strength."

"It's July, George. It's supposed to be hot. Last week was the eighty-fifth anniversary of the Declaration of Independence. Now we are fighting once again to be free men, not bound by the cords of tyranny from Washington."

"Yes, Sir. I wish I could go with you. I could care for your horse and make sure you always have provisions."

David looked back toward the porch where his mother stood with a kerchief to her mouth while Harriet had a hand on her arm. "No, your place is here. To take care of the farm and my mother."

David Rogers mounted the fine chestnut stallion, doffed his hat to his mother, reined the horse around, and started in the direction of Asheville. He never looked back. He sat ramrod straight in the saddle looking for all the world like a general. George stood at the gatepost and watched him until he was out of sight.

IT WAS THE FIRST day of April, 1863, when George heard from another slave in Webster where he was loading supplies for the farm that President Abraham Lincoln had signed the Emancipation Proclamation in January of that year.

"We're free," the slave whispered to George. "Emancipated."

George mouthed the word, *"Emancipated."*

"They can't keep us anymore. We're free," the other slave said again.

George glanced around toward the shopkeepers and farmers who were still left in Jackson County. The war had taken its toll. Now there were more young boys and women doing the work of men.

"I don't think the war is over," George said. "We're not free when there's no one here to enforce the *Emancipation Proclamation*. Besides, I'm about as free to do what I want to do as I could be. My master is gone off to war. His mother is on her deathbed. I farm. I tan hides. I make leather goods. I don't know anything else. I told Master David that I would take care of his mother and his farm until he got back from the war, and that's what I'm going to do." He threw some sacks on his wagon and headed back to the farm.

Polly Rogers died in late May. When her sons and daughters gathered for the funeral, David Rogers was still away at war as far as anyone knew. They had not heard from him by letter or report since October, 1861. If he was a casualty, he was buried on some battlefield as an unknown soldier. There was a rumor that he had been captured. His brothers and sisters presumed the worse but did not want to accept the inevitable burden of his death yet, especially with the passing of their mother.

Two of the sons, Hugh and Robert, lived on adjoining farms to David's and decided to let David's farm continue to be run by his slaves—George, Harriet, Lewis, now 12, and the little girl, Louisa, 10. They all could work, and George knew as much about caring for the farm as they did. Harriet could keep the house. It would all be there for David if he returned from battle. And if not, they would have another inventory to take and another division to make. There was no rush. Time would take care of things. And so, they laid Polly Berry Rogers to rest in the family cemetery at Cullowhee.

8

FOR THE NEXT TWO years, George and his mother, Harriet, ran David Rogers' farm as though it was their own. Harriet reminded her son of the Bible story about being good stewards of their master's property. They both took it literally and looked forward to their earthly master's return as well as to the real Master's return.

Life was hard. Fewer neighbors could afford to pay George for tanning services. They bartered. Three chickens, two ducks, a cured ham, cabbage, potatoes. Anything to eat, drink, or wear. They stayed warm through the winters and scraped out a living through the growing season.

News spread quickly in April, 1865, that the war had ended with Lee's surrender in Virginia. And shortly after, the news of Lincoln's death.

"What does it mean?" Harriet asked George. "Some are saying we're free now. Free from what? Where do we go? The other Rogers may throw us off the place now with the war over and no word of Master David."

George sat on a stool near the fireplace where his mother had placed a skillet of cornbread in the coals to cook. He looked out the open door to the mountains in the west. "We could go. I don't know where. Nobody around here could pay us to work. But I say we stay here until they throw us out. Better the devils we know than the ones we don't."

"Now, don't be going and saying that about the Rogers. They aren't devils. Master David has been good to us. And his poor mother was just like a sister to me."

"It's not them. It's the others."

ON THE FIRST DAY of September, 1865, George walked out of the barn after feeding the mules and hitching them to the farm wagon for a trip to Webster. He looked down the barren dirt road and far in the distance saw a man limping in his direction. He had a bag over his shoulder.

"It's Master David!" he shouted toward his mother at the door of the smokehouse. "I'd know that walk anywhere."

9

He jumped into the seat of the wagon and snapped the reins over the mules' backs.

When the distant man saw the wagon coming, he dropped down in the middle of the road and kissed the ground.

"Master David, Master David. We done worried ourselves sick about you," George said. He scooped up the emaciated master in his arms and carried him toward the wagon. He could feel ribs and hip bones through the tatters of clothing that David Rogers wore. He propped his master up on the inside of the wagon and looked at him. David Rogers was only three years older than George but now he looked almost as old as his father who had died eleven years before. What hair he had left was almost white. His eyes sat sunken in a face where the skin was taut over the cheek bones. His nose and forehead were red and rough from the sun and weather.

"George? Is that you, George?" he asked. His green eyes peered out like marbles in a cave.

"Yes, it's me, Master."

"How do I look?"

"You look great, Sir. But where's your hat, and your uniform, your horse, and your . . . your boots?" George looked down at his master's feet that were wrapped in rags.

Then a slight smile crossed David Rogers' lips and they parted. The teeth he had left were almost brown, but more than half were gone.

"My hat. My hat. George, my hat was the best meal I've had in two years. Good leather. It chewed well. My great horse was shot out from under me three months after I left here. I was a prisoner for the duration of the war. Some Yankee is wearing my boots.

"I'm surprised to see you still here, George. You're a free man."

"Yes, Sir. But I told you I'd take care of your place and I did." George started the mules and wagon back toward the house.

10

"George, take me to your cabin and wash me up before my mother sees me. I don't want her to see me the way I look. Do you have some clothes I could borrow?"

George looked at the gaunt man in the back of the wagon. "My clothes would fit you like they would a scarecrow, Sir. But we'll find you something."

"Don't let my mother see me until you do." Then David Rogers heaved out a small coughing laugh. "I rode out on the finest horse in the county. And I'm returning in a mule cart. Oh, how glorious is war."

David Rogers sat propped on a chair in George and Harriet's slave cabin and stared out at his own house when Harriet told him the news about his mother. She wiped his face with a cool, wet cloth and unwrapped the rags from his feet.

"Two years and four months ago?" David Rogers asked. "She died then?"

"Yes," Harriet said. "I sat with her all during her final illness. She knew it was coming. She had a great faith in the Lord."

"She had that dream before I went off. She said she would not see me alive again. I thought she was worried that I would die in the war."

"A dream's a dream, Sir," Harriet said.

"When I was in the prison camps, I dreamed I saw my mother on her knees praying for me."

"She sure did love you, Master David. She did pray for you. She prayed for you more than she prayed for herself."

A WEEK LATER DAVID Rogers stood at the gatepost with George. He stretched out his hand toward the mountains.

"You're free to go, George. You and your mother and your brother and your sister. You're free. To the west is Tennessee. Or you could go to Georgia or South Carolina. Virginia is to the north. And there are more states farther up north where there might be work. They've had free black men there for some time."

"I've heard the north is cold. I've heard about Tennessee. They say it's a lot like here. Georgia and South Carolina. I just don't think so, Sir. My mother, brother, and sister have talked about it. We'd just as soon stay on here. If you'd have us? We can work your fields and orchards."

David Rogers shook his head. "Times are rough. I'm broke, George. I couldn't pay you. But if you want to stay, we'll all try to work hard enough to have food to eat and a roof over our heads. There's not much for anybody here—black or white."

"Sir, we're willing to risk it."

"Well, you do have your tanning trade. I'll let you keep half of what you make from that in your spare time. You can use my tools and you can have a share of the crops and cattle we raise. How's that?"

"Good, Sir. That's good."

"We've got a deal then, George."

"Yes, Sir. But there's one more thing."

"What's that?"

"Now that we're free—my mother, brother, sister, and me—we need something."

"I told you, George. I'm broke. I have nothing. The war's ruined me. I have this land. That's all."

"Yes, Sir. I know that. What we need is not anything like that. Now that we're free, we need a name . . . a last name. Could we use your name—Rogers?"

David Rogers' mouth dropped open. "I had never thought about it. Yes, you do need a name. Rogers is fine, George. We'll have white Rogers and black Rogers. Now, never do nothing to disgrace the name. Understand?"

"Yes, Sir. We're proud to wear it."

12

1872

George Rogers had more than a last name by 1872. He had made a name for himself as an industrious and talented black man. Born into slavery in 1833, he remained true to his master until he was emancipated. He stayed on the David Rogers farm near Cullowhee after the war.

His reputation as a tanner brought him more and more business. He put back part of the money he earned for the future and used the remainder to support his mother, brother, and sister. Their needs were his needs.

As a free man, he had the right to take a wife and to own property. At least, that was what the law said. In 1867 at the age of 34, he married Eliza, the former slave who had been allotted to David Rogers' mother in the early division of the family property.

They had their first child in late 1868 and named him James Alonzo. Georgia was born in 1870. When the 1870 census was taken of Jackson County, it showed seven were living in the former slave cabin on David Rogers' farm. George was 37, his mother, Harriet, was 64, Lewis was 18, Louisa, 16, and both James Alonzo and Georgia were listed as infants. In 1872 another son, Wilson, was born.

George knew that something had to be done about their living arrangements. There were too many people in the small area. He needed a bigger place and land of his own.

Two miles down the pike toward Cashiers from the David Rogers' farm was the farm of his brother, Hugh. And

13

next to that was a farm owned by W. P. Wood. George did tanning work for Wood and had listened to him talking about moving to Texas. He would as soon as he could sell his farm.

One evening in early April, 1872, George Rogers found his former master, David Rogers, at the barn caring for the horses.

"Master David, I have something to ask you," George said.

David turned from where he was currying one of the horses. "What is it?"

"Sir, you know that my family is growing."

"Yes. You have some lovely children."

"Yes, Sir. I wanted to ask you. Would you mind me moving down the road a bit?"

"To where, George?"

"Mr. Wood has his place for sale next to your brother's farm. I could still do some work for you. But I think it's time for me to make provision for my family. I want to own some land."

David Rogers sat down on a stool and laid the brush aside. He looked up at George. "I guess I always knew this time was coming. That you'd have to leave. But we've grown up on this place together."

"Yes, and I could still do some work for you. Do you think Mr. Wood would sell his farm to me? A black man?"

"W. P. is only interested in one color, George. Gold. If you have the money, he'll sell you the land. I hear he wants five hundred dollars for that hundred acres. Part of it's rough mountain. Not too good a farm."

"Yes, Sir, but part of it is along the river. I could make a farm out of it."

"Where would you get the money? I don't have it to lend."

George pulled a draw-string leather pouch from his jacket pocket, opened it, and spread gold coins into the palm of his large left hand.

"I've saved, Sir. During the war and after. I never took Confederate money. Just gold. I don't read or write, but I can count. I have six hundred dollars in gold here."

David Rogers stood up and looked at the coins. "George, you've done well." He looked his former slave in the eye. "Yes, it's time for you to go . . . to own your own place. Offer W. P. four hundred for his place and see if he'll take it. Don't show him all your gold."

"And if he makes a deal with me, will you read the papers for me to be sure I'm getting the land?"

On the twenty-fourth of May, 1872, the deal was struck and the deed made. W. P. Wood, and wife, Jane, sold to George Rogers a hundred acre tract of land that bordered the farms of Hugh Rogers and Andrew Wyke for four hundred and fifty dollars. The farm was bounded by the Tuckaseegee River on the north and included a quarter mile of river bottom. On the south, it went to the top of a ridge from where George could see Cullowhee and the David Rogers' farm to the west.

David Rogers saw to it that the deed was properly written and recorded. So, within seven years of the end of the Civil War, George Rogers, the former slave, owned a tract of land that was worth about half of what he had been in the inventory of 1854.

As soon as he had built a house large enough to accommodate his mother, brother, sister, wife and children, George Rogers herded up the cattle and sheep that were his and drove them to his own farm in April 1873. He and Peter Gibbs, another former slave who bought a nearby farm, were the first black men to own land in Jackson County after the war. With the one hundred fifty dollars in gold that was left, George was able to buy enough lumber for his house and barn and add to his livestock.

George and Eliza had more children. Ida came along in 1873, Melvina in 1874, and Alfred in 1877. Tragedy struck when James Alonzo died from disease when he was only three. Then, Eliza, weakened by six births in seven years and still despondent over her first child's death, took ill in 1879 and died in the winter of the same year.

When the 1880 census was taken for Jackson County, George, 48, was listed as a farmer. His mother was 75. His sister, Louisa, had married and left the home. But his brother, Lewis, had married and brought his wife, Martha, to live at the house. George's children were listed as: Georgia, 10, Wilson, 8, Ida, 7, Melvina, 6, and Alfred, 3. Harriet and daughter-in-law, Martha, cared for the younger children while George and Lewis ran the farm.

On the nearby farm of Peter Gibbs, a daughter, Josephine, was then twelve.

"Sorry about your wife," Peter Gibbs told George one day when they met at church. "With those young children, you're going to have to find you another wife pretty soon."

"No. I can't even think about that now. My mother can help me. They're all weaned. We'll make it," George said.

"Well, I wish I had a daughter of marrying age to recommend to you, George. You're a good neighbor."

IN THE 1880s, TWO things came together to help the economy of Western North Carolina and Jackson County. People from other parts of the state and country travelled to that part of the state for the supposed restorative powers of mineral and hot springs. And the Western North Carolina Railway was completed with a line from Asheville to the new town of Dillsboro that was founded in 1882.

At about the same time, George Rogers seized an opportunity to add to the size of his farm. The state of North Carolina was selling some of the lands the state had gained from the Cherokees years before. George bid on one tract that adjoined his farm and bought the additional thirty acres in 1883 for three hundred dollars and eighty-seven cents. When David Rogers read the deed to George, he was doubly proud. The deed was signed by the governor of North Carolina.

William Allen Dills, the founder of Dillsboro, built the Mount Beulah Hotel—named for his daughter—in 1884. At the same time, he named the mountain facing the hotel Mount Beulah. The hotel was a two-story structure with wide porches that accommodated dozens of rocking chairs for the tourists who rode the train to the mountains and the surrounding springs. The hotel's restaurant became the official dining place for the railroad employees and its passengers.

Other hotels and boarding houses also sprang up in Dillsboro near the railway station.

For George Rogers and other farmers, these were new markets for their fruits, vegetables, and meats. From the time the hotels opened, George and Lewis made weekly wagon runs of whatever was in season to sell to the Mount Beulah Hotel and the others.

IN THE SPRING OF 1888, George noticed a new worker at the Mount Beulah Hotel. He was sure this young lady had not been there before. Someone that beautiful he would remember. However, there was something about this ebony angel that he thought he recognized. He stopped his wagon at the back to unload some cured hams and side meat.

"Just carry those on inside," the young lady said and motioned him toward the kitchen.

"I'm George Rogers," he said and laid one ham on a side table. "I haven't seen you before. Are you new here?"

"Just started to work for the Dills last week," she said and pushed the ham farther back on the table.

George didn't say anything but looked on. She was tall, her eyes flashed, and when she spoke, her words carried authority. But she was young, much younger than he.

"I didn't think I'd seen you before," he said.

The young woman straightened up and looked at him. For a second she smiled. "Oh, yeah, you've seen me before. And I know who you are, George Rogers."

George scratched his head and held his hat in both hands. He stared at her. "What's your name?"

"Josephine."

"Hm. Now that's a pretty name. How do you know me?"

"Because you're old enough to be my father. You visited my father's farm a lot when I was young, but I've been gone for a while helping out a sick aunt in Charlotte. I'm Peter Gibbs' daughter. I'm Josephine Gibbs."

George Rogers, if he was anything, was persistent. When he found something he wanted, he stayed after it like he had the dream of the farm. Later that year, George Rogers, 55, and Josephine Candice Gibbs, 20, were married.

For George and Josephine, 1889 was both a year of birth and death. Their first child, Earnel, was born on May 29. But on June 15, George's aged mother, Harriet, died at 84. She had been born into slavery in Virginia in 1805, sold to the Rogers of North Carolina as a young woman, and freed from slavery with the Emancipation Proclamation and the end of the war. She had taught her children about loyalty to family and to her Lord. George had learned the lesson well—always seeing to it that his mother had a place to live and was taken care of.

Things were also changing in Jackson County. On the edge of Cullowhee, between the David Rogers' farm and the George Rogers' farm, a local college called the Cullowhee Academy was formed. It was a place of higher education for the white population and another market for the food goods of George Rogers.

David Rogers never married and maintained his farm next to the academy as a gentleman farmer. Everybody now called him "Uncle Dave" Rogers. He maintained a friendship with his former slave, George, and always was watching to see how George did.

George and Josephine's family grew with the addition of John in 1892, David (named for Uncle David) in 1894, Pearson in 1896, McKinley in 1897, and Daisy in 1899.

18

The house grew to accommodate the family. In the 1900 census for Jackson County, George Rogers' family included him and Josephine, three of George's children by his first wife, their six new children, a daughter-in-law, and a niece. George was 66, an age that is now associated with retirement. But there was no rest for the farmer who was helping to support this big family. Everybody worked. With a hundred and thirty acres, there were chores for all.

George and Josephine were not through having children. Ada was born in 1901, Verdie in 1902, Hallie in 1906, and finally, a son named for his father, George in 1911.

Just because the family grew, did not mean that anybody moved out. They all clustered around George Rogers' home.

The 1910 census listed the following as living at George Rogers' farm: George, 76, Candice, 42, Earnel, 20, John, 18, David, 16, Pearson, 14, McKinley 13, Daisy, 11, Ada, 8, Verdie, 7, Hallie, 3, Wilson, 39, Eva, (daughter-in-law) 27, Sarah, (granddaughter) 10, William H., (grandson) 8, Ethel L., (granddaughter) 6, Anna M., (granddaughter) 3, and Matt Gibbs, (brother-in-law) 22.

ON AUGUST 24, 1912, George Rogers died. The former slave was the father of sixteen children, all but one living into adulthood. He was a farmer, a tanner, and a landowner. He lived all his life in North Carolina. Josephine, now forty-four, became the head of the household with the oldest son being Earnel.

"Uncle Dave" Rogers rode his horse the two miles to his former slave's house to pay his respects. He greeted Josephine and looked at the body of George laid out in the casket. "I asked him never to disgrace the name. He didn't. In fact he gave it an added dimension. I was always proud of George."

1917

Josephine, although a wealthy young widow by some standards, never considered remarrying. She had a house full to oversee and there were changes taking place in the county and country.

In 1913 the county seat was moved to Sylva from Webster and a great new courthouse was built atop the hill overlooking the town. From Main Street there were 107 steps leading up to the imposing building. Down the road at Dillsboro, the hotel where Josephine worked when she courted George had changed owners and names and was now called the Jarrett Springs Hotel.

On the national scene America was entering the Great War in Europe. Earnel joined the Army and headed off to war. Josephine remembered the stories that George had told her about "Uncle Dave" riding off to the Civil War and how Polly Rogers had cried not knowing what would happen. Josephine felt the same way. The times were uncertain. Her boys who were old enough tried to find work around Cullowhee and Sylva to supplement the income from the farm.

It was at a logging venture that McKinley had hired onto that he was killed in 1917, the same year that Earnel went off to war.

It was no wonder then that one day ten-year-old Hallie found her older sister, Ada, high up in an apple tree.

"You come down from there," Hallie yelled, "or I'm gonna tell Momma."

Ada just sat there on a limb looking off into the distance. She was sixteen—a young woman old enough to get married, according to local custom. But her mind was on the past as much as the future.

From the apple tree on her hill, she could see almost to Sylva where the courthouse sat high on another hill. She also could look across the Tuckaseegee River toward where the university sat that had been called the Cullowhee Academy but now had changed its name. What were the chances of a young, black woman going there? Even if she were smart?

She also pondered the past. Her father died when she was barely eleven. Now, McKinley, just four years older than her, was dead. She never would see her oldest brother, Earnel, again. War meant death. If he didn't die in battle, surely he would die going or coming from the place they called Europe. It was across the ocean. She had never seen an ocean, but she imagined it well—great waves crashing onto the ship. And they would throw Earnel over to appease the sea as the Bible said they had with Jonah.

She looked back toward the house where Hallie was walking down the steps with her mother. Oh, the orchard had always been a place of refuge. When she was eight, her father had shown her how to reach the highest apple on the tree by attaching a tin can to a long pole. He brought it down without a bruise and handed it to her. "You are the apple of my eye," he had told her.

It was always the orchard or walking barefoot across the Tuckaseegee where the water was no more than calf-deep most of the time that refreshed and renewed her. She would sit down and let the cool water run across her dark legs and think about far away places. Then she would look up at the mountains in the west and know that this was where she always wanted to be. This was home. Even if she could go across the ocean and not be eaten by some "great fish" like Jonah had been, she liked it best here near Cullowhee.

"Ada, you come down from there before you fall and get yourself hurt," her mother yelled up to her. "Come down to Earth, girl. What're you doing? Sitting up there day-dreaming? There's plenty of work to do. Get yourself down this minute."

And she did. Her mother was right. There were still fifteen mouths to feed. George Rogers had left all his land to his wife but there was little in the way of money. George and Josephine had even sold a few acres here and there from the edges of the farm when they needed a few dollars. There was a war going on and the things that she wanted were more scarce than ever. But it would all be worth it because this was "the war to end all wars." President Wilson said it, and Ada believed it.

Ada had even heard that there was a thing called a "horseless carriage" that moved its wheels on its own accord without being pulled by a horse. Now, she would like to see one of those if it ever made it as far as Cullowhee.

IN A LITTLE OVER A year Earnel was back home, the war was over, and the first automobile had putted its way into Sylva. Ada, along with most of her brothers and sisters, had walked to town to see the great event. Dogs barked and horses reared when they heard the putt, putt, putt of the motor that propelled the automobile.

On April 24, 1924, "Uncle Dave" Rogers died. The white Rogers who grew up with Ada's father and gave him his name left no wife or children—only memories with ones like George Rogers' wife and children who remembered the stories about the Civil War. One of David Rogers' last acts was to give his farm to be part of Western Carolina University. He was buried on a nearby hill in the family cemetery.

WITH THE ADDITIONAL LAND, Western Carolina University began to expand. New buildings went up brick by brick. Sylva and Dillsboro were also growing. The railroad brought tourists along with the automobiles that now populated the area. Josephine opined that it was just as well her husband didn't live to see this modern age. He would not have been at home in an existence where the services of horses, mules, and a tanner were shrinking.

Sylva was constructing a new water and drainage system. Workers were coming into the area from South Carolina and other parts of North Carolina. There was plenty of work laying the bricks for the deep and wide manholes in the system. Those with masonry skills could find a job in Sylva or at Cullowhee laying bricks for the new educational buildings.

WILLIS JAMES STREATER WAS born in South Carolina in 1891 and grew up in Chesterfield, South Carolina. His parents were "free born" but he had aunts, uncles, and grandparents who had been slaves. Some of them did not have masters as good as George Rogers did. But like George Rogers, they took their name from the master who owned them immediately before freedom came. There were white Streaters and black Streaters in Chesterfield County. Some spelled their name with two e's in the middle and some with the "ea." It was like the Tuckaseegee River in Jackson County—there were at least four accepted ways of spelling it.

Willis James Streater found work in Shelby, North Carolina, as a brick mason before he heard about all the buildings going up and brick work that was being done in Jackson County around Cullowhee and Sylva. In 1925 he moved to Sylva and began working as a brick mason on the buildings at the university at Cullowhee. It was there that he met Ada Rogers.

On February 2, 1926, Ada Rogers and Willis James Streater were married. They lived on the Rogers farm and helped there as they could.

In 1927 their first child, Margaret, was born. And during the next ten years, there were three more—Harvey, Herbert, and finally on March 8, 1937, Willis James Jr. was born.

THE GREAT DEPRESSION WAS little noticed in the Josephine Rogers' household when it hit in 1929 and continued into the 1930s. Actual money had always been scarce. But they had what they needed—food, clothing, a large house, a lot of land they could farm, and a large, loving family. Most of George and Josephine Rogers' children were working and married. Some left and some stayed at the home place.

In 1934, Josephine Rogers, then 66, deeded the farm to her oldest son, Earnel, knowing that he would see to it that his brothers and sisters received their shares when it was time.

On January 24, 1943, Josephine Gibbs Rogers died at the age of 75. She was the last direct connection that the Rogers and Streaters had to their slave heritage through her husband George.

THE STREATERS WOULD MOVE to Sylva but always remain closely connected with the Rogers farm where their roots in Jackson County remained.

Segregation was still the rule in education. But Margaret Streater, the first-born of Ada and Willis, was determined to get a college education—and more. She went to Fayetteville State University at Fayetteville, A and T University at Greensboro, and Western Carolina University at Cullowhee where she received her masters degree in early childhood education.

Willis James Streater Jr. found employment at the

24

papermills that were now sprouting up in Western North Carolina where there was an abundance of wood and water necessary for the making of paper. He married a young lady from nearby Franklin whose name was Shirley Ann Chavis.

On March 17, 1957, Ada's husband, Willis James Streater died. He was laid to rest in the cemetery of the AME Zion Church at Cullowhee near the graves of George Rogers and Josephine Rogers.

Within a couple of months Willis James Streater Jr. and his wife, Shirley, knew that they would be having a child. If it was a boy, he would be named after his father and his grandfather who had just died.

On December 17, 1957, a son was born. Mother and son barely survived. Shirley was only sixteen and a half at the time and had severe toxemia. Family who saw the child said he looked like "a little skinned squirrel" because he was so small. He had to stay several weeks in the hospital. But when James and Shirley took him home, they named him Willis James Streater III—and called him Jimmy.

Part of Jimmy Streater's Family Tree

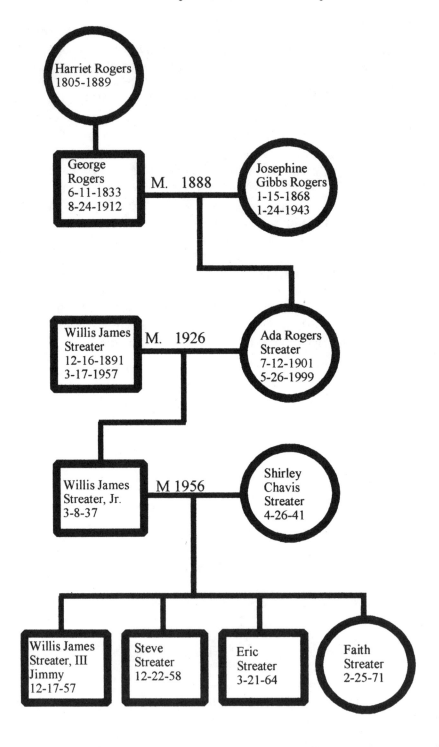

Harriet Rogers
1805-1889

George
Rogers
6-11-1833
8-24-1912

M. 1888

Josephine
Gibbs Rogers
1-15-1868
1-24-1943

Willis James
Streater
12-16-1891
3-17-1957

M. 1926

Ada Rogers
Streater
7-12-1901
5-26-1999

Willis James
Streater, Jr.
3-8-37

M 1956

Shirley
Chavis
Streater
4-26-41

Willis James
Streater, III
Jimmy
12-17-57

Steve
Streater
12-22-58

Eric
Streater
3-21-64

Faith
Streater
2-25-71

The Young Years

Jimmy Streater was born a hundred and three years after his great-grandfather was counted as property in the estate of David Rogers. In the intervening century many rights and privileges had been granted to blacks—on paper. They had been allowed to go to World War I, as Jimmy's great-uncle Earnel had. Jobs were available and the law said blacks could vote. But Jackson County, North Carolina, went with the rest of the state and the South in having segregated schools and other facilities. The major state universities were still segregated. But on a personal level, things went well between whites and blacks in and around Sylva, North Carolina.

Just a year and five days after Jimmy was born, his mother gave birth to another son—Steven Lydell Streater. Jimmy and Stevie would grow up almost like twins—playing together, fighting with each other, and, later, pushing each other to be the best they could be as athletes.

Jimmy's early memories center on his family and extended family. Grandmother Ada Streater still lived on the family farm purchased originally by George Rogers.

"I'd go out there and my grandmother would cook for all of us. I remember those meals well. I liked to explore. I climbed the ridge on the back of the farm, and I would go down and wade through the Tuckaseegee River. I would fish. There were rainbow trout in there. Those were good times."

Although, Jimmy had a large family, he often went

alone to the river to be by himself and imagine what he would be when he grew up. The cool, running water of the river below his grandmother's house provided an excellent getaway.

Then when he came back to family there was always plenty of encouragement. Aunt Margaret and Uncle Ray Miller lived next door. Uncle Harvey and Uncle Herbert weren't far away. And on his mother's side, Aunt Mary Chavis and Uncle Lockwood Chavis were a few miles farther down the road over in Franklin.

Jimmy learned family values at an early age. Everywhere he looked, his family members worked and stayed close. His father got on at the local paper mill and stayed. There were layoffs and name changes for the company, but James stayed employed at the papermill for practically all of Jimmy's youth.

When he started school, Jimmy only had to walk two blocks from his house to the Jackson Elementary School where his Aunt Margaret taught the first grade. "I knew the black kids went to that school and the white kids went to Scott's Creek. I was too young to really know why. It was just the way it was."

Thinking back on it in later years, Jimmy understood that there was official segregation in the town of his youth, but he also knew that most everyone got along.

"Our vacations usually consisted of driving to an uncle's place near Washington, D.C. where he worked as a policeman. I don't remember ever going to the ocean when I was real young or going anyplace else just for a vacation. I understand why now. The accommodations were still segregated. It was hard to find a motel or know which restaurant to go to when you were away from home."

Even in Sylva there were separate accommodations, but blacks were welcomed as customers—if they went to the right door. "Yeah, I remember on Sundays sometimes we'd drive to a restaurant to eat. But instead of parking and going in, my dad would drive around the building and pull up to the back door. They'd bring our food out to the car, and we'd take it home and eat. I guess it was one of the first drive-throughs.

"Aunt Margaret was my first grade teacher, but when it was time for second grade, they integrated. I went to Scott's Creek Elementary. I don't remember any race problem then or ever while I was in school."

Integration came as easily and smoothly to Sylva and Jackson County as the fog rising from the Tuckaseegee River when Jimmy was ready to go to the second grade. It was probably as little protested as anywhere in the country according to some who lived there then and live there now. Perhaps it was because the population of blacks was always less than five per cent. Or it may have been that the heritage of Jackson County had people of all colors working together.

At the time of the Civil War, the Cherokee population was greater than the number of slaves. Then, into the Twentieth Century the black population remained low in Jackson County. So when integration came, it was no great leap for children and adults to start going to school and eating with those they had known and worked with for years. It was a stable and peaceful society.

Blacks and whites lived sometimes side by side or at least within the same block. They worked together in the mills.

Boyce Deitz, who would later be an assistant coach at Sylva-Webster High School when Jimmy was there, remembers living within a couple of blocks of where the Streater family lived. "They were just plain good people. Although I was nine years older than Jimmy and Steve, I remember watching Jimmy and Steve play little league ball and remember just watching them play in the neighborhood. I was older and because of that didn't actually play with them. But I remember the Streaters always being fine, hardworking people."

Children never saw in black and white according to

The Jimmy Streater Story

Jean Hartbarger who, along with her husband and sons, runs the Jarrett House Hotel and Restaurant. She had sons who were close in age to the Streater boys.

"All the kids wanted to play with the Streater boys. It didn't make any difference—black or white. If the adults would just leave the kids alone, there never would be any race problem."

The perspective from the black side is similar. "Oh, it's just a few of both races who get liquored up that cause all the problem. We get along here. There's never been any real problem," Jimmy's uncle, Ray Miller, said recently.

The county made an easy transition. The all-black elementary school where Jimmy went to the first grade is now the board of education building. Aunt Margaret Miller was transferred to the integrated elementary school nearer to Cullowhee where parents—black and white—requested that their children be in her class. She compiled a record of teaching no telling how many first graders over a 39-year career before she retired.

Another son, Eric, was born to Shirley and James Streater in March of 1964. Eric was six years and three months younger than Jimmy and five years and three months younger than Steve. So, while Jimmy and Steve grew up almost as twins and went off to elementary school, little brother Eric was left at home with his mother, always looking up to his older brothers and wanting to be as good as they were at whatever they did.

WHAT JIMMY AND STEVE did most and best during their growing up was playing ball. It didn't really matter what season it was because they played them all as youngsters—baseball, football, and basketball.

After Jimmy and Steve graduated from sandlot ball or kicking the football around in a neighbor's yard, they were welcomed as members to the local Little League baseball teams and the Pop Warner type youth football.

Their dad coached Little League baseball. As a

prerogative of being a coach, any father was allowed to have his own sons on his team. For the Streaters and Sylva, this almost automatically meant that the team coached by James Streater would be one of the best, if not the best. Jimmy played shortstop and pitcher while Steve played second base and pitcher.

"If Jimmy or Steve got on base, either one was so fast that you knew it wouldn't be long until they'd steal second and third and then score," Coach Deitz remembered.

"We had a good team," Jimmy recalled. "I would pitch some, but Steve was a better pitcher. We'd usually win our league. There were a lot of good players who wanted to be on my father's team."

After the main season was over in this type of youth baseball, an all-star team was chosen with the league's winning coach also coaching that team.

Here again, the Streater boys excelled. Their father and an assistant coach or two would choose the best players to build their Little League all-star team around Jimmy and Steve who made up most of the infield and who swapped out pitching.

They won and won and won. They weren't defeated until they were just one game shy of going to the Little League World Series.

"It broke my heart. We fell just one game short of going for it all," Jimmy recounted years later. "I loved baseball."

JIMMY COULD GAZE ACROSS the street and see what a great athlete looked like. Tommy Love, the greatest football player in Sylva-Webster history to that time, lived there.

"Tommy should have been the first black athlete to play at the University of Tennessee," Coach Babe Howell remembered years later. "But Tennessee was recruiting Albert Davis of Alcoa, and it never worked out. Tommy went to Michigan State, and Albert Davis never played for the Vols." Tennessee recruited Lester McClain at the same time to be Davis' roommate, and he did star for the Vols.

Tommy Love died of a heart attack at age 22. He had broken Michigan State's all time rushing record for a sophomore and had been named national player of the week for his effort against Notre Dame.

AND IT WAS IN football that Jimmy was destined to make his mark when it came decision time.

However, if his first day of organized football was to be an indicator of his whole career, it would be catastrophic.

"I had to talk my mother into letting me play football. I was always real skinny with legs that looked like bird legs. She thought I might get hurt."

His mother finally relented and Jimmy hit the practice field. On the first day of practice he broke his arm without being hit by any other player.

"I just fell funny and broke it. I was out for the whole season. But I went out again the next year. My mother just said, 'Go on. You know what happened last time. You want to try it again. You just go on.' "

As Jimmy and Steve grew and continued to play, they also occupied their time with other activities.

Church was always important. The family attended Liberty Baptist just down the road and near Scott's Creek. His great-grandfather George Rogers and some of the family had attended the Mt. Zion AME Church in Cullowhee. Then grandmother Ada Streater was first with Mount Carmel Baptist, before the family moved to Sylva, and then with Liberty Baptist. Jimmy's ancestors on the Rogers' side of his family are buried in the Mt. Zion AME Church Cemetery at Cullowhee.

Jimmy's outgoing personality and singing ability were noticed at church. He soon became part of the choir.

When he wasn't playing ball and going to church, there was the occasional movie at the Ritz Theatre downtown or more fishing out at his grandmother's.

Sylva–Webster
1973 and 1974

Richard Nixon was President when Jimmy Streater began high school at Sylva-Webster in 1972. The President was gearing up for a re-election run in September and October while the thoughts of many at Sylva-Webster were on the football team. Earlier in the summer, there had been a burglary at a building in Washington that was named the Watergate at the offices of the Democratic Campaign Committee. Little notice or mention had been made of it.

In the South in the '70s football was king. It was no different in Jackson County, North Carolina, where high school football was represented by the Golden Eagles of Sylva-Webster. High schools have special rivalries and one of those for Sylva-Webster was neighboring Swain County High.

Swain County itself was actually cut out of Jackson County years before. Bryson City, part of the Smoky Mountains, and Cherokee, North Carolina, all lie in Swain County.

After three boys had been born to James and Shirley Streater, Faith came into the family on February 25, 1971.

Jimmy, then a seventh grader, was delighted to have a little sister.

AS A FRESHMAN IN the fall of 1972, Jimmy only sat and watched at the varsity games. He honed his skills on the practice field and in junior varsity games. But by watching this great Golden Eagle team, he learned what was expected. Sylva-Webster expected to win and win big. There was no place for losers on the Golden Eagles. As the name implies, they soared and glittered.

Coach Charles (Babe) Howell pushed all the right buttons. He had good assistants, including Boyce Deitz who came on as line coach in 1971 fresh out of college.

What Jimmy saw in 1972 was a Golden Eagle team that went undefeated and won the state AA championship. Jimmy had to sit and wonder when he would get his chance. With such good talent, would the Golden Eagles ever need a skinny kid with legs that resembled a stork's more than an eagle's?

"I ALWAYS WANTED TO be the quarterback," Jimmy would recall years later. "My idol growing up was Joe Namath of the Jets. And when I watched Joe, I also noticed Emerson Boozer. I wanted to throw like Joe and run like Emerson."

However, the coaches at Sylva-Webster had a good stock of quarterbacks and running backs entering the 1973 season. Both Jimmy and Steve dressed with the varsity and saw playing time. But it would be on defense that Jimmy would shine. The coaches were yet to see the potential of a Joe Namath or Emerson Boozer.

Coming off an undefeated 1972 season, Coach Babe Howell merely re-tooled for the 1973 campaign.

Ronnie Smith, David Allen, Terry Smith, and Dickie Woodard would all receive more opportunities to run the ball than Jimmy and Steve put together. Allen and Smith would also throw more passes. Sylva-Webster was deep, tough, and fast at running back. They had experience at quarter-back. Jimmy barely weighed a hundred and forty pounds. He looked frail when he was on the field with juniors and seniors.

On the passing side of the offense, David Allen and Dickie Woodard would be the quarterbacks who received the most playing time, with Jimmy being on the third-string.

But as the season progressed and the Golden Eagles remained undefeated, the coaches began to notice something. When Jimmy Streater touched the ball—as a runner, passer, or defender—good things happened.

It was mid-October when Sylva-Webster took on Rosman. It seemed like every time the Rosman quarterback threw a pass, it found a player's hands. However, it wasn't Rosman's players who were catching the ball. Jimmy Streater had four interceptions for the night. His interceptions helped to lead Sylva-Webster to a 55-0 victory, racking up twenty-eight straight wins without a loss.

The coaches would begin to find more ways to get Jimmy around the ball.

Jimmy returned kickoffs from the opposing team. These were few because the opposing team rarely scored. He threw passes. He ran. He caught passes from his quarter-back. He intercepted passes from the opposing quarterback. He kickedoff. In short, Jimmy was talented in most aspects of the game and there wasn't much he couldn't do. Quite a dilemma for the coaching staff in deciding where to play Jimmy the most.

They gave him jersey Number 40 which indicated he would be a running back and defensive back. Jimmy still wanted to be the quarterback, but it wasn't yet to be.

On the final game of his sophomore regular season, Jimmy's Sylva-Webster's Golden Eagles defeated rival Swain County 61-10 as a tune-up for the state play-offs.

The play-offs seemed as easy or easier than the regular season. Sylva-Webster won the semifinals by a score of 78-7 and the finals 43-18 to finish the season with fourteen victories and no defeats and extending the streak without a loss to thirty-one.

College coaches came calling to see the great Sylva-Webster team. They wanted to mine this mother lode of talent. Three seniors—David Allen, Ronnie Smith, and David Alston—signed with Clemson. Smith was the leading rusher in 1973 with 1546 yards on 204 carries for an average of seven and a half yards per carry. He scored twenty-seven touchdowns by carrying the ball. David Allen rushed for eight touchdowns and threw for eleven.

While the college coaches had their eyes focused on these three seniors when they watched the games, they couldn't help but notice the young, skinny sophomore with the elusive moves and instincts to know where to throw or run. They jotted down his name and number for future reference. It looked like they would know the road well to Sylva before Jimmy Streater's high school career was over.

When they totaled up the statistics for the 1973 campaign of Sylva-Webster, the team as a whole had outscored its opponents by 628 to 116—an average score of 45 to 8. Seniors Smith and Allen led in rushing and passing respectively, while junior Woodard was second in passing.

Jimmy Streater's sophomore stats put him third on the team overall in yardage. He had 401 yards rushing, 121 yards passing, and 320 yards receiving. On the scoring side, he had seven touchdowns running, one throwing, and four as a pass catcher. He also returned three interceptions for touchdowns and ran back a kickoff for another. That added up to sixteen touchdowns for 96 points and total yardage of 846, not counting the kickoff returns and pass interception return yardage.

Jimmy Streater looked forward to his junior year, hoping that he would get more opportunities to play his favorite position—quarterback—and trade his jersey number for one more fitting for a quarterback like Namath wore, or at least anything below 20.

Chris Cawood

JIMMY TURNED SIXTEEN IN December of 1973, and like all young men and women, he was anxious to get his driver's license and a car. It was okay to jog home from football practice in the summer and fall, but a car would be real nice to have too.

On those long runs from the football field to home, Jimmy pushed himself as he ran along main street, up the 107 steps to the courthouse, and back down and around the road along Scott's Creek toward his home. He had time to daydream. He was going to be a quarterback some day and he was going to college. Maybe it would be Clemson to re-join his teammates or North Carolina or Alabama where Joe Namath had played.

"Oh, yeah, I wanted a car too. But I had to earn money to get one. On Saturdays I would sell tickets and popcorn at the Ritz Theatre. During one summer I worked for Mr. and Mrs. Hartbarger at the Jarrett House. I bussed tables. They had great food there. The Hartbarger boys—Buzz and Scott—went to Sylva-Webster too, but they were a little younger than me."

Dillsboro, where the Jarrett House served tourists and locals, and Sylva, where Jimmy lived, were next door to each other. Things had changed since William Allen Dills founded Dillsboro and William Sylva left his namesake town for the frontier of Texas in the 1800s. There were more tourists, more locals, more paper mills, more lumber mills, and more traffic.

This side of the Smoky Mountains was attracting tourists by describing itself as the "Quiet side of the Smokies."

Great-grandfather George Rogers would hardly have recognized what had been small villages. One thing had not changed though. What was now the Jarrett House still served the best food. The structure looked practically like it did when George sold vegetables and fruit to the hotel and met Josephine. Only modern conveniences had been added—electricity, a newer plumbing system, and more bathrooms. Upstairs, though, guests could step into a room furnished in 1800s' decor.

The football field of Sylva-Webster lay toward Cullowhee from Sylva. Just three miles beyond the field was George Rogers' old farm. That was still the refuge where Jimmy visited with his Grandmother Ada, took long walks along the river and up the mountain, and listened to stories from uncles and aunts. This was the land they had owned for a hundred years now.

Everybody had to have an anchor—a place they knew they belonged—and, as for many Southerners, the land of the ancestors was it for Jimmy. When he looked up at the mountains and down at the lovely Tuckaseegee, he knew he always wanted to live there or in a place like it. No wonder his great-grandfather had not walked away when he was freed. His roots were here in Jackson County and so were Jimmy's.

Jimmy earned enough money to buy an eight-year-old 1966 Ford Fairlane the next year, which he later traded for a 1967 Camaro, and then a 1970 Nova. He learned practically every backroad of Jackson County.

He could always work at the Ritz on Saturdays. Then in the summers he was either bussing tables at the Jarrett House or working at a lumber mill up past Scott's Creek Elementary. Nothing came easy or was given. The Streaters had four children and everything, it seemed, was expensive. But two things were priceless in the Streater household—family and education. James and Shirley Streater decided early on that they wanted all their children to go to college, to be educated, and to remember their family.

If James had to work overtime at the mill and Shirley had to work in daycare, so be it. Their children would do their part too. No one would be a shirker.

"I said it. You heard it. You'd better believe it!" would always be Shirley's admonition to her children when she was making a point about doing or not doing something.

That settled it. There would be no arguing the point. The boys, and Faith too, could play sports if they wanted, but education and citizenship came first.

WHEN FALL PRACTICE BEGAN for the 1974 football season in August, Jimmy had bulked up to 155 pounds. The coaches looked at him and knew he wouldn't be their power runner, but when they saw him run with the elusiveness of a deer, they threw him jersey Number 40. He would still be their running back who would skirt the corners and outrun the opponents along the sidelines.

Before two-a-days were over, everybody in town was talking about something besides football. President Nixon had resigned on August Ninth and flown off to California, leaving new President Gerald Ford in the White House. But Jimmy's thoughts were still on football. When he looked around, he saw the same thing as the coaches. There was too much experience at quarterback ahead of him.

His dream of being the quarterback for the Golden Eagles would have to wait. Dickie Woodard was back. Woodard was experienced, tough, and could dish the ball off to whomever the coaches called. There would be a lot more runs for the Golden Eagles than passes anyway. Coach Howell ascribed somewhat to the old theory that three things can happen when you throw the ball and two of them are bad.

Jimmy wished the hot practices were over and the season would begin immediately. He would do whatever the coaches and team needed him to do, but he would still keep that dream of being the one to take the snap from center. He could run or pass then. Why was there a need for an intermediary? "Just give me the ball." The coaches were even practicing Steve as a back-up quarterback in case of an emergency. They wanted Jimmy at running back where they believed he would be more of a threat with his running ability than his passing.

The season started with a win—but a close win. The

Golden Eagles flew by Tuscola by a score of 23 to 22. Something was wrong here. Sylva-Webster was supposed to win by larger margins.

The coaches opened up more the next game and saw to it that Jimmy touched the ball more. The result was a 67 to 0 thrashing of Hayesville. In the game, Jimmy threw for a touchdown from his running back position, returned a punt for a touchdown, and kicked eight of eleven kickoffs into the opponent's end zone where there would be no return.

So, all was well in Golden Eagle territory entering the third week of the season and the game with Murphy. The streak was now thirty-six games in a row without a defeat and twenty-nine straight victories.

Then disaster struck. Early in the game, quarterback Dickie Woodard injured his knee. When they helped him off the field, the coaches knew he would not return to the game. They huddled and decided to try sophomore Steve Streater at quarterback. He had been practicing as the backup in case of an emergency. This was definitely an emergency.

Steve played heroically, passing to his brother for a touchdown. But Murphy ended Sylva-Webster's streak with a 22 to 13 decision.

The ensuing week was one of decision for the coaches at Sylva-Webster. Which Streater to put at quarterback?

Jimmy was obviously the best athlete on the team. This Sylva-Webster team wasn't as deep with talented players as the previous year's team. The decision came to put the best athlete and the older Streater at quarterback. They would see if he could help carry the team at quarterback. Jimmy would touch the ball on every play. Maybe there would be some magic in those hands, those legs—those moves. Jimmy would make his first start at quarterback against Franklin.

He practiced his new position all week. The coaches were not disappointed with the decision as the team rallied around their new quarterback to trounce Franklin 60 to 7.

In the next game, the local paper—*The Sylva Herald*

and Ruralite—noted that "Jim Streater hid the ball on his hip for a 30-yard run around end." This would become a familiar phrase for those watching Jimmy's ball carrying over the next several years. The Golden Eagles defeated Robbinsville 44 to 26.

Jimmy was beginning to feel at home at his new position by his third start, but he still could not shuck his running back jersey for one with a number appropriate for a quarterback. "And at quarterback, Number 40, Jim Streater," the P. A. announcer would intone. The programs had been printed and there was no need to change a jersey number during the middle of the year. They won 56 to 12 over Swain County High.

Near the close of the next game at Andrews, someone in the press box leaned over and said to his neighbor, "At least Andrews is getting a lot of kickoff return practice."

On one series, Jimmy passed thirty-five yards to Jim Robinson. Robinson then scored on a two-yard plunge. Jimmy later ran 44 yards for a touchdown, intercepted a pass to set up a field goal, and ran for another touchdown.

By the eighth game of the 1974 season, Jimmy was proving he was something special at quarterback—not so much for his throwing as for his running. For the season, his running attempts would outnumber his passes by a three to one ratio. When they could, college coaches were already watching him and writing. If there were any scouts at the next game with Rosman, they saw something spectacular.

Jimmy scored seven touchdowns—one about every way that could be imagined. He rushed for five of them, caught a pass from his brother for another, and picked up a fumble and returned it for six points on another play. He had 169 yards rushing with another 70-yard run called back because of a penalty. The pass from Steve covered 68 yards in all counting pass, catch, and run. This set an individual scoring record for Sylva-Webster.

He accomplished all this in a game that was shortened in the second half to eight-minute quarters from the regulation twelve minutes because of the lopsided nature of the score.

Teammates Ronnie Black, Gary Melton, and Bill Scott added other touchdowns while Bruce Evans kept busy kicking extra points.

The very next week, Jimmy made the coaches look like the wisest men since Biblical times. Although he was playing from the quarterback position, he set a new record for Sylva-Webster in rushing yards against Cherokee. On twenty-eight carries, he ran for 311 yards—an average of over eleven yards per carry.

He didn't score as many touchdowns against Cherokee as against Rosman—only four. Brother Steve scored the other two with Bruce Evans kicking the extra points.

Jimmy's yardage gained against Cherokee pushed him above the 1000-yard mark for the year. He was one of only five Golden Eagles to have accomplished that in a season in the history of the school. Among his runs were ones for 56, 46, and 24 yards. Jimmy was also a recipient of a 46-yard pass from brother Steve.

Certainly, all the Streater family sitting in the stands could be proud of the two brothers who not only grew up like twins but were now playing and scoring like twins. It was a Streater night.

But Sylva-Webster was by no means a two-man team. Others contributing included Phillip Howell, Ronnie Sutton, Ty Smith, Tim Shuler, and Evans with his extra points. For the first time in thirteen quarters, the punter for Sylva-Webster had to trot onto the field in the second quarter.

THE LAST GAME OF the season was another match with Swain who Sylva-Webster had beaten earlier 56-12. This game would be an even worse drubbing for Swain as fifteen seniors for Sylva-Webster finished their careers on a high note by pounding Swain 60-0. Those fifteen seniors were: Ronnie Black, Gary Melton, Paul Bowers, Doug Fox, Ty Smith, Kole Clapsaddle, Gene Thornburg, Tim Shuler,

Bill Scott, Charles Blackburn, Ted Jamison, Jim Huskey, Mike Smith, Bruce Evans, and Dickie Woodard.

J. D. Pruett scored the first touchdown for Sylva-Webster on a fumble recovery and run. Jimmy Streater ran 36 yards for the next and the rout was on. Phillip Howell punched in from five yards out for the third TD. Jimmy ran for a second touchdown by him in the first quarter. Bill Scott, Pruett, Ted Jamison, and Jimmy added other touchdowns while Bruce Evans continued kicking extra points.

In all that evening, the Eagles racked up 417 yards rushing and only six through the air. Jimmy gained 114 yards and Steve carried for 22. Swain netted only three yards rushing for the whole team.

Because of the early season loss to Murphy, the Sylva-Webster Golden Eagles could not go to the play-offs and finished their season with nine wins and one loss.

Jimmy was the total offense leader. His season statistics showed that he gained 1126 yards on 108 carries for a 10.4 yard per carry average. He threw for 474 yards and was 14 for 39 in attempts. He scored twenty touchdowns—19 rushing and one receiving—and threw for four more.

Steve—a sophomore—had 239 yards rushing, 206 throwing, and 116 receiving. He had eight touchdowns and threw to Jimmy for another.

When college coaches looked at Jimmy's statistics and watched him play they had a problem. At what position would he play in college? Would he be recruited as a quarterback, running back, or receiver?

Jimmy knew what he wanted to play and that was quarterback. So, when the colleges and coaches came calling, he always wanted to know if he would get a shot at quarterback. The ones who said "yes" would get a further look and those who said "no" could look elsewhere.

He also knew that a quarterback in college was expected to pass more than run. His stats at Sylva-Webster for his junior year had his running yardage at seventy per

cent and his passing at thirty. Those numbers would have
to be reversed his senior year if he were to be taken seriously as a major college quarterback.

AS SOON AS FOOTBALL season was over in 1974,
Jimmy jumped into basketball. Football would be his college
ticket but he enjoyed the flow of basketball and the outdoor
spring time of baseball and track.

It was after football season and during basketball
season that Jimmy could occasionally glance over to the
spectator section and see faces of men who were not from
Sylva. College football coaches would come to watch him
play basketball and let him know that they indeed were
interested in him.

Among those watching him was the University of
Tennessee head football coach, Bill Battle. Coach Battle
would later comment, "It was back when Jimmy was a
sophomore in high school, and he was playing in a hostile
gymnasium. He took charge of the game and showed me
enough right then in courage and quickness that I would
have signed him to a football scholarship on the spot."

As soon as basketball ended, Jimmy was on the
baseball diamond at short-stop. His skills were so good
there that the recent world champion Cincinnati Reds
invited him to a camp near Cincinnati for a tryout. They
were impressed and kept Jimmy on their list for drafting
after his senior year.

HOWEVER, PERHAPS WHERE JIMMY'S pure
athletic ability was on display most was at the annual state
track meet. "I ran the hundred, two-twenty, and some of the
relays. We really didn't have an experienced track coach. I
just went and ran as fast as I could and jumped as far as I
could."

Jimmy ran a 9.9 in the hundred.

But it was the long-jump, without any coaching,
where he would just run and jump, that he broke the

regional records. In 1974, 1975, and 1976 he jumped farther than anybody in the state.

"Sylva-Webster would finish among the top teams in the state just because Jimmy and a couple of other guys would go down to the state meet and win all those medals," Coach Deitz later recalled. "If he had had a real track coach in the long jump, he could've been Olympic caliber."

What Jimmy did in the long jump was merely to run and jump for a record twenty-three feet and four inches. To put that into today's perspective, from the top of the circle on the basketball court where the three-point line runs to the baseline at the end of the court is about the same distance. What he was doing was jumping that distance without being coached. Even twenty-five years later, that distance would rank among the tops in most states.

Senior Season

At the beginning of football season in 1975, Jimmy received what he had been wanting for two years—a football jersey with a quarterback's number on it. He traded in Number 40 for Number 19. Now all he had to do to impress college coaches as a potential college quarterback was to prove that he could pass as well as run.

About his running ability there was no doubt. His sophomore and junior seasons combined allowed him to carry the ball for 1527 yards and 21 touchdowns.

"Jimmy was as elusive as anybody I've ever seen. He would just toy with the opposing players. They thought they had him hemmed up and he would just skirt around them. He would give them a leg and take it away. His moves were like a scared calf in a barn lot. Impossible to catch," Coach Deitz recalled years later.

In fact, he and brother Steve were so good on the ground that there was little reason to pass during his sophomore and junior seasons.

But 1975 would be different. All the opposing teams knew who they had to stop to have a chance to beat Sylva-Webster. "Corral Streater," were the watchwords. Also, the Golden-Eagles had moved up in classification voluntarily.

"We had been beating the AA schools so badly that we decided to move up to AAA and see how we would do. It was a struggle. In 1975 the total team quality was down and we had to rely more on the Streaters," Coach Deitz said.

There was a lack of seniors on the team. Just six in all—Jimmy, Neil Setzer, Ray Swayney, Tony Cunningham, Jim Wilson, and Ronnie Bumgarner. Jimmy, Neil, and Ronnie were selected as captains.

SYLVA-WEBSTER OPENED THE season against the Tuscola Mountaineers at Waynesville. This was the debut of the Golden Eagles in AAA classification.

The Mountaineers' strategy was clear from the beginning. They weren't going to let Jimmy Streater beat them by running around end. After Jimmy returned the opening kickoff 42 yards, the Golden Eagles had to pound it up the middle with fullback Phillip Howell running behind Ronnie Bumgarner, Neil Setzer, Ray Swayney, and Jim Wilson.

On their second possession, Jimmy threaded a pass through the arms of three Tuscola defenders to Steve Streater for a 29-yard gain. Howell later carried the ball into the end zone.

After being held on the next possession to little gain, Steve punted the ball 57 yards to back the Mountaineers up to their 26-yard line. There was no further scoring in the first half with Steve snuffing out a Tuscola threat near the end of the half with an interception that he returned 40 yards.

On defense to open the second half, Jimmy intercepted a pass on the first play from scrimmage but the possession ended with a punt. On their next opportunity Jimmy and Steve teamed up to put some yards on the stats. Jimmy carried for nine and then threw to Steve for fourteen. Jimmy also threw on fourth down to Tony Cunningham to keep the drive alive. Howell banged across for his second touchdown. Jimmy threw to Steve for the two-point conversion. Jimmy later found James Bowers for a 52-yard gain. Sylva-Webster won 14-8.

This was the coming out party for Jimmy as a passer.

For the third straight year, the Golden Eagles beat

Tuscola's Mountaineers. Jimmy was four for eight passing, for 101 yards. He only netted eleven running, but he had started to show his skill as a passer.

THE NEXT WEEK SYLVA-WEBSTER had the opportunity to avenge the loss to Murphy from the previous year that had kept the Golden Eagles out of the play-offs. They did it in a runaway, 40-20.

However, Jimmy was forced to revert to his running abilities because of the defense of the Murphy Bulldogs. While Phillip Howell was plowing up the middle on 22 carries for 176 yards, the defense let Jimmy skirt around end for 91 yards on 13 tries.

His only pass completions were a pass to Steve on a two-point conversion and another two-pointer to James Bowers.

But the main thing was to have fun, and Jimmy did. He ran for a touchdown. He tackled the Bulldogs' quarterback in the end zone for a two-point safety, and he kicked off so far on one occasion that the ball zoomed over the crossbar of the opposing team's goal posts before kicking up dirt when it landed out of the end zone. He also returned a punt for 48 yards. All in all, Jimmy accounted for twelve of the points. His passing yardage was only 58.

Brother Steve only had to punt one time—for 46 yards. The important thing was that they won and kept in contention for the play-offs.

FRANKLIN WAS THE HOME town of Jimmy's mother. He had relatives on her side of the family still living there. So, it was always special to go down and play the Panthers where he could show off his skills before another group of relatives.

Sylva-Webster only had three plays from scrimmage in the first quarter of the game but two were for touchdowns. On the first play after Franklin had scored, Phillip Howell blasted through the center of the line for seventeen yards. On the next play, Jimmy reverted to the play that gained him so many yards the previous year, hid the ball on his hip, faked a hand-off, sailed around end, and outran Franklin defenders sixty-three yards to the end zone.

He then kicked off into the end zone.

The next time the Golden Eagles had the ball, Howell surpassed Jimmy's run by going straight up the middle for sixty-six yards and a touchdown. Jimmy passed to Steve for the two-point conversion.

The Eagles recovered a Franklin fumble on the next series. And on the first play from scrimmage, Jimmy took the ball all the way for another touchdown by zig-zagging across the field with Franklin defenders missing tackles or falling by the wayside for 53 yards. Howell ran the two-point conversion. So, on three consecutive plays from scrimmage, the Golden Eagles had scored each time.

Jimmy and Howell would go on to score three touchdowns each and beat the Franklin Panthers by a score of 48-13. Jimmy's last touchdown came on a 62-yard punt return. This time he ran the two-point conversion himself. Jimmy had 123 yards on eight carries while Howell had 224 yards on 15 tries.

But when Jimmy looked at the statistics, he saw that he had only thrown seven times for two completions and twenty-four yards. Those would not be numbers that would impress college coaches to recruit him as a quarterback.

Already there was letter after letter arriving for Jimmy at school and at home from college recruiters reminding him that he was on their list. The coaches also came and watched when it was allowed by rules. The pressure was growing on Jimmy to make a decision even before the fourth game of the season. The number of colleges contacting him grew by the week from thirty, to forty, to fifty, and beyond.

TAKING A PAGE OUT of Bear Bryant's book by poor-mouthing his own team, Coach Babe Howell acted worried about the next week's game with Mountain Heritage High when asked by a local reporter to share his perspective of the coming game.

"They throw the ball a lot more than we do. We'll have to play better defense than we did at Franklin or somebody's going to whip us," Coach Howell said.

His concern was a bit overstated as the Golden Eagles soared over Heritage the next Friday by a score of 60 to 6.

The demolition of the Cougars was behind a balanced ground and air attack led by Jimmy Streater. Jimmy ran for three touchdowns on nine carries for 103 yards. He passed for two others to his brother Steve and ran three two-point conversions. All in all, Jimmy accounted for thirty-six points. This time when he looked at the stats he was more pleased. The team won and he had thrown for 192 yards, completing nine of 22 attempts.

Steve, beside catching two touchdown passes, had thrown for another, intercepted a pass, and made several key tackles.

It was a good night for the whole team. Phillip Howell gained 85 yards on nine carries; Charles Allen, 24 yards on six tries; Ronnie Sutton, 21 yards on five attempts; Eddie Adams, 28 yards on four carries; Steve Streater, six yards on three attempts; and Kent Dillard, three yards on one try.

Now when Jimmy jogged down Main Street, up and down the courthouse steps, and along the winding road by the creek to his home, he could imagine himself as a college quarterback. He would throw passes and run when he couldn't find anybody open. Maybe Steve would be on the receiving end of those aerials too.

THE NEXT FRIDAY NIGHT could have been headlined as the Jimmy and Stevie Show. While there was once again a complete team effort, the Streater brothers put on quite a scoring show against the Patriots of Madison High.

Jimmy returned the first punt of the Patriots for a 52-yard touchdown run. On the second half kickoff by Madison, he ran 92 yards to the end zone, going around and through their eleven defenders on the way. He ran another touchdown in from seventeen yards and threw to Steve for another.

By halftime the Golden Eagles led 28 to 0 and Coach Howell inserted second-stringers on both offense and defense. The bad news for Madison High was that Steve Streater was the second-string quarterback. He proceeded to run for two more touchdowns, pass for a two-point conversion, and throw for another touchdown.

With the Streaters running, passing, and catching, they had been involved in all of the scoring except for one touchdown by their friend Phillip Howell. The result was another rout—58 to 0.

Halfway through the season the Golden Eagles were 5 and 0, having outscored their opponents 220 to 47.

AT HOME IN THE afternoons or on Saturdays and Sundays, Jimmy would relax with his brothers and friends by playing basketball on the goal out beside the driveway.

It was there on one afternoon when he was in a hot game of horse with Steve that his mother came to the door and yelled for him. "There's a coach on the phone wanting to talk to you, Jimmy."

"A coach? Who?" Jimmy asked and shot the basketball off the backboard and through the net. "See if you can beat that, Stevie Boy."

"He told me his name. But I forget. Some coach."

"Where's he from?" Jimmy asked and watched Steve make his shot.

"I don't know. Now do you want to talk to him or not?"

"Okay, I'll be right there."

"Hurry, he's been hanging on for several minutes now."

Jimmy shot one last time from twenty-five feet and swished it through on his way to the door. "See if you can match that. And you tell me the truth when I get back out here."

Jimmy reached for the phone when he got to the kitchen and put the receiver to his ear. "This is Jimmy."

"Jimmy, this is Coach Paul Bryant from the University of Alabama."

Jimmy dropped the phone to the floor but quickly picked it back up. He caught his breath and gave his mother a hard stare. "Some coach," she had said. This was *THE* coach. The *BEAR*.

"Coach Bryant, excuse my time in getting to the phone. I was outside shooting a little basketball."

"Yes, that's what your mother told me."

Jimmy listened to the deep, gravelly voice on the other end of the line. Coach Bryant sounded just like he did when Jimmy had heard him interviewed on television.

"Jimmy, I want you to come visit us at Alabama. We've been following your career at Sylva-Webster. I know you're a good student and citizen as well."

"Thanks, Coach. I can only visit six schools and I haven't decided on which ones yet."

"Yeah, that's why I'm calling. I want you here. Jimmy, we're going to have a good recruiting year. I think we have the young men who can win. Somewhere down the road during your college career we can win a national championship. I believe that."

"I'm honored, sir, by your calling. You know that I want to play quarterback in college, don't you?"

"Yes, Jimmy. It's time. We'll give you a shot at quarterback. We don't promise anybody where they'll end up or how much playing time they'll get. You'll have to earn it. But it's time now that we can play you at quarterback."

They talked for a few minutes more, and then Jimmy returned to his game of horse with Steve in the driveway.

"Who was that on the phone?"

"Coach Bear Bryant of Alabama," Jimmy said and shot one toward the goal over his shoulder.

"Sure," Steve said. "They want a black, North Carolina kid to play quarterback for the University of Alabama? You're kiddin' me."

"No, it was Coach Bryant and yes, they want a black kid—not just any black kid—they want Jimmy Streater to play quarterback for them."

"Sure. And they're going to make the Reverend Martin Luther King's widow the new president of the university." Steve laughed and shot the basketball off the backboard and through the net.

"Coach Bryant said, 'It's time,' and I believe him," Jimmy said. He ran, jumped, and grabbed the rim. "I'm going to be a college quarterback."

THE HENDERSONVILLE BEARCATS CAME to town the following Friday with ideas of shutting out the high-flying Eagles of Sylva-Webster and did a good job of it the first half. It was 0 to 0 at halftime.

The locker room was abuzz at the intermission. Coaches reminded the players of their play responsibilities and the players encouraged each other to reach down and do something for the team. They had averaged 44 points per game up until this time and they didn't want to stumble now and miss the play-offs one more year. Bad things had already happened in the first half. Jimmy had returned a punt 86 yards for an apparent touchdown, only to see it called back on a clipping penalty.

It didn't take long after halftime though. Jimmy returned the kickoff to the 32-yard line. Phillip Howell, from his fullback position, dove nine yards over tackle. Then Jimmy put the ball on his hip, skirted right end, and sprinted down the sideline 59 yards to pay dirt.

Three plays later, Steve intercepted a Hendersonville pass and returned it to the opponent's 22-yard line. Howell, two plays later, burst up the middle for a 15-yard touchdown run. Jimmy threw to Charles Allen for the two-point conversion.

On Hendersonville's next series, they went backwards—with Jimmy, on a safety blitz, catching the opposing quarterback at his own 1-yard line. After a punt by the Bearcats and a short drive by Sylva-Webster, Jimmy ran it in from the five-yard line. He threw to Steve for the two-point conversion.

The Golden Eagles had scored 22 points in the third quarter and left it at that. The Bearcats, coming in looking for a shutout, were shut down themselves, losing 22 to 0. Jimmy had gained 130 yards on 14 carries. He fell back to only 2 of 7 in passing for 46 yards.

Besides doing much of the running, passing, and catching, the Streater brothers also handled the kicking for Sylva-Webster. Jimmy kicked off, with most of them going into the opposing end zone. Steve punted and averaged 41.5 yards against Hendersonville.

THE WEST HENDERSON FALCONS were to be the next victims of the Golden Eagle onslaught. It was to be expected that Falcons could only aggravate and pester Golden Eagles after all.

Coach Howell warned his players that West Henderson was big along the front line and could give his team a challenge.

And it was true, for a while. There were no long runs from scrimmage as the big line of the Falcons narrowed the alleys through which Phillip Howell and Charles Allen ran. They cut off the corners on Jimmy. But the Falcons couldn't stop the sustained pounding of Howell and Allen. It took twelve plays to go 71 yards for the first touchdown. Jimmy then threw to Steve for the two-point conversion.

If they couldn't go by ground as fast as they had in the past, the Eagles found that the flight patterns were open. Jimmy hit Steve on a 60-yard catch and run in the second quarter, and Howell finished it off on a one-yard plunge. It was Streater-to-Streater again for the two-point try after touchdown.

The Falcons scored a touchdown, but when they kicked-off, Jimmy slithered through the defenders and around them for an 84-yard touchdown run. Allen scored another touchdown on a run after a pass by Jimmy to Tony Cunningham kept the drive alive. Jimmy forsook throwing it to Steve for the two points and ran it in himself.

The scoreboard read 30 to 12 at game's end. Jimmy had run for only 14 yards from scrimmage, but added 101 yards by passing, along with his kickoff return for the TD. Sylva-Webster was 7 and 0 and had won 14 in a row.

The Golden Eagles had not lost since Jimmy Streater became the starter at quarterback.

THE NEXT TWO GAMES were shutouts for the Golden Eagles who beat Mitchell County 46 to 0 and Owen's Warhorses 38 to 0.

Jimmy was held out of the Mitchell County game with a bad arm, except he was allowed to kickoff and kick extra points. He kicked two extra points while Steve got to start at quarterback. Besides passing for 85 yards, Steve ran for 47, punted for 53, and intercepted a pass.

Jimmy, though, had to preserve the shutout by making a one-armed tackle after a kickoff when he was the last defender between the Mitchell runner and the goal line.

By the game with the Owen Warhorses, Jimmy was able again to use both arms. This proved to be the undoing of the Warhorses. Within a period of eleven plays during a ten minute time span, Jimmy either ran or passed the ball on nine of the eleven plays. The Eagles scored four times during that brief time to rein in the Warhorses and put them into the stable.

Jimmy had gained 92 yards on nine carries and passed for 156 yards with five completions out of thirteen attempts.

The Jimmy Streater Story

ONLY THE EAST HENDERSON Eagles stood between Sylva-Webster and a perfect regular season. The Golden Eagles had previously disposed of Hendersonville and West Henderson. East Henderson had a highly touted defense but the Golden Eagles were not about to let mere Eagles interfere with their goal of a third undefeated season in four years.

On the second play from scrimmage, Jimmy faked a handoff, hid the ball on his hip, and then threw to brother Steve who caught the ball around the East Henderson 40-yard-line. Steve continued to run across the field to pick up blockers and then speeded toward the end zone. The catch and run covered 67 yards.

Phillip Howell scored the Golden Eagles' next touchdown on a nine-yard run after a sustained drive of ten plays and 67 yards. Jimmy ran the two-point conversion to make it 14-0.

Charles Allen was the recipient of Jimmy's pass on the next drive. This one covered 69 yards but a fumble on the next play killed the scoring opportunity.

Steve got to show off his golden foot for the Golden Eagles with a 55-yard punt after the next possession failed to budge East Henderson.

If Steve could punt, Jimmy could return punts. And that's just what he did on East Henderson's next one. His return of 56 yards was one yard farther than his brother had punted. Jimmy then threw to Steve for a fifteen-yard gain before Howell slammed four yards into the scoring zone.

There were just thirty seconds left until halftime when East Henderson took over. Instead of running out the clock and regrouping, they tried a pass on second down. Jimmy saw it spiraling toward him like a peach on a tree ready for the picking. He stepped in front of the receiver, intercepted, and ran it 70 yards for a touchdown.

In the first half, Jimmy had thrown for a touchdown, run for a two-point conversion, and intercepted a pass for another TD. The only thing left in the second half for him to do was to run for a TD from scrimmage. This he did in the fourth quarter. It was a spectacular run of 64 yards.

The Golden Eagles won 32-8. They also won the Ivy Division of the Mountain Athletic Conference and closed out another undefeated season. The team had a seventeen game winning streak—the longest in North Carolina. Jimmy had 67 yards on five carries to go with his 165 yards of passing. The play-offs awaited.

AN EARLY SNOW BLANKETED Western North Carolina the following Thursday night and forced the first play-off game for the Golden Eagles to be moved from their home field down the road to Western Carolina's Whitmire Stadium. The field there was Astro-turf and was easily clearable of the snow.

The Bunker Hill Bears came in to challenge Sylva-Webster but they might as well have stayed in hibernation. Jimmy, Steve, and Phillip Howell found out that they liked to play on the artificial surface. They bounced the Bears 57 to 0.

Howell got the first touchdown, with Jimmy running a two-point conversion, and the rout was on. The Bears were backed up to their own goal line the whole first quarter. They made punts from their own three and ten-yard-lines. After one of the short punts and a quick drive, Howell burst up the middle for another TD run of seven yards.

On the Bears' next possession, Jimmy intercepted a pass and returned it 38 yards to set up the third touchdown. Charles Allen got the honors this time. Howell ran the two-point conversion to make it 22-0.

The Bears' only luck was bad. They fumbled on the next series and Ronnie Bumgarner recovered for Sylva-Webster. Howell ran twenty-one yards for his third touch-down just a bit later. He rubbed it in by running for the two-point conversion.

Sylva-Webster's Jim Wilson recovered the Bears' next

fumble at the Golden Eagles' twelve-yard line. On the next play from scrimmage, Jimmy made the longest run of his career and tied a school record that had been set by Tommy Love in 1966.

The run of 88 yards had Jimmy rolling-out and running through and around the eleven opponents all the way to the end zone. It was like the ones he had done before—only longer. He was tired and winded by the time he reached the end zone. But the cold air in his lungs and the snow that was heaped up in banks would not cool down his exuberance and enthusiasm.

Tommy Love was a hero of Sylva-Webster from the last decade. He had died early. Now, Jimmy had tied his record on a field that once belonged to the farm where his great-grandfather George Rogers had stood on a stump to be appraised over a hundred and twenty years before. The most valuable one there this evening was Jimmy.

But brother Steve and fullback Howell competed for the same distinction. Steve had three interceptions on the night and a touchdown. Howell had four touchdowns and three two-point conversions for a total of 30 points. Charles Allen and Ronnie Sutton tallied the other two touchdowns.

The win put the Golden Eagles in the quarterfinals.

PISGAH HIGH SCHOOL OF Canton was a school that Sylva-Webster had not played recently. Both had a tradition of good football teams. Both had individual stars which included the Streater brothers for Sylva-Webster and David Singleton for Pisgah. Singleton and Jimmy Streater both played quarterback for their respective teams. The game would be on Pisgah's home field some thirty miles from Sylva. Fans gathered as though they knew this would be a classic. Before the first kickoff, 9500 people had assembled in the stands and huddled around the fence to witness this spectacle.

In the press box, college coaches and scouts hunkered over to watch the explosive offense of Sylva-Webster and the more methodical ground game of Pisgah. There was talent on the field and it didn't take long to be noticed.

On the opening kick, a Sylva-Webster player received the ball on the twenty-five yard line and took off. Pisgah's faithful immediately saw that their team had made a mistake—they had kicked to Jimmy Streater.

It took Jimmy thirteen seconds on the scoreboard clock to weave his way down field, elude some would-be tacklers, and shake others off before he reached the end zone. He ran the two-point conversion to give the Golden Eagles an 8 to 0 lead.

The Black Bears took the next kickoff back to the 28-yard-line and then drove 55 yards in a dozen plays before yielding possession at the Sylva-Webster seventeen.

On the Golden Eagles first play, they fumbled, Pisgah recovered and was back in business deep in the Eagles' territory.

But when Singleton threw into the end zone on fourth and four, Jimmy Streater intercepted and returned the ball to the Pisgah 43-yard-line.

Two plays later Singleton returned the favor by picking up another Sylva-Webster fumble and running it back to the Eagles' 35. Eight plays later Singleton scored on a one-yard plunge. At the end of the first quarter, both quarterbacks had shown their stuff and the score was 8-7, Sylva-Webster.

On the next possession, the Golden Eagles moved the ball to mid-field before Jimmy was hit on a blind side tackle and fumbled with Pisgah recovering. Nine plays later Singleton punched over from the two to give Pisgah the lead at 14-8.

Sylva-Webster was not to be denied on the next possession, driving from their own fifteen to Pisgah's end zone in a sustained drive. Jimmy gained five yards, Charles Allen eight, and Phillip Howell seventeen. Jimmy passed to Steve for 34 yards and then found Allen in the corner of the end zone for an eighteen-yard touchdown pass. Jimmy ran the two-point conversion putting the Golden Eagles back ahead 16-14.

Jimmy kicked off while his adrenaline was still flowing and the ball sailed 70 yards, going out of the end zone. But the Black Bears drove 62 yards from their twenty and positioned their kicker for a field goal attempt which was successful. Bears 17, Eagles 16.

The Eagles surged back and got another TD. The points-after attempt failed. Eagles 22, Bears 17 at the half.

Neither team scored during the third quarter.

But on a possession that covered part of the third and fourth quarters, the Golden Eagles showed that they could mount a sustained drive of their own, going 79 yards in a twenty-play drive with Allen going the final yard for the touchdown. Jimmy ran the conversion for two points making it 30 to 17.

Pisgah picked up the challenge and drove down the field 66 yards after the kickoff with the score coming on a 23-yard pass by Singleton to a wide-open receiver—30-24.

Disaster struck the Golden Eagles when another fumble—the fourth of the night—was recovered by Pisgah at the Eagles' 49-yard-line. Eleven plays later the Black Bears were in the end zone with the extra point giving them a 31-30 lead.

With time running out, the Golden Eagles had to punt. Their defense tried every trick to knock the ball loose from the Black Bears. The Bears caught Sylva-Webster in a blitz. Singleton skirted through the defenders and ran 49 yards for an insurance touchdown. When the Bears kicked the extra point there were only 29 seconds left, and the score was 38-30.

Jimmy didn't quit. He threw to Tony Cunningham for 28 yards. Ran for another fifteen. Time, the season, and Jimmy's high school career ran out with him still trying to find a receiver for the tying score. The ball fell incomplete.

Even today, nearly a quarter century later, people in Canton and fans in Sylva still talk about the classic battle in

1975 between the Pisgah Black Bears and the Sylva-Webster Golden Eagles. It was a game for the ages in high school football lore. While the game was being played out, old-timers in the press box uttered words such as *fantastic, superb,* and *unbelievable* when they watched Jimmy Streater and David Singleton perform their magic for the night.

Sylva-Webster's six seniors—Jimmy Streater, Ronnie Bumgarner, Neil Setzer, Ray Swayney, Jim Wilson, and Tony Cunningham—had been on teams during their four years that had won 47 games, lost two, and tied one. They had won two state championships.

With Jimmy at quarterback, the Golden Eagles had lost only one game—the last one. He had led them to seventeen victories from the quarterback position.

Jimmy's career statistics included 38 touchdowns rushing, thirteen passing, and five receiving. He had total rushing yardage of 2335 and passing of 1606. He ran six punt returns, four kickoffs, and four pass interceptions back for touchdowns. With his two-point conversions added in, Jimmy scored 389 points in his career.

Now, for Jimmy, it was time to move on.

Awards
and
Recruitment

Moving on meant, first, just going from a football uniform to a basketball uniform. By the time that the football play-offs were over, basketball season had begun. Jimmy went from quarterback to guard or wing on the basketball court.

Coach Babe Howell felt bad for his football team, though, and for Jimmy in particular. He wanted his star player and star citizen to go out with another state championship. But it just had not been. A great team like Pisgah's could sometimes beat a good team with a star athlete like Sylva-Webster's.

Coach Howell was still nursing the loss the following Tuesday when Jimmy played in his first basketball game of the season.

Coach Deitz remembers the scene well. "We were playing our biggest rival in basketball just after losing that tough game to Pisgah in football. We were down by like four points with about twelve seconds left in the game. Jimmy stole the ball two or three times in a row and put it back in to tie up the game. There was a big dispute about how much time was left in the game.

"Coach Howell and I were sitting here watching.

Coach Howell got angry, and when he gets angry he turns completely white. Here he was just the football coach, and the next thing I remember, he was in the middle of the basketball court arguing with the officials about how much time was on the clock.

"And I know what it was. Coach Howell loved Jim Streater so much and he was so hurt about him not getting to play farther in the play-offs. Then it was as though somebody was messing with the basketball game. He just couldn't take it. I mean he had to go out there and defend him right on the court. The basketball coach wasn't out there. It was the football coach arguing with the officials."

It wasn't unusual for the coaches, teachers, and students to like the Streaters—Jimmy and Steve, and later Eric and Faith. They earned a loyal following.

"Those kids were as good as citizens and students as you would ever see," Coach Deitz added. "In fact, they were more special as people than as athletes.

"Jimmy and Steve never cut classes. They made good grades, behaved themselves, and excelled as athletes.

"I had Heath Shuler later as a quarterback at Swain County High. Heath and Jimmy were different as quarterbacks but they were identical in citizenship. First class."

"Just fine folks," Gene McConnell said recently about Jimmy and the other Streaters. McConnell is a former junior varsity coach and former athletic director at Smoky Mountain High School which is the renamed high school that combined Sylva-Webster and Cullowhee. "I thought Jimmy would end up as a state senator or something like that. He, his brothers, and sister were all good citizens."

Jimmy was chosen as a co-captain of the basketball team and continued to average 14 points per game over the season.

His classmates chose him and Molly Vodak as the Most Popular seniors. They were also chosen as Mr. and Miss Golden Eagle in recognition of athletics and citizenship.

Football awards began to roll in. Jimmy was chosen

to quarterback his side in the Shrine Bowl. There was district, regional, and state recognition as an all-star.

College coaches and recruiters were becoming more persistent. Letters piled up every day at home and at school. Phone calls interrupted him at home. And home visits seemed like they were occurring every day. In the back of his mind though, Jimmy was thinking about baseball too. The Cincinnati Reds wanted him to come to their organization right out of high school. They would draft him and offer him a $40,000 signing bonus. Sylva-Webster had won the state titles in 1974 and 1975 behind the hitting, fielding, and pitching of Steve and him.

"No. I've said it. You've heard it. That's the way it's going to be." Jimmy's mother's words were emphatic. He was going to college. There would be no signing to play baseball now even if he had to give up what looked like a whole lot of money.

"Well, I want to go to a college that will let me play football and baseball then so that I can give baseball a try after college if I want to," Jimmy said.

"That's fine. You work it out with the coaches. I just know that I want you to go to college and get a degree. Period."

The first task for Jimmy in deciding where he was going to play football in college was to pare down to six the list of 85 schools that wanted him and visit them.

It wasn't easy for Jimmy to say "No" to college coaches. When it came down to it, he would have to say "No" to close to ninety colleges and "Yes" to only one.

All of the nation's powerful programs wanted him, including Notre Dame, Alabama, and Ohio State. The schools of the Southeastern Conference and the Atlantic Coast Conference, which were right on his door step, were all besieging him.

After a lot of thought and consultation, Jimmy cut the list down to six. He decided not to visit Alabama. "Coach Bryant was persuasive. But when it came down to it, I couldn't see myself as the first black quarterback at Alabama. Maybe I was a little scared. I don't know. But I decided not to visit so I wouldn't fall under the powers of persuasion of Coach Bryant."

A few years before Coach Bryant had shot straight with Condredge Holloway who was from Huntsville, Alabama. "Coach Bryant said he wanted me at Alabama but the time wasn't right for a black quarterback yet," Holloway remembered years later.

Although Bryant had assured Jimmy that things had changed in five years, Jimmy was not persuaded. Indeed, Alabama did not have a black quarterback to start until Walter Lewis in 1981. But the words of Coach Bryant to Jimmy were hauntingly accurate and prophetic when he told him, "We want you to come and be our quarterback. I believe we can win the conference title a couple of times during your career and a national championship." Alabama won the conference championships and national championships in 1978 and 1979 during Jimmy's career but without him. Jimmy was another quarterback who just said "No" to Alabama.

North Carolina, Clemson, Ohio State, Notre Dame, Kansas, and Tennessee were the schools that Jimmy chose to visit. All the others would have to look elsewhere for a quarterback. Coaches at these six schools indicated to Jimmy that there would be no problem with him pursuing baseball as well as football. "Yeah, they all said I could. Clemson said I could do anything I wanted. They wanted me bad. They had recruited Sylva-Webster players before. Clemson was the closest school and that would be a factor in my final decision. I wanted my parents and other family to be able to see me play." Kansas turned out to be too far away.

Honors rolled in from throughout the nation. *Scholastic Magazine* said Jimmy was "a quarterback you can build a team around." He was named to the Orlando *Sentinel*'s 56th Annual All-Southern team.

The Jimmy Streater Story

The all-star honors only added to the interest of the other five schools he had selected. Although it was the state school, North Carolina was eliminated by Jimmy when he got the feeling that they may have wanted him more as a receiver than quarterback.

When he visited Notre Dame, "I didn't have a good feeling. They were so much different than what I grew up as. It was Catholic and cold. I was Baptist and from the warmer South. I saw a river frozen over on my visit and I just started to shiver."

So, the top three finishers came down to Ohio State, Clemson, and Tennessee. Tennessee was working him hard. Coach Bill Battle, who had been head coach since 1970, told his assistants Dal Shealy, Fred Malone, and Wayne Stiles that he wanted Streater. The heat was on. There had been constant criticism about Tennessee's recruiting.

Tennessee had finished the season with seven wins and five losses. (They played twelve games because the game with Hawaii didn't count against the eleven game schedule limit.) There had been no bowl game. And what was worse, UT had lost for the fifth straight time to it's most dreaded rival—Alabama—by a score of 30 to 7.

Condredge Holloway, who was believed by many to have been Battle's best recruit to date, was enlisted to help recruit another black quarterback—Jimmy Streater—to the Volunteers. "Condredge had already paved the way for a black quarterback to start at Tennessee. He was positive in what he said about the Vols," Jimmy said.

"Condredge came to Sylva and visited me and my family. On my trip to the University of Tennessee, Condredge was the one who showed me around."

When Jimmy visited Ohio State he again found it cold. In addition, he was not overly impressed with Coach Woody Hayes. "He appeared more like a drill sergeant. And their offense was famous for the phrase 'three yards and a cloud of dust.' I was more interested in a wide open offense."

So, it came down to Tennessee and Clemson.

Chris Cawood

THERE WERE TWO MAJOR sports stories in different places of the Knoxville *News Sentinel* on Sunday morning, December 28, 1975. They both would be important to Jimmy Streater, but he probably looked a lot closer at one than the other.

The renowned sports editor of the paper, Tom Siler, at the top of the sports section, wrote in his column that 1976 would, in effect, be the make or break year for Bill Battle as head football coach.

"Tennessee fans are apprehensive about the football future. They have a right to be. The Vols have lost prestige in recent years.

"The offense was sporadic at best last year. The defense was fair. The won-lost record was 7-5-0, but those conquests of Colorado State, Utah, and Hawaii fooled nobody. Maybe the one big plus of 1975 was that the Vol partisans, shelling out $8 per seat, got a bellyful of 'sweetheart' football. Wonder if AD Bob Woodruff got the message?

"Tennessee's decline began with recruiting four or five years ago.

"The staff recruited one quarterback of rare talent in five years, one Condredge Holloway."

Siler knew the heat was on from alumni and continued by saying:

"YEAR OF DECISION: Thus, the recruiting must be revamped, the talent must be upgraded, the offense and defense must move up to old Tennessee standards.

"This is the year of decision for Battle. Many of the more sensitive fans deplore such a system. So do I. I would be the first to admit that college football is much too big, much too important in the lives of alumni, much too important to school officials who use it for their own prestige. College football will be cut back, but the time has not come yet.

"But in the current system the stakes are high. The

67

stadium must be filled. The coach who jumps into this whirlpool accepts the terms. Battle, like all the others, balances a high pressure job with a dubious future against the limelight, high salary, TV and glamor. All in all, bigtime football is an ego trip and the coach pays an awful price for what he gets. But that's the system. . . .

"The time has come to put some points on the board . . . until then there is nothing to shout about."

With that kind of pressure on Coach Battle, rival recruiters could make it known to prospective recruits that Battle might not be at Tennessee very much longer. "Don't take a chance," they would whisper. "Avoid Tennessee. Go with us."

What drew Jimmy Streater's attention was not the column on Coach Battle but the listing of the *Parade* All-America High School Football Team that was included as a supplement to the Knoxville *News Sentinel*.

Being a *Parade* All-American was the highest honor in American high school football. This was the magazine's thirteenth year to make the selection.

When Jimmy saw the magazine, his finger started down the list of 50 high school players from 24 states who had made the team. His finger didn't stop until it got to the bottom of the page. His was the last name listed and he was chosen under the category of receivers. It didn't make any difference though. It did not douse the fire of his joy. Just to be there was enough.

It was a present and honor that came three days after Christmas. Coach Howell had told him before Christmas that he thought he was going to make the team, but he couldn't believe it until he saw it in black and white.

Others chosen the same day included Mark Malone, Curtis Dickey, Vagas Ferguson, Matt Suhey, Anthony Munoz, Scott Brantley, and Lance Taylor. Some of these, he imagined, he might play against in college.

Jimmy did not know that Coach Battle was in trouble at Tennessee when he was being recruited. "He was very nice. I liked him. My family liked him. He seemed to be honest with me. He said I could play baseball and football at Tennessee. I would get my shot at quarterback."

CLEMSON AND TENNESSEE WORE different shades of orange. Jimmy had worn orange and black uniforms at Sylva-Webster that were styled after those of Clemson. "I was overwhelmed with the amount of orange there was when I went to a game at Tennessee. It was like floating in a sea of orange."

Clemson was close and players from Sylva-Webster had gone there before. So, when it came time to make a decision, Jimmy talked with his parents and with Coach Howell. It was going to be tough, and he wanted to be sure. Signing day would be in February, and Jimmy wouldn't announce his decision until then.

Tennessee fans had turned their attention away from the downtrodden football program by the first of February, 1976. They were concentrating on an exciting basketball team coached by Ray Mears. The Ernie and Bernie show was in high gear. On the last day of January, the Vols had destroyed an Alabama team coached by C. M. Newton and led by Leon Douglas and T. R. Dunn, 80-74. Both teams came into the game with identical records and tied for the league lead.

Bernard King scored 37 points and pulled down 18 rebounds. Ernie Grunfeld got 20 points and many assists along with John Darden. Tennessee was 14-2 overall and 7-1 in the Southeastern Conference. They were at the top of the ten-team league. Kentucky was uncharacteristically in fifth place.

The fans had been rowdy at Stokely Center. Ice and oranges were thrown onto the floor. Police removed one offender but C. M. Newton wasn't pacified. "The orange throwing is a disgrace. I don't feel like we incited the crowd," he said.

Kentucky was coming to play the Vols on Saturday,

The Jimmy Streater Story

February 7. So, football recruiting did not receive much attention in the local papers. Jimmy Streater cast his lot with Tennessee over Clemson and signed papers on Sunday, February 8, because of the football reputation of the school, the nearness, and his impression of the coaches and followers of the Vols. He could play baseball and football and his family would only have to drive a couple of hours across the mountains to see him play.

The signing drew only four paragraphs in Marvin West's sports wrap-up column the following day that included stories on basketball and baseball.

He wrote: "Jimmy Streater, generally considered the best prep footballer in the state of North Carolina, says he will sign with Tennessee Sunday.

"Jimmy is a quarterback from Sylva, maybe six feet tall and 165 pounds. He was durable enough to run and pass for more than 2000 yards last season. He also can kickoff and run back kicks, play dazzling basketball and hit .500 and pitch and play shortstop in baseball.

"Instead of waving a flag about what he can do, Streater has tried to avoid the spotlight. He said 85 or 90 schools had shown a recruiting interest but 'I don't want it to go to my head.'

"*Scholastic Magazine* referred to Streater as 'a quarterback you can build a team around.' "

Jimmy had earned the designation of outstanding athlete of the year in the Carolinas which was awarded by the Charlotte Athletic Club on a ballot by North and South Carolina sports writers and broadcasters. That was the same honor that Stanley Morgan had earned four years before. He had gone to Tennessee and played tailback.

"Jimmy is the same style athlete as Condredge Holloway," Coach Battle said. "He runs the 100 in 9.8 and is extremely quick. He could play any skill position on a football team, but quarterback is where we want him."

And quarterback for the Tennessee Volunteers was where Jimmy wanted to play.

70

Part Two:

Football
at UT

1976—1979

Bill Dyer's last *DyerGram*

1976

Other things were happening in the country besides football in 1976 when Jimmy Streater arrived in Knoxville at the University of Tennessee with the other freshmen in August. The country had just celebrated its bicentennial. Alex Haley's *Roots: A Saga of an American Family* was being released and would take the country by storm.

Jimmy Carter was running against Gerald Ford for president. Ford had risen to the vice-presidency and then to the presidency without being elected to either. He happened to be in the right place at the right time to be appointed vice president when Spiro Agnew resigned as vice president and then, in 1974, to become president when Richard Nixon resigned from the presidency before facing impeachment.

Jimmy hoped he was in the right place at the right time for Tennessee football.

Other news on the local and national scene in 1976 included Pat Head, the new young coach of Tennessee's women's basketball team, captaining the U. S. women's basketball team to a silver medal in the Montreal Olympics. Big John Tate had won the bronze in the Olympic heavyweight boxing competition.

A deadly outbreak of a virus, later named Legionnaires' disease, hit a Harrisburg, Pennsylvania, convention of the American Legion. Later in the year Patricia Hearst was sentenced to a seven-year jail term for her role in bank robberies with her supposed kidnappers. The Tennessee Valley Authority won approval from the courts to begin

73

limited construction on its Tellico Dam project.

The Sunday paper in Knoxville was the *News-Sentinel* where two great writers, Tom Siler and Marvin West, kept readers informed on sports. Don Whitehead and Carson Brewer wrote columns for the front page of the feature section. And Bill Dyer continued his *DyerGrams* of Tennessee football games which he had been drawing for 40 years.

Afros were in for young black men and leisure suits were a stylish fad in men's clothing.

The three main college head football coaches that Tennessee fans were watching and talking about were Bill Battle at Tennessee, Doug Dickey at Florida, and Johnny Majors at Pittsburgh. Battle was on the hotseat at Tennessee. Dickey was eyed with both hate and respect by different segments in Volunteer land. Some felt he deserted Tennessee and therefore held ill will toward him. Others respected him for what he had done at Tennessee and was now doing at Florida. Johnny Majors was a player-hero from the 1950s at Tennessee and was moving into national prominence at Pittsburgh as the head coach. Already, there were those working to bring him back to Tennessee.

Coach Battle had the unfortunate position of being compared to both Dickey and Majors. Dickey had given Tennessee respect in the conference and many thought Majors was the man to return Tennessee to that prominence.

The National Collegiate Athletic Association was beginning to cut back on the number of coaches allowed on a staff and the number of scholarship players on teams. Scholarships were now limited to 30 per year.

Oklahoma, under Coach Barry Switzer, was the national champion—and also champion in the number of assistant coaches they had on staff. Oklahoma skirted the new rule, which allowed only eight full-time assistants, by signing all of their thirteen assistants to long-term contracts before the rule went into effect.

Tennessee's Battle would have to work with fewer. Dal Shealy and Ray Trail labored on offense while Larry

Jones, Robbie Franklin, and Lon Herzbrun took care of the defense. Fred Malone, George Cafego, Bill Baker and Jon Conlin were other full-time coaches, but before fall, Battle would have to cut one back to part-time to comply with the rules.

Tennessee's schedule for 1976 was: Duke, Texas Christian, Auburn, Clemson, Georgia Tech, Alabama, Florida, Memphis State, Mississippi, Kentucky, and Vanderbilt. Coach Battle couldn't see any "gimmes" on that list.

His recruiting class looked good, but freshmen weren't going to win the big games in the SEC. In this class he had Streater, another highly recruited quarterback in Wilbert Jones, a defensive back from Ohio by the name of Roland James, a running back from McMinn County in Hubert Simpson, and Tim Irwin, a big lineman from Knoxville. Mike Jester, Brad White, Billy Berrian, and Jim Noonan were others who also showed promise.

The varsity already had proven stars in Stanley Morgan, Larry Seivers, and Randy Wallace. But Battle knew more were needed. Joe Hough and Pat Ryan, who had been teammates at the same high school in Oklahoma, were pressuring Wallace for the quarterback position.

COACH BATTLE BELIEVED IN testing the incoming freshmen as to their athletic abilities in five different tasks. "If the NCAA would approve just these five skill tests, it would eliminate a lot of recruiting errors," he said. "With the scholarship limit at 30, schools certainly need to recruit more efficiently." Battle did not advocate the old tryout system. He said college recruiters must discover from games and film whether a prospect hits with authority.

"These tests reveal athletic ability you simply cannot evaluate in most football games," he said.

The tests were: vertical jump (for explosion), an obstacle course (for agility), a stool jump (to measure quick feet), line touches a few feet apart (reaction), and a pair of

880 runs (conditioning and endurance).

Roland James barely edged Streater among all freshmen. They both definitely were athletes.

James was big and fast at 6-4 and 190 pounds with 9.8 speed. Bill Higdon had recruited James from the doorstep of Ohio State. He told him he could play sooner at Tennessee. James would be to the defense what Streater would be to the offense. Their high school records sounded the same.

Higdon said, "Roland was a wingback and cornerback in high school, an outstanding basketball player, and almost a one-man track team. He scored 26 points in the state track meet and the team that won got 29. James would have won the team title by himself if he hadn't had such a sorry day in the long jump." He could have used Jimmy Streater's state record in the long jump.

Roland James would become a useful measuring stick for Jimmy. Roland was bigger but Jimmy knew if he could do some of the things that Roland did, he would improve his own abilities. "Roland helped me a lot. He was a great athlete," Jimmy remembered years later. Jimmy and Roland became roommates that first year at Gibbs Hall and pushed each other. They also consoled each other and helped one another to forget that one was from North Carolina and the other from Ohio. Now they both were Tennesseans and *Volunteers*.

The adjustment to a new home was not easy. This was the first time that Jimmy had stayed any lengthy amount of time away from his home in Sylva. Knoxville was larger and school wasn't in session yet. Time was filled with everything related to football. But when he looked to the east, Jimmy could see the mountains. On the other side were his mother and father, brother Steve, who was going into his senior year at Sylva-Webster, brother Eric, who was twelve now, and little sister Faith, who was five.

THE FOOTBALL TEAM HAD its first scrimmage of

the season on the last Saturday of August, two weeks before the opening game with Duke.

"It was better than I expected," Coach Battle reported. "I liked the effort and the hitting."

The *News-Sentinel*'s Marvin West wrote that, "Wilbert Jones jumped ahead of Jimmy Streater in the freshman quarterback sweepstakes, hitting a TD pass to Bill Berrian and snaking through a scattered defense and outrunning the pursuit for a 46-yard touchdown.

"Streater threw crisply but his targets had no hands. Jimmy did direct a scoring march, capped by a Hubert Simpson dive from the 5, an Olympic-style flight."

Randy Wallace was in the driver's seat to be the starting quarterback and if Pat Ryan or Joe Hough couldn't oust him, it was certain a freshman wasn't going to.

Jimmy couldn't have been pleased to read in the Sunday paper that he was at the fifth-string position at quarterback.

But a story on the inside of the sports section perked him up. Dr. Charles Holland, a statistics expert at the nuclear facilities in Oak Ridge, had rated the top 100 incoming college football freshmen in the nation. Jimmy was in the top ten at number nine. So, while *Parade* magazine had not tried to rank their list of 50 where Jimmy appeared at the bottom of the page, he now was believed to be among the top ten in the nation.

Ahead of him were Curtis Dickey of Texas, Scott Brantley of Florida, Anthony Munoz of Southern Cal, Vagas Ferguson of Notre Dame, and four others. Somebody still thought he was good. If they thought he was among the top ten, he was not going to let them down. It just meant he would have to work harder. Get his mind off of being homesick and concentrate on football—on what he did best. He would run, he would elude, he would dance around defenders, and he would perfect his throwing skills.

WHEN THE PRE-SEASON POLLS came out,

77

Tennessee was ranked 15th by *Sports Illustrated*. Michigan was ranked No. 1 and Alabama No. 2. Johnny Majors' Pittsburgh team came in at No. 10. Of Tennessee's opponents for the season, only Alabama and Florida, at No. 13, were rated in the Top Twenty. In the Associated Press poll Nebraska was first with Michigan second. Alabama was sixth and Pittsburgh No. 9. Battle looked at the ranking in *Sports Illustrated* and shook his head. He knew if the Vols didn't meet or exceed that ranking, his job would be in jeopardy. To make matters worse, the *News Sentinel*'s sports editor, Tom Siler, picked the Vols to finish third in the ten-team conference.

IN THE SECOND SCRIMMAGE, Jimmy improved his performance. He showed he could pass by airing one out to sophomore tight end Bo Arthur for a 60-yard touchdown strike. In the last scrimmage before the Vols played their opening game against Duke, Jimmy showed his versatility. Against a defense that was supposed to look like Duke's, he put on a showy 89-yard run that included what observers described as "Houdini-type" moves. He then threw a touchdown pass to Jim Duvall.

Battle got caught smiling. "I guess I grinned a little on that run," he said. Then he added, "Our Duke defensive team wasn't quite as good as the one we'll see on Saturday."

BATTLE'S WORST FEARS WERE realized with the opening game on September 11, 1976. The crowd was there—82,687—but they were quiet. They had a lot to be quiet about. Assistant police chief Albert Caldwell said, "It was one of the quietest, most peaceful crowds I have ever seen." The crowd got to see the new 10,000-seat upper deck addition to the south end zone which now made the whole horseshoe configured stadium double-decked. The north end zone was still just bleachered, awaiting further expansion. Now, though, it didn't appear that they would need more seats. The Vols lost to Duke 21-18.

Chris Cawood

On the front page of the Knoxville paper the next day was an aerial shot of Neyland Stadium and beneath the photo, a listing of top ten scores. There was little consolation that Alabama had also lost its opener to Ole Miss. What Vol fans noticed was that Johnny Majors' Pittsburgh Panthers had beaten Notre Dame, 31-10. Ugly pranks and words were already beginning to haunt Bill Battle and his assistant coaches.

Battle would later relate that even before the first kickoff fans were on his assistant coaches. "My coaches have gotten harassed. Before the Duke game, which was before we even played, my coaches started to the press box and fans got after them bad while they were going up there. They came back down for halftime and it was worse. We were behind, 14-12, then. They didn't even come back down after the game."

BEFORE THE NEXT VARSITY game the following Saturday, the junior varsity went to Lexington, Kentucky, to face the Wildcats and see how the two freshmen quarterbacks—Jimmy Streater and Wilbert Jones—would react and play under game conditions. Both freshmen got a touchdown. Nate Sumpter got the other one on a one-yard plunge as the Vols won, 21-14.

Jimmy's 54-yard touchdown run was described by Wilbert Jones who was watching from the sidelines. "It was a beauty. Jimmy sprinted out to the right and cut back across the grain. He put some moves on those cats." Jimmy was the leading passer and the second leader in rushing with a total of 68 yards.

FANS PAID LITTLE ATTENTION to junior varsity success, though, unless it carried over to the varsity. Coach Battle had little to celebrate. The Texas Christian Horned Frogs were coming to town, and if the Vols lost this one, he could start packing.

The coach didn't have to start packing—yet. The Vols

won in a shutout, 31-0. Both the defense and offense played well. Veterans like Randy Wallace, Stanley Morgan, Larry Seivers, Andy Spiva, Russ Williams, Kelsey Finch, Bobby Emmons, and Thomas Rowsey, led the way. On defense, though, Tennessee started a talented freshman at safety—Roland James. He recovered a fumble.

When Tennessee pulled far enough ahead, Coach Battle put in the second-string quarterback—Pat Ryan, and then the third-string quarterback—Joe Hough, and then the fourth-string quarterback—Wilbert Jones, and finally for a series, the fifth-string quarterback—Jimmy Streater. Jimmy threw a 17-yarder to Billy Arbo and then ran off tackle himself for a first down. However, on the next play, Jimmy retreated and found no place to run. He was dropped for a 20-yard loss.

Jimmy saw that he had a long way to go. But it was his first varsity appearance and his first stats that would start to accumulate. He had 17 yards passing and nine running. Freshman running back Hubert Simpson had two carries for four yards.

All-American Larry Seivers was moving up the ladder in Tennessee's reception records. He moved up to fourth in the Texas Christian victory with 74—one behind third-ranked Ken DeLong. He already held the record for career receiving yardage—then at 1325.

FOR COACH BATTLE THE problem was that the euphoria of the shutout victory lasted only one week. When the Volunteers went to Birmingham on September 25, 1976, to play Auburn they were soundly beaten, 38 to 28. Johnny Majors' Pitt Panthers, behind the running of Tony Dorsett, kept winning and his name kept popping up in the newspapers amid constant speculation about the coaching job at Tennessee.

A moving van was sent to Coach Battle's house. Exterminators were sent to his office. For Sale signs were put in his yard. Derogatory bumper stickers were stuck to his car and mail box. And this advertisement appeared in the UT student newspaper *The Daily Beacon* under employment: "Position soon for football coach, Southern university, large staff, antique athletic director, also post game show. Send win-loss record to General Neyland. Bill what'sis name need not apply."

Battle finally had had enough from the arm-chair critics and "Gay Street quarterbacks" as he termed them. He called a news conference on Thursday—the first he had ever called—and blasted away. Representatives from 70 news organizations attended.

Battle had come to Tennessee in 1966 as an assistant coach and been elevated to head coach in 1970 at the time of Doug Dickey's departure. "There have been some excellent years when we won 10 or 11 games, some decent years when we won eight or nine games, and a couple of catastrophes when we have won seven games. . . . We have been to nine bowl games. . . .

"I have never reacted much to the garbage-dump thinking that has been going around. . . . I am tired of standing and being quiet and taking it. I am tired of the negative people who call themselves supporters of Tennessee. I am tired of the Gay Street quarterbacks. If they knew as much about their business as they think they know about mine, they would be on Wall Street instead of Gay Street. . . .

"The easy way out at this point and probably a year ago and two years ago would be to quit. I happen to enjoy coaching football. I happen to believe in my staff and my team. . . . I also happen to be too stubborn or either too ignorant to quit. . . .

"If Tennessee needs a new head coach, get one. But don't tear down the whole Athletic Department while you're trying to do it. . . .

"I would like for the Tennessee people who are supporters of Tennessee, the real supporters, the positive ones, to stand up and be counted. I am not going to quit. I am going to do the best I can. If that is good enough, fine. If that is not good enough, that is fine too."

It was true that Tennessee had been to nine bowl games during Battle's ten years. The only year they hadn't been was 1975. It was also true that only twice during his ten years as an assistant or head coach the Vols had won as few as seven games per season. However, the old saying of "What have you done for me lately?" was also true. It was 1974 and 1975 when the seven-win seasons came. Volunteer fans wanted to return to the top of the Southeastern Conference. They saw the drop-off as permanent and not a temporary aberration.

The junior varsity would have a game against Lees-McRae at Banner Elk, North Carolina, on Friday before Clemson came to town on Saturday.

Junior Varsity coach Robbie Franklin was becoming impressed with freshman Tim Irwin who stood 6-7 and weighed 240. Battle noticed too. "I like his attitude. When we recruited Tim, we kept hearing he was a hard worker. Well, this past summer he spent many hours building his strength. He was really motivated."

Jimmy Streater, however, would still be playing behind Wilbert Jones on the JV offense.

On a rainy, windy afternoon the JVs lost to Lees-McRae, 13-0. Jimmy hit an early pass to Billy Berrian but the threat was snuffed out. Wilbert Jones led the team in rushing with 92 yards. John Chavis and Steve Hatfield were standouts for the Tennessee defense.

The varsity rallied around their beleaguered coach and put away Clemson by two, 21-19.

The following week the Vols improved their record to 3 and 2 with a 42 to 7 victory over Georgia Tech at Atlanta.

However, the third Saturday of October was approaching and that meant the annual rivalry with Alabama. If Battle could coach the Volunteers past the Crimson Tide of his alma mater, he might be able to preserve his job for another year. Tennessee hadn't beaten Alabama since

Bobby Scott quarterbacked the Vols to a 24 to 0 victory in 1970. If they lost this year, it would be the longest string of losses to Alabama since the dark ages of 1905 to 1913 when the Vols failed to score against Alabama in seven consecutive games. It was make or break. Do or die.

In national sports news, the World Series was underway. Cincinnati was going for two championships in a row against the New York Yankees. Jimmy Streater could sit back, watch the television, and wonder where he would have been in the Cincinnati organization if he had taken their offer out of high school. Would he have been fielding with Pete Rose, Joe Morgan, and Johnny Bench? That $40,000 signing bonus looked good now. Baseball couldn't be as difficult as college football. Here the linemen were bigger and faster than in high school. Reading defenses and learning all the plays was tough.

The Reds rolled to a 5 to 1 opening game win and went on to sweep the Yankees for their second championship. Jimmy went back to football practice.

The Vols lost to Alabama, 20-13, on Saturday, October 16, in Knoxville. Despite heroic efforts by Frank Foxx, Greg Jones, and kicker Jimmy Gaylor, the Vols went down, and so did the prospects of Coach Battle. Now, it was just a matter of finishing out the season.

Doug Dickey brought his Florida team to Knoxville the following Saturday and also scored 20 while holding the Vols to 18. That proved what the critics had been saying: "Battle can't or won't beat his alma mater, Alabama, and can't beat his mentor, Doug Dickey." The statement wasn't true, of course, because Battle's teams had won over Alabama in 1970 and over Florida in 1970 and 1971. But truth didn't really matter to the critics because they could always say that the victories were with "Dickey's recruits" who remained when he left after the 1969 season.

THE MEASUREMENT OF HOW far the football program had fallen was the amount of ink that was given in the newspaper to basketball the week after the Alabama defeat—and women's basketball at that!

Pat Head, Tennessee's young coach, was featured. She had played on the Olympic team that had taken the silver medal. The Lady Vols first regular season game would be against Kentucky. Pat had recruited a fellow player from the Olympic team to come to UT in Trish Roberts. Roberts and freshman Holly Warlick would provide a strong base upon which to build a team.

"This past summer was great for me," the coach said. "I had always wanted to play international basketball and to make the Olympic team. I felt it would benefit me as player and coach.

"Yet, right now I have no desire to get back on the floor as a player. I'm really enjoying coaching." Pat Head was just two years out of UT Martin and ready to start building a career at Tennessee

TENNESSEE HAD AN OPEN date on the last Saturday of October, so the Junior Varsity played Vanderbilt at Neyland Stadium. JV Coach Robbie Franklin decided to get his two freshmen quarterbacks—Wilbert Jones and Jimmy Streater—into the game at the same time. This he did by putting Jimmy at wide receiver. The combination proved explosive. The junior varsity Vols won, 38-6. Jimmy had scoring runs of 42 and 36 yards off deep reverses while Jones streaked 84 yards for another.

Wide receiver was not the position that Jimmy wanted to play. He had turned down several colleges that had mentioned that as a possibility. But on this Saturday, he gave it a shot and enjoyed it. He hoped, though, that this wouldn't be a permanent change.

IT WAS ALMOST AS if artist Bill Dyer chose the open date in Tennessee's football schedule to die. The beloved artist and cartoonist for the Knoxville *News-Sentinel* *DyerGrammed* his last game the week before.

Dyer was an institution at the newspaper and had drawn the weekly football summary of scores and plays for over 40 years. East Tennessee fans always looked forward to following the flow of action in Saturday's game by turning to the *DyerGram* in the Sunday sports section of the *News-Sentinel*.

Dyer played high school football in Johnson City and then in college at Washington and Lee. He joined the newspaper in 1935 and spent the next forty years entertaining people with his great talent. He also taught cartooning classes at UT and served as a football official.

JIMMY STREATER WAS KEPT at wide receiver in the following week's practice after his success in the junior varsity game. A reporter wrote, "Jimmy is pleased with the opportunity to help the varsity. He is disappointed with his progress as a quarterback."

ON SATURDAY, NOVEMBER 6, Tennessee defeated Memphis State at Memphis, 21-14, to even its record at four wins and four losses for the season. In the following Tuesday's edition of the *News-Sentinel* on the front page of the sport's section just above Tom Siler's column was a photo of Johnny Majors next to the UPI and AP football polls for the week. Pitt had moved to the top of both polls with a 9 and 0 record.

Siler's column was headlined, " 'Ara Come Back' Buttons Amidst Irish Followers." Notre Dame had fallen to 18th in the AP poll with a 6 and 2 record. Dan Devine was under pressure. But the hint was implicit and "Johnny Come Home" buttons would soon be outwardly adorning the coats of many Volunteer fans.

ONE OF THE FEW bright spots of the otherwise dismal season was the continued success of wide receiver Larry Seivers of nearby Clinton, Tennessee. Seivers had been named All-American in 1975 and would receive the same honor in 1976.

He caught his first pass for Tennessee at the Auburn game in 1974. Condredge Holloway threw it. He would go on to catch 116 more and finish his career with 1924 receiving yards and eight touchdowns. He was Tennessee's top receiver of all time and would remain so until edged out by Tim McGee in 1985. He and Stanley Morgan would go on to play in the Hula Bowl and Japan Bowl.

TENNESSEE BEAT MISSISSIPPI AT Knoxville on the next Saturday, 32-6, to edge to a 5 and 4 record.

But on Saturday, November 20, Kentucky shut out the Vols 7 to 0 to drive the final nail into the coffin of Bill Battle's career.

Although athletic director Bob Woodruff told the press there would be nothing to say on Battle's future before the season-ending game with Vanderbilt, columnist Tom Siler wrote in Sunday's paper following the Kentucky game that "Bob Woodruff has a problem."

Kentucky's defeat of the Vols was the first by the Wildcats since 1964. Tennessee's won-loss record was the worst since 1964—Doug Dickey's first year as head coach.

"If you want the key statistic," of the Kentucky game, Siler wrote, "it's this. Craig Colquitt was called upon to punt 14 times. That translates into impotence of the offensive platoon." Kentucky signed after the game to go to the Peach Bowl. Tennessee would finish at Vanderbilt where the Commodores wanted to make it two in a row over the Vols.

BUT ON MONDAY, NOVEMBER 22—the thirteenth anniversary of John Kennedy's assassination—Coach Bill Battle made it official. "Bill Battle has quit. Tennessee is now free to open negotiations with John Majors," wrote Marvin West in the *News-Sentinel*.

John Majors still had a final season game with Penn State. "I have not been contacted by the University of Tennessee," Majors said. "I simply am not interested in discussing any situation until the regular season is concluded. My entire effort this week will be devoted to the Pitt-Penn State game." When told there was a report that his brother Joe was negotiating for him, Majors said, "Nobody speaks for John Majors except John Majors."

Majors had been at Pitt for four years. The Panthers went 6-5-1 his first year; 7-4 in his second; 8-4 in his third; and were 10-0 and Number One in the nation when Battle resigned at Tennessee.

Majors was a tailback at Tennessee in the mid-1950s. The Vols were 4-6 his sophomore season; 6-3-1 as a junior; and 10-0 in the regular season of 1956. The Vols finished runner-up to Oklahoma for the national championship in both polls in 1956. At that time the polls were taken before any bowl games. Tennessee lost to Baylor 13-7 in the Sugar Bowl. Majors also finished runner-up in the Heisman Trophy balloting.

Before Pitt, Majors was head coach at Iowa State and amassed a 24-30-1 record, which was thought to be good. He had also served as assistant coach at Arkansas, Mississippi State, and Tennessee.

COACH BATTLE RETURNED TO the practice field to prepare for Vanderbilt. This game would decide if he would go out with a winning or losing season. He closed the practice to the press and all spectators. He said he wanted to be alone with his players and coaches for this last week. Then when Saturday came, the Vols barely beat back the Commodores by a score of 13 to 10.

Battle's coaching career at Tennessee was over. In actuality, his entire coaching career was over. He never returned to the sidelines for any college. He went on to become a wealthy businessman who oversaw licensing of college and NASCAR sports-related items through his company in Atlanta. There, he had his family near him, didn't have to worry about disgruntled fans writing letters to local newspapers, face moving vans sent to his home, or watch his car for demeaning bumper stickers.

What if Battle had beaten Alabama more often?

"I don't think there is any question about it. Wherever you are, you have to beat your biggest rival in a certain amount of time or you aren't going to be around. If I lose six, or Johnny loses seven in a row, or if Tennessee beats Alabama seven times in a row, I promise you, they aren't going to have the same coach there. That's life in the big city," Battle reflected years later.

Interestingly enough, Battle finished his career with 59 wins at Tennessee for a winning percentage of 71.1. His predecessor, Doug Dickey, finished with a winning percentage of 70.8. And the coach who followed Battle, John Majors, would finish with a winning percentage of 62.4.

ON DECEMBER 3, 1976, the front page headline of the Knoxville *News-Sentinel* shouted: "It's All but Official: Majors Coming."

Only the details had to be worked out. He had resigned at Pittsburgh. His contract at Tennessee was reported to be a five-year deal that would pay him $42,000 per year plus television revenue and other benefits that would send the entire package to over $60,000. This was thought to be a tremendous amount of money in 1976. Battle's contract ($48,000) for the following year would be bought out.

JIMMY STREATER SAT IN his dorm room and read the news. What now? He was recruited by Coach Battle. He liked Coach Battle. In 1976, Jimmy was the fifth-string quarterback. He had gotten into the huddle of the varsity for a total of eight plays during the whole season. He had seven yards rushing and seventeen passing—hardly impressive statistics. Now a new coach who didn't know him and whom he didn't know.

Where would Jimmy Streater fit into the plans of Johnny Majors?

1977

New head coach Johnny Majors made it a point to talk with each player on the football squad in January 1977. They needed reassurance, and he didn't need a bunch of players abandoning ship. He had come in too late to do much with the latest recruiting class. Some who had committed to Coach Battle came and some turned to other schools.

"Jimmy, I think you have talent at quarterback. You need to push yourself. You were fifth-string at the end of last season. Spring practice will be a telling time where you can prove yourself and be in the running for some playing time in the fall," Coach Majors told him.

Jimmy sat in the office wide-eyed. His jaw must have dropped.

"What's wrong, Jimmy?"

"Well, Coach Majors, I was told I could play baseball in the spring when I was recruited. I wanted to keep sharp there. Cincinnati offered me a signing bonus out of high school."

Coach Majors shook his head. "I didn't recruit you, Jimmy. I'd like to have you play on our football team though. You have talent. But you have to prove yourself to me in the spring. Understand?"

"Yes, coach."

THE ONLY BASEBALL JIMMY would experience in the spring of 1977 would be to hear about his brother Stevie at Sylva-Webster pitching 26 victories out of 28 games—two in the same day at the state tournament. Stevie went on to be named a high school All-American in baseball. But, he, too, was told by his mother to get a college education. While all the turmoil was surrounding the Tennessee football program, Stevie signed to play football with the University of North Carolina as a defensive back and punter. One of his teammates would be Lawrence Taylor.

WHEN SPRING PRACTICE OPENED in April, Jimmy had moved up one position thanks to Randy Wallace having finished his career. With "Waldo," as Wallace was known to his teammates, leaving, Jimmy saw an opportunity. He would have to beat out senior Pat Ryan, junior Joe Hough, and fellow-sophomore-to-be Wilbert Jones.

PERSEVERANCE was the big word for it, but Jimmy just knew it by the term "sticking to it." In high school he didn't get his shot at quarterback until an injury forced the regular quarterback out. When he got his chance there, he took it. Now would be no different. Indeed, he would take the advice of now kicking coach George Cafego, "If you ever get your chance, take advantage of it. Be ready to play when you're called on. Take advantage and do your best."

By the time of the first spring scrimmage, Jimmy found he had another competitor in David Rudder. It seemed as though everybody wanted to be quarterback.

Coach Majors had tapped Bobby Roper to be defensive coordinator and Joe Avezanno for the offense. Pat Ryan was the first-string quarterback until someone unseated him. He took the first team 70 yards on the second possession for a TD in the scrimmage. David Rudder scored two touchdowns. Streater had runs of 10 and 18 yards and a 12-yard pass to Kyle Aguillard. Jimmy also ran for a two-point conversion.

But the best Majors could say was, "Our quarterbacks were inconsistent and we really need help at receiver."

Jimmy's chance to move up when the coaches moved Wilbert Jones to receiver for some work was set back by a nagging ankle injury. It seemed as though Jimmy's legs were as fragile as those of a Thoroughbred race horse. He was always getting nicked up.

Majors opened a major scrimmage to the public and 4000 came to watch. Both Ryan and Jimmy missed the scrimmage with injuries. Joe Hough and David Rudder did most of the quarterbacking.

But by the day of the spring Orange and White game, Jimmy had recovered enough to have practiced for the preceding week. He also had read the newspaper reports about how well some of the other quarterback prospects were doing. He had incentive.

Marvin West in the *News-Sentinel* had written that, "Joe Hough . . . as in tough . . . has jumped another giant step closer to No. 1 quarterback at Tennessee." Coach Majors told the paper that, "The two older guys (Hough and Ryan) have been clearly ahead."

The Orange and White game would go a long way toward deciding the depth-chart position for all players going into fall practice.

It turned out that the game was an exercise in ineptness. Both the Orange and White fumbled five times. Ryan hit Jeff Moore on a long pass. Then Ryan ran in for the TD himself.

On defense Jim Noonan and Johnny Chavis led their respective teams in getting in the way of the opposing offense.

Quarterbacks fell like ripe apples from a tree. First, Joe Hough was hurt, necessitating Jimmy changing sides and shirts. Ryan went down in the fourth quarter, and Jimmy went back to the Whites. He was injured on the next play. Rudder missed the game because of an ankle injury. The Whites won, 14-0.

Despite all the confusion and injuries, Coach Majors said, "Streater showed poise. I'm so glad Jimmy got to practice the last week. He may have gained a lot from the game."

There would still be a five quarterback race in the fall

with Ryan, Hough, Jones, Rudder, and Streater all trying for the top job.

THE SCHEDULE FOR 1977, Johnny Majors first year at head coach, appeared daunting. There would be seven games beginning Saturday, September 10, without an open date. Then after one free Saturday, the Vols would finish with four games in November. There would be six conference foes and five non-conference games that included California, Boston College, Oregon State, Georgia Tech, and Memphis State. The six SEC opponents would be traditional rivals Auburn, Alabama, Kentucky, and Vanderbilt, with two floaters in Florida and Mississippi.

Majors knew he was without an experienced quarterback and the top receiver of all time, Larry Seivers, had used up all of his eligibility.

As fall practice opened, Joe Hough was running Number 1 at quarterback with Pat Ryan hot on his heels. After a couple of practices, Jimmy moved up to third. "Jimmy Streater looks alive in the QB scramble. David Rudder is listed No. 4," Marvin West wrote late in August.

In a big scrimmage just two weeks before the opening game, Jimmy made his move. He directed two scoring drives and had another one that was called back because of an official's whistle that was blown prematurely. He ran for another TD on his own. Coach Majors wouldn't comment on individual performances, but other observers on the field were amazed.

They compared Jimmy's touchdown run of 45 yards to Condredge Holloway. He had started right on a called pass play, but when he found all the receivers covered, he broke back the opposite direction and ran to the end zone untouched. Also helping Jimmy in the coaches' minds was the inept play of those ahead of him. Hough was unable to lead the team down the field. Ryan had one TD drive but also was intercepted.

After reviewing the scrimmage over the weekend,

Jimmy was moved to first-string quarterback on Monday. Majors figured that with the lack of quality receivers and a questionable offensive line, he needed someone at quarterback who could scramble out of trouble and create something on his own.

The depth was so lacking on both offense and defense that for the second year in a row, a freshman was put at first team safety. Roland James, Jimmy's roommate, had played that position in 1976 but was being moved to cornerback. Val Barksdale, a rangy 6-2 kid from just down the road at Harriman, was getting the look. Barksdale was mature beyond his years. He had been a three-year starter in high school, a standout in basketball, a trombonist in the concert band, and a preacher for his church.

Other freshmen making a move included Reggie Harper at tight end, Clark Duncan and Junior Reid, both at cornerback. Jeff Olszewski was the leader among freshmen quarterbacks.

On Tuesday the Vols went at each other again. Jimmy lived up to his Saturday's performance by leading three touchdown drives of 50, 75, and 70 yards. On one play he ran for 30 yards down to the 5-yard-line and then flipped the ball to a trailing Billy Arbo.

"Purty, purty! That was very purty," Coach Majors yelled along the sidelines.

Reggie Harper was the recipient of a 48-yard toss-and-run by Jimmy that helped move Harper farther up in the race for the tight end position.

Coach Majors still wasn't ready to install Jimmy as his starting quarterback even with just ten days until the first game. "Jimmy's showed us some nice work in the past few days, but I'm not going to say he'll start against California. But if he keeps improving, well . . . ."

The practices were getting spirited. In one practice noseman Johnny Chavis, a walk-on from South Carolina, who stood 5-10, and weighed 220, squared off with guard Bill Marren, 6-4, 240. "That was a good day for me," Chavis remembered years later. Coach Majors was looking for players who had a fire in their bellies.

The last scrimmage before the first game did nothing to instill confidence in Coach Majors. There were more mistakes and injuries than the coach could tolerate. He delivered a blistering half-time message. Streater was off his previous performances. Roland James limped off with a knee injury. Jimmy Gaylor missed a 29-yard field goal attempt. The offensive line was as porous as a sieve.

"Just think. As bad as we looked, we have to play on this field in public in one week," Majors said.

AS THE OPENING GAME approached, there was other news in the sports world of interest to Tennessee sports fans. Johnson City Science Hill High graduate Steve Spurrier was back in Florida, having signed to play backup quarterback with the Miami Dolphins. He had been released by the Denver Broncos the preceding week.

David Pearson won the Southern 500 at Darlington, South Carolina, in a Mercury.

At the University of Arkansas, new head coach Lou Holtz was complaining as much as Johnny Majors was at Tennessee. He said some of his players were so bad, "It would have been easier for them to have paid $8 at the gate and got in for the games. We don't have a quarterback problem that switching to the single wing wouldn't cure."

On the political scene, Governor Ray Blanton said he had mixed emotions about the prospects of a proposed 1982 Energy Expo in Knoxville that had been promoted by Jake Butcher for the past two and a half years.

THERE WAS NO WAY to put off the game with California. So the Vols steeled themselves for the school's first game ever with the visitors. Roland James' knee was still day-to-day, so there was the possibility that Tennessee would start two freshmen in the secondary—Val Barksdale at safety and either Clark Duncan or Junior Reid for James.

For Coach Majors, the National Championship ring on his finger from Pitt would mean little when the Vols opened on Saturday. He was 42-years-old, had been to the top of the mountain, and was ready to make the climb again.

The Vol Navy and a total of 84,421 fans showed up for the night opening game. It was a sell out at $9 each per ticket. This game would produce the richest gate in Neyland Stadium history. The Tennessee Walking Horse, Sundance Superstar, ridden by Bill Mullins of Knoxville, stumbled and fell in the north end zone on its circuit of the field—perhaps a bad omen for the Vols.

But the crowd's enthusiasm could not be dampened. The 84,000 rose to their feet as one when the band formed a giant T for the Vols to run through from the east side line to their places on the west side. High above in a press box booth, John Ward and Bill Anderson were beginning their tenth season of broadcasting the games on the radio.

Jimmy Streater would start his first game for UT at quarterback. He had a quarterback's number—6—and thought he was ready. He was nervous, anxious, excited and every other emotion that could be tight-wired into his slender frame. He watched the kickoff sail to returner Gary Moore who almost broke the return all the way. Jimmy snapped the strap to his helmet and ran onto the field. Somewhere in the south end zone sat his high school assistant coach Boyce Deitz.

Someone on the offensive line jumped early. The penalty set the Vols back five, but Jimmy responded with a 15-yard scramble for a first down. Craig Colquitt booted a punt down to the Cal one-yard-line when the drive bogged down. For the remainder of the first quarter it was a feeling out and defensive struggle between the Golden Bears and Vols. On one drive, the Vols stopped Cal at the Vols' one-yard-line. Lyonel Stewart, Greg Jones, Dennis Wolfe, and Val Barksdale made key hits in slowing the drive. Pert Jenkins and Jesse Turnbow put the final lick on ball carrier Oliver Hillmon.

The Jimmy Streater Story

Star UT linebacker Craig Puki was helped off the field in the first quarter with a knee injury and never was able to return to the playing field during the game.

Cal scored first in the second quarter with a 42-yard field goal.

The Vols were intercepted on a deflected pass on their next possession. The Golden Bears' try for another field goal failed, and UT took over on the twenty.

After a first down try that went nowhere, Jimmy came to the line for second and ten. The call was to be an option to the left with Jimmy pitching to fullback Bobby Emmons. But when Jimmy slid down the line, Cal overplayed the pitch and invited the wiry sophomore to run off tackle and take a hit from a mean linebacker.

However, no one was able to touch the shifting legs of Jimmy as he darted through the line and cut back to the outside for an escort down field by Emmons and wingback Jerome Morgan. Split end Ken Sanderson aided in the blocking brigade. Jimmy didn't stop running for eighty yards. His heart pounded. The roar of the crowd vibrated through his helmet to a deafening pitch. It was his first Tennessee touchdown. It was the team's first touchdown under Coach Johnny Majors. Nobody could take that away.

Coach Deitz, high in the stands, jumped to his feet when he saw Jimmy slide through the line. He had seen it so many times in high school at Sylva-Webster that he knew they would never catch the sprinter. He pounded the air with his fists in time with Jimmy clipping off five yards after five yards. When the run ended with the touchdown, Coach Deitz turned to an unknown Vol fan next to him, punched his side, and shouted, "I coached him! I coached him!" The fan gave the coach a wary look and turned away.

"It was like that was my son out there who had just scored," Deitz said.

John Chavis had seen the Streater moves in practice from the viewpoint of a defensive tackle. "If Jimmy didn't want you to touch him, you couldn't lay a hand on him. He just made life miserable for linemen or linebackers who chased him around to make plays. He seemed to enjoy doing that. It was something he was doggone good at." This time Chavis got to watch Jimmy do it to California.

The 80-yard TD run was the fourth longest scoring run in UT history and the longest ever by a Vol quarterback.

The euphoria was short-lived as California came back and converted a fumble into a touchdown to take a 10-7 lead.

On the kickoff, Jerome Morgan returned it 34 yards for UT. Jimmy, still feeling it from his 80-yard run, faked a pass and then scampered another 38 yards through the Cal defense to the Golden Bears' 28-yard line. The drive stalled after a sack set Tennessee back. Jimmy was able to throw to freshman Reggie Harper to set up a Jimmy Gaylor 23-yard field goal. At the half it was, 10-10.

The pace of the game and the energy expended was unbelievable to Jimmy. In the locker room at halftime, he became dizzy and so weak he had to lie down. He began to throw up uncontrollably. When the team went back out for the second half, the trainers worked trying to get Jimmy re-hydrated with liquids.

Pat Ryan would have to start the second half if Jimmy wasn't ready. But California got the ball first and scored on a 58-yard pass. Ryan went in and hit a couple of 13-yard passes to Billy Arbo but lost a fumble that resulted in a field goal by Cal. Under Ryan's direction the Vols drove down field eighty yards in ten plays on the next possession for a touchdown by Kelsey Finch.

Roland James was sidelined with an injury, forcing freshman Junior Reid to cover punts. He fumbled one when the Vols had held Cal. From the Vols' 14, Cal quickly drove in for a clinching TD, making it 27-17.

Jimmy came back in for one play but fumbled. Ryan finished out the game for the Vols as they were forced to pass on practically every play. The opener was lost, 27-17.

Despite playing just one play in the second half, Jimmy had led the team in rushing with 150 yards on 14 carries. He also had passed for 25 yards. He had directed the drives for ten of the Vols seventeen points.

"Streater did some nice things. So did Pat Ryan. There were times when Ryan needed more help," Majors said. "We just gave it away with fumbles."

"Jimmy is one of the few quarterbacks in this league who can make something happen. And he didn't play as well as he will in games ahead," offensive coordinator Joe Avezzano said.

Coach Mike White of California also had some nice things to say about Streater. "I didn't know if he was injured or what. I was glad when I didn't see him out there. He totally disarmed us. Streater's gonna be great. He kept us completely off-balance when he was in there. We never knew what he was going to try next.

"Streater runs well and Ryan throws great. They've obviously got to decide what they want to do, run or throw."

Cal assistant Fred Malone, who had been a Vol assistant in 1976, was given a game ball by coach White. "Fred was a definite edge for us. He knew Tennessee's personnel. He knew their qualities."

Jimmy was pleased with his first half effort but wondered about what happened to him. Was he too frail to play college ball? What was this mysterious dizziness, weakness, and throwing up? Would he be able in the near future to put two halves of football together? When would the illness strike again?

ONCE THE SEASON STARTED there was little time to think about anything but the next game. Sunday was spent resting and recovering from Saturday's game, and when Monday came, it was time to start getting ready for the next opponent. This time it would be Boston College.

It seemed like a game of give-away more than football when the game was over. Boston College had turned it over eight times on fumbles and interceptions while the Vols had turned it over four times.

98

Coach Majors came out of the dressing room after the game clutching the game ball to him, representative of his first victory as a coach at UT.

"I guess that means I've got the best hands in the house," he said. "Wasn't that a work of art, a thing of beauty? But let me tell you . . . a win is a win is a win."

Jimmy had started his second game, but when he struggled, Pat Ryan came in. Jimmy had not been able to lock up sole possession of the quarterback position.

The good things included a seven-play, 64-yard touchdown drive he directed. He had a nice 16-yard pass to John Murphy, and Kelsey Finch had finished it off with a 35-yard TD run.

Later Jimmy was intercepted on one possession, fumbled on another, and was sacked on another. He didn't get sick at halftime, and found the strength to direct a fourth quarter touchdown drive that ended with a tough throw to Billy Arbo.

Tearaway jerseys were a popular item with running backs, receivers, and quarterbacks. Jimmy changed between plays one time while the twenty-five second clock was clicking down.

"We prepare for the tearaway jersey," Jimmy told a reporter. "We're ready to change in a hurry. I'd a done it quicker but it got caught on my helmet."

Val Barksdale, Roland James, Jimmy Noonan, and Lyonel Stewart were defensive standouts.

The coaches around the SEC, which included Bear Bryant at Alabama, Doug Dickey at Florida, Vince Dooley at Georgia, Fran Curci at Kentucky, Fred Pancoast at Vanderbilt, Charley McClendon at LSU, Ken Cooper at Ole Miss, and Doug Barfield at Auburn, were keeping an eye on the Vols and quarterback Streater—especially Barfield since Auburn would be coming to Knoxville next.

The 24-18 victory over the Boston College Eagles was a good win to start with, but those Eagles were nothing like the War Eagle battle cry of Auburn. But Streater, the former Golden Eagle, knew that all birds were relative.

DAL SHEALY WAS AN assistant at UT in 1976 but
went to Auburn with the hiring of Majors at UT. For the
UT versus Auburn game of 1977, Shealy was on the victori-
ous side as the Tigers snatched a 14 to 12 win from the Vols.
He was the second former Vol assistant—Cal's Fred Malone
being the other—to help pin a loss on their former team in
a period of three weeks.

It seemed like everything went wrong, and when it
came down to the final play, time wasn't on Tennessee's side.

The Vols had a chance to win with a 36-yard field
goal attempt on third down. They had no time-out left.
Coach Majors said he could have asked Streater to throw the
ball away on third down but it was risky to ask that of a
sophomore. It could be intercepted or completed with no
time left. Instead, the ball was snapped to Arbo who was
holding for Jimmy Gaylor's attempt, and Gaylor missed.

"The game is 60 minutes long—not 14 seconds," Arbo
said in the dressing room, defending his kicker. "The blame
doesn't belong on Gaylor."

Streater blamed himself. "I was unable to get the job
done in the final two minutes."

It was another game where Streater and Ryan both
saw plenty of action—almost an equal amount.

Coach Majors said there was no plan to divide
quarterback time. "It just worked out that way. They give
the defenses different looks. We're always hunting for the
hot hand. We changed at the half, hoping Pat could give the
team a spark. We changed at the end, thinking Jimmy
might scramble away from the rush."

Among the miscues in the game were a fumble at the
Auburn goal line by Ryan as the Vols were ready to score a
touchdown, two delay of game penalties, two early contacts
by Noonan along the defensive front, and a rarely called
penalty. Bill Marren was flagged for helping to pull Streater
toward the goal when he was falling to the turf near the

five-yard-line. "I knew I was falling. Then I felt somebody dragging me on toward the goal," Jimmy said. It wasn't a miraculous hand that had come down from the clouds but those of guard Bill Marren who just wanted the Vols to score.

THE VOLS WERE A seven point favorite over the Oregon State Beavers of coach Craig Fertig. But in this game another Craig—the one in orange and white—would get the headlines.

"In this era, and in the framework of this Tennessee team, Colquitt's punting Saturday was the greatest," said kicking coach George Cafego, speaking of punter Craig Colquitt's efforts. He should have known. He saw Johnny Majors' quick kick against Georgia Tech in 1956 and other great punters through the years.

"I've never seen a kicker kick like that," said coach Majors.

"I've never seen a guy punt the ball like No. 28 did," Coach Fertig said.

Colquitt had six punts for an average of 52 yards. His long was 71, and he had one that rolled out at the Oregon six-yard-line.

Jimmy Streater was not as fortunate. He had a miserable day. Despite it being band day with 2500 area students given tickets for the game and the pre-game prancing of Tennessee Walking Horse Royal Copy ridden by Jerry Derryberry of Kingston, Jimmy's work in the first quarter was terrible.

Pat Ryan replaced him and had his best game ever. Ryan scored two touchdowns rushing and threw for another. Ryan gained 26 yards on the ground and 136 through the air. He was a fifth-year senior and he finally scored his first touchdown.

The Vols won 41 to 10. Jimmy celebrated with the team, but he had nothing to be jubilant about as far as his personal statistics. He ran for two yards and threw for none.

101

"From my standpoint, Pat should be the starter next week. I won't make excuses about just a bad day or the weather. I just didn't play well," Jimmy said and hung his head.

PAT RYAN GOT HIS first start the next week against Georgia Tech, but it was Jimmy Streater who came off the bench this time to put a spark in the Volunteers.

It was the Vols' fifth home game in a row, and if the Tech game was any indication, this was not a show to take on the road. The Vols lost 24 to 8.

The heros from the previous week failed in their efforts. Ryan threw an interception that was returned for a touchdown. He threw two other interceptions. Colquitt punted one for a mere fifteen yards and Tech turned it into a field goal. Jimmy Gaylor missed another field goal attempt.

Coach Pepper Rodgers' Techsters won in remarkable fashion—without throwing a single pass.

Jimmy came into the game in the third quarter without success himself. But in the fourth he rallied the Vols with a drive that included four pass completions and a run by him of 38 yards for a touchdown. He also ran for the two-point conversion. It was not satisfying to lose, but Jimmy had some personal reassurance from his fourth quarter performance. However, he had to limp off the field with a slightly injured knee.

THE VOLS STOOD AT three losses and two wins for the season when they traveled to Birmingham on the third Saturday of October for the annual clash with Alabama. There were games and there were BIG GAMES. On the schedule every year, Alabama was the big game. Dominance in Southern and national football would always have to pass through Alabama. And until Tennessee could beat this foe, it would have no chance at a Southeastern Conference championship.

Bear Bryant was now 65 but he intended to keep coaching for some time.

IN OTHER SPORTS AND entertainment news, Texas' Earl Campbell was the front runner in the Heisman Trophy race. After three games, the Yankees led the World Series, two games to one, over the Dodgers. Bing Crosby died on a Spanish golf course at age 73. Ray Mears, the Vols' basketball coach for the past fifteen years, was reported ill again. Associate coach Cliff Wettig was put in charge.

Veteran NBC sportscaster Joe Garagiola said he thought the ABC crew of Tom Seaver, Howard Cosell, and Keith Jackson was "butchering" the World Series.

THERE WAS NOTHING THAT Jimmy Streater wanted to do more than play Alabama and win. He had quickly learned the meaning of this game and the tradition. But more than that, he took it as a personal challenge to show Coach Bryant that he was not wrong in recruiting him. He wanted to play his best game.

For players who had not grown up in Tennessee, such as Streater and Chavis, there were two things they learned early on in their football tenure as Volunteers. "First of all you were taught to hate Vanderbilt. And as far as the Alabama thing, it took only one season of being here to find out what the Tennessee-Alabama tradition was all about. The third Saturday in October. That says it all," defensive coordinator John Chavis commented recently, reflecting on his playing days at Tennessee.

On Friday when the Vols left for Birmingham, Jimmy's health, as it related to his knee, was questionable. Trainer Tim Kerin listed Jimmy as "probable" for the game. Tennessee was a 20-point underdog. In this series, the underdog usually lost because both sides took the game so seriously that they weren't going to think beyond the third Saturday of October.

"This situation recalls the 1964 season. Alabama was

on the way to a national championship, led by a gimpy-kneed Joe Namath. Yet Alabama was only a ten-point favorite on UT, which was starting anew under Doug Dickey," wrote Tom Siler in the Knoxville *News-Sentinel.*

Pat Ryan would start and Joe Hough would back him up if Streater couldn't go, according to Coach Majors.

Alabama opened an awesome running attack behind Johnny Davis, Tony Nathan, Lou Ikner and several others. They ground out a total of 347 yards for the day and passed for another 82. Tennessee managed only a total of 181 yards by air and by land.

When Ryan couldn't move the team, Jimmy was unable to go in, so Joe Hough got baptized under fire. He responded well and threw a 13-yard TD pass to Kelsey Finch in the third quarter.

Alabama quarterback Jeff Rutledge scored on runs of four and nine yards and threw a TD pass to Ozzie Newsome. The Tide rolled, 24-10.

Jimmy Streater could only stand along the sideline and watch. He wanted to play so badly that he almost became ill again. But as strange as it sounds, his not playing against Alabama set him up to start the following week against Florida. Ryan had led the team for a fruitless 27 minutes where the Vols had not gained one first down. Ryan was 0 for 5 in passing. Joe Hough fought valiantly, but Coach Majors didn't believe he would fill the bill in the long run. It was back to Jimmy in the week-to-week saga of who was going to direct the team.

FLORIDA WAS NOT A regular opponent on the Vols' schedule. They were one of the SEC teams that appeared for a two-year set and then disappeared for several years. The two teams wouldn't play again until 1984. The rivalry arose because of the connection of coaches and athletic directors between Tennessee and Florida. Florida Coach Doug Dickey had been Tennessee's coach from 1964-1969. Florida Athletic Director Ray Graves had captained Tennessee in

1941. Tennessee Athletic Director Bob Woodruff coached at Florida, coached Doug Dickey as quarterback there, and hired Doug Dickey as Tennessee's coach in 1964. It was almost like an in-bred Appalachian family. They were either fighting each other or loving each other all the time.

By now the Tennessee players didn't care that Doug Dickey was a former UT coach. That was ancient history. Most were in grade school when Dickey coached the Vols. This was just the next opportunity to win a conference game. That's what they wanted.

Majors announced early in the week that if Jimmy Streater was healthy, he would be the starting quarterback. He gave the Vols a chance at an occasional big play. "It's hard to play three quarterbacks and be fair in the amount of playing time. I guess we'll just let them fight it out in practice," Majors said. The QBs were now aligned in opposite order of their class standing. Streater, the sophomore, was first. Hough, the junior, was second. Ryan, the senior, was third.

A TEAM DISASTER WAS barely averted on the Vols' ride to the game. They had stayed in Silver Springs to avoid the confusion of a hostile college town. The team and official party, including school officials and some reporters, traveled from Silver Springs along State Route 315 in a convoy of three buses with police car escorts. Rolling along at a good clip and feeling secure with the escort, the bus drivers didn't notice a speeding Seaboard Coast Line train heading for a crossing a short distance ahead. The police cars and the first bus of the three made it through the crossing, but the other two bus drivers had to slam on their brakes and come to a screeching halt just as the train sped across in front of them.

Just twelve years before and two days after the Alabama game, three UT assistant coaches, Bill Majors, Bob Jones, and Charlie Rash, were killed in a car-train crash in Knoxville. But this time it was not a disaster—just close.

JIMMY WAS INDEED THE starter when the teams lined up in Gainesville. The Vols struggled in the first half, going in at the break trailing 3 to 17.

The third quarter was electric. Gary Moore returned the second half kickoff 64 yards, Kelsey Finch gained eleven, and three more plays gained seven. But Florida held.

Tennessee also bent but didn't break as Thomas Rowsey made several key stops on Florida's possession. Streater and the Vols took over 78 yards from the Florida goal. They drove all the way on five of seven passing by Streater. He hit Arbo for eleven, Reggie Harper for eight and fifteen, Ken Sanderson for eleven, and finally Harper again on an eighteen-yard touchdown strike.

Florida quarterback Terry LeCount came back throwing to Wes Chandler and Derrick Gaffney. As Florida neared Tennessee's goal line, a pass skipped through Gaffney's hands and was intercepted by Rowsey at the one-yard-line. This set up a historic and record-setting run.

Jimmy tried a sneak to move the ball out far enough from the goal line to give punter Craig Colquitt some room. His skinny frame was unable to move the ball ahead even an inch. The Vols came back with an off-tackle dive by tailback Kelsey Finch. "It was the very play that Bud Wilkinson used for years at Oklahoma," Coach Majors explained later.

"We had one on one blocking, and when I broke through the line, I knew I could go all the way," Finch said. Florida was up close, and when Finch did get through the line there were few left to stop him.

Florida's free safety, Chuck Hatch, appeared to be in position and have the angle on Finch.

"I knew somebody was coming, but I didn't know who. I'm no 9.5 or 9.6 man, so I cut back on him a couple of times. I knew I had the touchdown because I had the room to maneuver. There was no way he was going to catch me," Finch explained.

No one did catch Kelsey Finch. His name is etched

in the Tennessee record book. His 99-yard run against the Gators will stand forever since no one can ever have a 100 yard run from scrimmage in the way that runs are now measured.

With the extra point, Finch's run tied the game at 17.

Florida failed on its next drive. Streater came back throwing. Drives got close, but always bogged down when the goal line loomed near.

Johnny Chavis had one of his best games. After battling Jimmy Noonan for the nose tackle job, he moved to defensive tackle. At Florida he threw quarterback LeCount and his replacement for two successive losses.

Florida came back and scored a field goal and another touchdown to make it 27-17 with time running out in the game.

Kelsey Finch's record setting touchdown and what happened as the game ended are what fans and players remember most. Florida called time out with three seconds remaining and near the Vol goal line. When LeCount came back to the huddle from a conference with Coach Dickey on the sideline, he announced a play that would for years rankle Vol fans. Instead of taking a knee with the snap of the ball and going away a ten-point winner, LeCount rolled out and threw to Chandler beneath the goal post. Chandler caught it but was ruled out of bounds as time expired.

Tennessee players, led by Joe Hough, rushed toward Florida's sideline. There were words and then there were fists. The fight went on for what seemed like fifteen minutes.

Majors was hot in comments after the game. "I don't know who had the idea of that last pass but if they need it that badly, God speed. Our day will come. Our day will come." But Majors' day of a win over Florida wouldn't come for thirteen more years until 1990.

Danny (Pert) Jenkins told a reporter, "Coach Majors told us not to pop off, but I have one comment. I used to have a lot of respect for Coach Dickey. He recruited me five years ago. Now I know how Alabama wins the championship even when Florida has better players."

John Chavis, now defensive coordinator for Tennessee, says the Florida game is the one he remembers the most in his career because of the fight. "We had us a heck of a fight. And Kelsey had that long run. We were setting the ground work for better things to come."

Doug Dickey would be gone as Florida's coach when the teams would meet again in 1984. In 1985 he came back to UT as athletic director with John Majors still the head coach of the Vols. Had either Majors or Dickey forgotten the 1977 Tennessee-Florida game? Or have they yet?

For Jimmy Streater, it was his first game in which he was the only quarterback who played for the Vols. He only netted one yard running, but Jimmy completed 17 of 29 pass attempts for 168 yards. "Kelsey's run really fired us up, but we got bogged down again. Just a couple of more breaks and we would have won."

Scot Brantley, Florida linebacker who was among the top ten players in the country when he was recruited in the same class as Jimmy, said, "Streater was better than we expected. He would throw those short passes and bring up our defense. Then he'd go long."

THE FLORIDA LOSS MADE the Vols 2 and 5 for the season with no SEC victories. They would have a week off before they finished with four games in November and a chance of salvaging something from the season. Texas, Alabama, and Oklahoma were the top teams in the polls. But November opponent Kentucky, although on probation, was ranked seventh—the highest they had been in years.

There was other news in Tennessee besides football as Halloween turned to November. President Jimmy Carter was being urged by state and local politicians to authorize $80 million for the Clinch River Breeder Reactor project near Oak Ridge.

O. J. Simpson, playing with the Buffalo Bills, was put

out for the season by a knee injury.

At Burgin Dodge in Knoxville, a new 1978 Dodge Monaco with a V-8 engine was selling for $4955.

Two weeks after beating Tennessee, Florida Coach Dickey was reported to be on the hotseat with alumni and fans because of the 3-2-1 season record.

Coach Majors took advantage of the off week to do some recruiting and to visit Alabama's practice field. There he watched from the tower with Coach Bryant as the Tide prepared for their next game.

MEMPHIS STATE CAME TO Knoxville on the first Saturday of November with a 5-3 record and hopes for a shot at the Hall of Fame Bowl. The Vols had spirited practices leading up to the game, including four fights at Tuesday's practice.

Jimmy Streater, having established himself as the premier quarterback of the Vols in the Florida game, was hoping for another good game. He wanted to win. The Vols would be state champions if not SEC champions. To do that, they had to defeat both Memphis State and Vanderbilt during the last four games.

They took care of Memphis State by a score of 27-14.

In a chilling rain, Jimmy ran for two touchdowns. One was a one-yard sneak and the other was a daring and classic Streater run of 25 yards off tackle.

Jimmy cemented his quest for the No. 1 quarterback position with 52 yards running and 140 passing. He was now relaxed enough that he could find receivers Jeff Moore, Reggie Harper, and Billy Arbo easier.

In Monday's *News-Sentinel*, sportswriter Marvin West wrote that, "Jimmy Streater is beginning to look exactly like a quarterback."

Bill Cox, quarterbacks coach, said, "Jimmy has made fine progress. He started to show some confidence in the Florida game. Now I'm sure I see more. Jimmy has ability. He dominated as a high school quarterback."

Coach Majors said part of Jimmy's success was due to the improvement of the offensive line in pass protection. "Joe Avezzano is the best pass-protection coach in the country."

MISSISSIPPI MASSACRED THE VOLS the following Saturday in Memphis. The Rebels had seventeen points before the Vols had a first down. The score was 30-0 at the half.

"We looked like the Keystone Kops," Coach Majors said after the game. The Vols tied a school record with eight fumbles, losing five of them.

Jimmy did help to account for the Vols' 14 points in the 43-14 loss. He scored on a twelve-yard run and hit Billy Arbo on a 72-yard pass play. Both came in the third quarter and that was it. It was the most points Ole Miss had scored on the Vols in 30 years. Tennessee was now 0-4 in SEC play and had lost six games in the season. The Vols had never lost seven games in a season in the history of the football program.

"They had our game plan down pat. They were ready for everything we were going to run. I don't think they'd been watching our practices but they sure were ready," Jimmy said after the game.

KENTUCKY MADE IT A historic day when they handed the Vols their seventh loss of the season the next Saturday in Lexington by a score of 21-17.

This one wasn't decided early as the game with Ole Miss had been. The Vols held on, fought, and scratched until the end. Jimmy Gaylor hit a record-setting field goal of 57 yards and the Vols were on top 17 to 14 in the fourth quarter but couldn't keep the Wildcats out of the end zone.

Tennessee got one more chance, but Jimmy fumbled when assaulted by Kentucky's Art Still and the Big Blue recovered.

Kelsey Finch got both of the Vols' touchdowns but

Jimmy played well, often setting up Finch on the option.

On one classic drive, Jimmy ran for ten yards, threw to Reggie Harper for nineteen, ran for another gain of thirteen, and then handed off to Jesse Briggs for five.

With the win, Kentucky finished with a 10-1 season and pushed the Vols to 3-7 with Vanderbilt waiting. Kentucky athletic director Cliff Hagan said he would begin negotiations with coach Fran Curci about increasing his salary from the present $35,000 per year.

IT WAS THE GAME of the cellar dwellers when Vandy came to Knoxville for the final game of the season for both teams. The Vols dressed in orange pants and jerseys for the first time that season. Vandy had won two games and the Vols only three, but when they met, the Vol seniors were determined to go out with a victory. They did, 42-7. "The first thing you learn when you come to Tennessee," John Chavis said later, "is to hate Vanderbilt."

As the clock ticked down, Tennessee students began to shout, "We're Number Nine, you're Number Ten!" Senior linebacker Greg Jones from Bristol took out all his hostilities and frustrations on the Commodore ball carriers and receivers. He had 19 tackles, six assists, a pass interception, and a fumble recovery for the day. "There was no way Vanderbilt was going to beat us in my last game at Tennessee," Jones said after the game.

"Our offense finally started clicking. We were confident we could move the ball because we did on Alabama, Florida, and Kentucky. Yes, I checked off a couple of times when I saw their safety coming," Jimmy told reporters. He had run for three touchdowns and passed to Jeff Moore on a 51-yard bomb for another.

Coach Majors said, "We're going to play more games like this, the kind you can really enjoy, in years to come."

JIMMY STREATER'S SOPHOMORE SEASON was over. He had gained an appreciation of how competitive the

The Jimmy Streater Story

Southeastern Conference was. He also learned there were other players waiting to take his position if he didn't perform well. He had never been on a losing team until now. He wanted more than anything else for that to change.

Individually, he had done well. He had 397 rushing yards, second only to Kelsey Finch. He had completed 59 of 105 passes for 742 yards. His total yardage for the season had moved him into eleventh place in the Tennessee record books for total yardage in a season, just ahead of Coach Majors.

Jimmy had scored eight touchdowns rushing and had thrown for four others, accounting for twelve of the Vols' twenty-seven TDs for the season.

His dazzling runs had earned him the nick-name of the "Sylva Streak" by John Ward in the radio booth.

The question he asked himself, though, was, "Have I established myself as Tennessee's quarterback for 1978 so that I can play baseball in the spring instead of 'proving myself' again in spring football practice?"

1978

C oach Johnny Majors gave Jimmy Streater the good news early in 1978. Jimmy could play baseball in the spring and not be concerned with spring football practice. Coach Majors didn't say it, but Jimmy knew that meant the coach was only looking for a backup quarterback that year in spring practice and wanted to keep Jimmy healthy for the fall campaign.

After a year out of baseball, Jimmy found his skills rusty and worked the whole season trying to get them back. The more he played, though, the more he realized that he liked football a lot better than baseball—if he was the quarterback. He looked around, and even at the biggest of baseball games there would only be a hundred or so fans.

On football Saturdays at Neyland Stadium there were 85,000 when the stands were full—most wearing orange and most screaming for him to do something. He had to admit it. He enjoyed the attention, the drama, and the shouts of a football Saturday. Football would be his future, at least in college.

SO WHEN FALL FOOTBALL practice opened and Jimmy was at the top of the depth chart at quarterback, he was ready. Wilbert Jones, Jimmy's freshman competitor, was switched to defense permanently. So was Joe Hough who then dropped out of football. David Rudder was Number Two and Jeff Olszewski was Number Three.

Sportswriters said Jimmy had the starting job sewed up—at least for the first game. He had a baseball arm, snap in his delivery, and zip on the ball. He could deliver the sideline cut from the opposite hash line. He could throw long—60 yards in a recent scrimmage.

113

The Jimmy Streater Story

Jimmy survived in the land of giants along the line and around linebackers with quick feet and a quick mind. He repeatedly dove under heavy blows as if protected by a sixth and seventh sense. Tanks, in the form of defensive linemen, could be coming from different directions to crush him and he felt them before they arrived.

He was a Baryshnikov with cleats and a helmet. His running style had no herky-jerky movement. He glided along and then darted through openings. His speed was deceptive because of the fluid motion. Defenders would think they had the angle to take him out, and then Jimmy would look back at them falling along the wayside as he shifted up a gear. "He was so smooth," Jimmy's high school coach Charles Howell remembered years later. "He was a phenomenal athlete."

SCHOOL OFFICIALS WERE LOOKING at financing plans to expand the stadium again. Talk was about 20,000 more seats. Dr. Joe Johnson, executive vice-president of UT, said the university could solicit substantial cash gifts or place a surcharge on season ticket holders to help finance any expansion. Tickets were going up to $10 each. There were 50,000 season ticket holders and a surcharge of $15 per season ticket holder could raise money that would go a long way toward servicing a bond debt for construction, Johnson explained.

Also, as the 1978 season was nearing, there was a move within the NCAA to outlaw tearaway jerseys. Tennessee had used them for years on quarterbacks, running backs, and receivers. Very often defenders would end up with a souvenir piece of orange cloth in their hands instead of a tackle as they watched the soles of cleated feet waving goodbye to them on long runs and passes.

ANOTHER CALIFORNIA FOOTBALL TEAM came to Neyland Stadium for opening day in 1978—this time it was UCLA, coached by Terry Donahue, and not California.

UCLA and Tennessee had begun a sporadic rivalry back in 1965 in a game that Vol fans will always remember as the "Rose-Bonnet Bowl" because UCLA was headed for the Rose Bowl and Tennessee for the Bluebonnet Bowl when they met in the final game of the regular season. The Swamp Rat—quarterback Dewey Warren—and company led the Vols to a 35-34 victory in Memphis that set the tone for future games in the series.

This time a record crowd of 85,897 roared when the Vols stormed onto the field for the first game of the season on September 16. Muhammad Ali had beaten Leon Spinks in New Orleans in a comeback bid the night before, but at Neyland Stadium and on Shields-Watkins Field it was "FOOTBALL TIME IN TENNESSEE."

UCLA lived up to its Number Nine national ranking by shutting out the Vols 13 to 0.

It was not the way either Jimmy or Coach Majors wanted to open the campaign. Jimmy was intercepted twice by UCLA free safety Kenny Easley and was credited with a fumble on an errant pitchout to Kelsey Finch.

UCLA got its touchdowns on a 54-yard gallop by fullback Theotis Brown in the third quarter and a quarterback keeper by Rick Bashore in the fourth.

On the defensive side, Tennessee played hard. Chris Bolton, Brad White, Craig Puki, Jimmy Noonan, and Johnny Chavis were standouts. Chavis blocked UCLA's first extra point attempt.

Streater thrilled the home folks and caused UCLA Coach Donahue heart palpitations.

"That Streater is just magnificent. He reminds me of Condredge Holloway. He gives you heart failure every time he gets the ball," Donahue said after the game.

"We knew at halftime that we had to control Streater. So we used our linebackers to help shut off the outside. Streater is still one of the best triple-threat quarterbacks we'll face," said Easley. He was still remembering two remarkable runs that Jimmy had made in the first half.

115

On one play beginning at the Vol 17-yard line, Jimmy faked inside, kept off right tackle, streaked down the sideline, and finally pitched to Frank Foxx for a total gain of 42 yards.

Later, from his own 13-yard line, Jimmy took the same play to the left, cut back on two Bruins, and wasn't stopped until he had covered 58 yards.

"We proved we can move the ball. If we can move it on UCLA, we can move it on anybody. But the name of the game is getting it in the end zone. That's what we weren't able to do," Jimmy said in the locker room.

For the day, Jimmy finished with 93 yards rushing and hit seven of 17 passes for 79 yards.

A sideshow of the game was the match-up between Vol center Robert Shaw and Bruin noseguard Manu Tulasosopo. In the dressing room after the game, Tulasosopo said, "He (Shaw) was everything I thought he'd be and more. He's quick and strong . . . a really fine center. I'm just happy it's over."

THE VOLS HAD BEATEN Oregon State, their next opponent, by 41 to 10 in 1977. In 1978 they were favored to beat them again even though Roland James was out with a broken thumb.

Marvin West was most prophetic when he wrote in the *News-Sentinel* a few days before the game, "Before us are some basic ingredients of upsets. Tennessee is favored. They remember last season and the 41-10 romp over the Beavers. This is dangerous. Even a slight decrease in defensive intensity could be deadly."

West was right. Oregon State jumped out to a 13-0 lead at halftime on a rainy night in Knoxville. Tennessee battled back in the fourth for a 13-13 tie. To Oregon State Coach Craig Fertig it felt like a defeat, and across the way in the Tennessee locker room it did too.

For the first time that Jimmy Streater could recall, instead of cheers from his fans, there were boos.

116

George and Josephine Gibbs Rogers

Willis James Streater and
Ada Rogers Streater

Jimmy at about age 2 on grandmother Ada Streater's knee.

The Streater Family

The Streater Siblings

Jimmy

Eric

Steve

Faith

Jimmy as
High School
Senior

Basketball captains - Jimmy and Alton
Owens.

Mr. & Mrs. Golden Eagle - Molly
Vodak and Jimmy.

1975 Sylva-Webster Football Seniors - Jimmy,
Neil Setzer, Ray Swayney, Tony Cunningham,
Jim Wilson, and Ronnie Bumgarner.

Football captains - Jimmy, Neil Setzer,
and Ronnie Bumgarner.

Sylva-Dillsboro Scenes

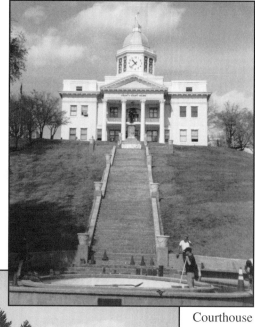

Courthouse

Jarrett House

Ritz Theatre

Scotts Creek Elementary

Coach Babe Howell,
Jimmy, and
Coach John Majors

Jimmy in
baseball uniform

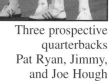

Three prospective
quarterbacks
Pat Ryan, Jimmy,
and Joe Hough

Jimmy handing off
to Hubert Simpson
against Notre Dame

Tommy Love, "a Greek god in a football uniform." Jimmy's idol as a youth.

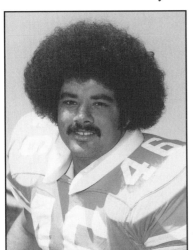

John Chavis as player in 1978 and now as UT Defensive Coordinator.

Jimmy looking baaad!

Jimmy's jail cell

Jimmy's room now

Cap given by
Heath Shuler

Midnight

Jimmy's Precious Possessions

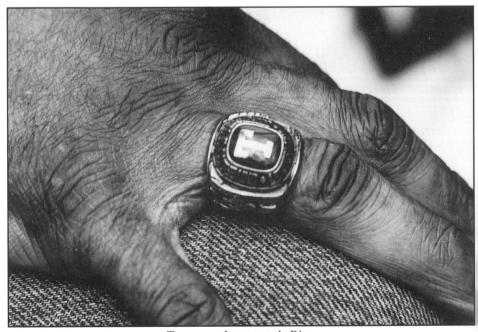

Tennessee Letterman's Ring

"I don't blame them. I felt the same way they did. I would have booed too," he said after the game. "The boos don't bother me." But they did. Or at least the reason for them did. He had fumbled twice, thrown an interception, and generally had a poor game. He finished with a net of two yards rushing and 173 passing. He did account for both of UT's touchdowns on the two-yard run and by a 44-yard pass to Jeff Moore set up by a Dennis Wolfe fumble recovery.

In other football news, former Vol Pat Ryan, who had started only two games in his career at UT, had found a home as the backup quarterback for the New York Jets. New Florida State Coach Bobby Bowden had moved his Seminoles into the top ten with an impressive run-pass offense.

POPE JOHN PAUL I died two days before Tennessee's next game with Auburn after only 34 days as Pope. In the same week America also lost a great entertainer with the death of ventriloquist Edgar Bergen. For the Vols, their obituary for the 1978 season hadn't been written yet, but several newspaper scribes had pen in hand. With a record of one loss and one tie, the Vols now entered the rough part of the schedule with three SEC games over the next five weeks.

WHEN YOUR PUNTER IS the top player in the game, coaches know that you're not likely to be on the winning side. Dale Schneitman punted seven times for a 44.4 yard average for the Vols. Auburn's Tigers throttled and humiliated Tennessee by a score of 29-10, and it wasn't that close.

Auburn offensive coordinator and former Vol assistant Dal Shealy especially enjoyed tormenting his former team. Behind the running of James Brooks, Auburn piled up 349 yards on the ground and 113 through the air on the arm of Charlie Trotman. Tennessee had only 69 yards on the ground and 146 in the air on Jimmy Streater's passing.

"We planned on 500 yards in total offense and 30 points," Shealy said after the game. "We came up a few yards and one point short, but we'll take it."

But Tennessee running back Kelsey Finch wasn't taking it when Auburn linebacker Harris Rabren delivered what Finch thought was a late hit to friend Jimmy Streater after Jimmy had thrown an interception. At first it was thought Jimmy's jaw was broken and he would miss the second half, but he came back to direct the drives for the ten points.

"It was a lowdown, cheap, rotten shot," said Finch after the game, not hiding his feelings. "The referee looked at it as it was happening, looked at me, and did nothing. He knows he was wrong. I got mad. I got hot." He also got a 15-yard penalty for arguing with the referee.

Jimmy wasn't as sure. "I don't know whether it was a clean blow or a late hit. A lot of people said it was a cheap shot. It was a long time after I threw it. I got knocked down. I was up and saw that we had tackled the fellow who had gotten the interception. I turned around and headed for the sidelines. The guy coldcocked me.

"That's football. I'm not complaining."

Auburn was undefeated after the win. Tennessee did not yet have a win for the season.

When football is bad early, newspaper sportswriters start writing more about the upcoming basketball season. In the next day's *News-Sentinel* there was a photo of new Tennessee head basketball coach Don Devoe with Harriman High School coach Richard Pickell and Austin-East coach Clifford Ross taken at the Vols' coaches' clinic.

ARMY WAS THE EXACT tonic that Tennessee needed in order to get into the win column. The next week the Vols took out some of their earlier frustration by slamming the Cadets 31-13. The win gave the Vols and Cadets identical records of 1-2-1.

Both the defense and offense finally came together for

a game and contributed to the win over a well-coached Army team. The kicking team and return team were added pluses. Gary Moore from Meigs County almost had an opening kickoff return for a touchdown, but he was ruled out of bounds at the Army 39. The Vols drove on in from there with Frank Foxx punching it into the end zone.

Two series later Tennessee's Clark Duncan recovered a fumble to put the Vols back in business. When the drive stalled, Alan Duncan came in and kicked a 32-yard field goal. Former quarterback Wilbert Jones, now a defensive back, had an interception in the second quarter. It was 10-7 UT at the half.

In the third quarter, after taking over at their own twenty, the Vols put together a ground and air game that culminated in a TD off a 47-yard run by Streater. Later in the same quarter, Jimmy added another score on a three-yard sweep.

Greg Gaines picked off another pass in the third period, on the series after Jimmy had scored on the sweep, and ran it back for a 31-yard TD. Gaines also had eleven tackles for the day. The 21 points in the third gave the Vols a commanding lead. Army scored in the fourth but could mount no other serious threats.

It was just what the Vols needed. A convincing win with a week off before they had to host Alabama. Jimmy ran more than he threw. He had 81 yards on the ground on 17 attempts—just one yard behind leading rusher Hubert Simpson—and 67 yards through the air on six completions in eleven attempts.

The following day, it was reported that UT had grossed $5.7 million from athletics—$3.5 million of it from football—during the 1977-78 year, leaving a deficit of $631,000. Bob Woodruff was the athletic director.

THE WORLD SERIES STARTED and finished between the Army and Alabama games. The Yankees beat the Dodgers four games to two.

The Jimmy Streater Story

FOR A BOY GROWING up in Tennessee caring about football, the week of the Tennessee-Alabama game had special meaning. Fall was in the air by the time the third Saturday in October rolled around. The World Series was either being played or just over. Leaves on trees were even reflecting the colors of the game—crimson and orange. The air and hitting were both crisp as the players collided on the field.

David Rudder and Tim Irwin were both Knoxville boys who had attended local high schools at Bearden and Central, respectively. They had listened to or watched the Vol-Tide series with interest for years and now were both on the Volunteer team for different reasons.

Irwin was a highly recruited lineman who had a 6-7 frame that now carried 256 pounds of muscle. Rudder was a volunteer in the true meaning of the word. He was a walk-on quarterback who was battling with scholarship recruit Jeff Olszewski for the backup QB position. Irwin was a sophomore, and Rudder was a senior in school but a junior in eligibility.

In the week leading up to the Alabama game, Irwin was featured in the local newspaper as the only Vol who was playing both defense and offense—both in the trenches of the line. Nothing was written about Rudder. But the two shared a common interest—they wanted to play well when they got their chances. Very few fans—except their mothers and fathers—kept a constant eye on an offensive lineman or a backup quarterback who was holding a clip board and standing near the coach. Being Tennessee boys though, both Irwin and Rudder relished the Alabama game.

Billy Arbo was another senior and local product from Knoxville's Webb High School. Arbo felt he had been slowed of late but looked forward to the Alabama game as his last chance to defeat the Tide in his college career. "A year ago, as a junior, I guess I was in for every offensive play against Alabama. I was right at home, even if it was a big traditional game," Arbo said.

Alan Duncan of Powell, Reggie Harper of Hartsville, and Hubert Simpson of McMinn County were other young men from Tennessee who had witnessed the Vol-Tide series from their youth and were hoping for big games personally and a big win for the team.

For other young men like Kelsey Finch and Robert Malone, who grew up in Alabama and now played for the Vols, the game also had a special meaning. They had to go home and listen to the trash talk if they lost. And Tennessee had lost a lot lately to Alabama. The record was 1-7 in the 1970s—seven losses in a row.

Alabama came to Neyland Stadium on October 21 with a 5-1 record, ranked fourth in the nation, and aiming to stay among the top teams.

THERE WAS NUDE DANCING, cigar smoking, and laughter in the Alabama dressing room after the game. None of it was pretty. Trainer Jim Goosetree, who once worked for UT, did his version of a Tennessee Fast Step adorned only in his birthday suit. Alabama assistant Ken Donahue who was a former Vol player under General Robert Neyland joined in the dance. Coach Bear Bryant passed out the cigars. The laughter came from the Alabama players. The Tennessee game was still special to them. They had just won their eighth in a row, 30-17.

Alabama rushers had accumulated 279 yards on the ground behind Tony Nathan and Major Ogilvie so that quarterback Jeff Rutledge only had to throw six times.

One of the few golden nuggets among the dross of the defeat was that Tennessee had won the fourth quarter 14-0. The players didn't quit when they were down 30-3. And it was done primarily by the Tennessee native sons on offense. Jimmy Streater had gone out in the third quarter with a bruised hip. He had passed complete five times on fourteen attempts for 45 yards and rushed for 48 yards on ten attempts.

121

Into his place stepped David Rudder who then played a remarkable game. Rudder led two drives of 78 and 69 yards. He was eleven of twelve in passing attempts and threw for 122 yards and two TDs. His touchdown passes were a six-yard pass to Hubert Simpson and a nine-yard one to Reggie Harper. Alan Duncan kicked five points on a 27-yard field goal and two points after touchdown. Billy Arbo had three receptions for 33 yards.

"This makes it all worthwhile. I have received my reward for walking on at UT," Rudder said. "I wish so much we had won. Naturally, I'm disappointed, but I am thankful the Lord gave me a chance to play. And I'm even more thankful that I was able to contribute a little."

Rudder had played eight plays in the Auburn game and he thought he had not performed well. "It made me wonder if I belonged on the team. All my life I've wanted to be in a big game like this. Doing well certainly helps my confidence.

"Jimmy Streater is a tough quarterback, a great one. He'll be back. I'm just glad I could help when I was needed."

TENNESSEE WAS 1-3-1 GOING into their sixth game of the season. Already fans were growing impatient with Johnny Majors' rebuilding program. He had told supporters it would take at least four years to rebuild, but after two more losses to Alabama were piled onto the stack, fans hadn't seen much improvement. They were growing restless.

"They said when John Majors came back to Tennessee from Pittsburgh, he would turn the program around," wrote one Vol fan. "But I didn't think this was the turn and the direction he would take us."

The schedule ahead didn't look very promising to produce a winning season. Mississippi State, Duke, Notre Dame, Mississippi, Kentucky, and Vanderbilt lay ahead in October and November. Jimmy Streater had 311 yards rushing with three touchdowns and 518 yards passing with another touchdown. Tennessee as a team had only eight touchdowns in five games.

JIMMY STREATER'S SORE HIP and David Rudder's tremendous showing against Alabama in the final quarter earned Rudder a start at quarterback the next week against Mississippi State at Memphis.

Many fans had already given up on the Vols for the year. Three thousand tickets were returned unsold. The attendance at the game was a mere 40,879. That would have been good at Pittsburgh, but for Tennessee it was devastating. But maybe the fans weren't so dumb after all. The Vols lost, 34-21.

Marvin West wrote that the Bulldogs, "Humbled the stumbling Volunteers for three quarters . . . . It was a mismatch, the worst of the season. . . . State's fourth play was a 67-yard run by James Jones, its fifth a touchdown by Len Copeland."

The previous week's cheers for David Rudder were short-lived. He was intercepted on his second attempt. He did some good things though, including a run for 25 yards and passes that kept drives alive. Kelsey Finch and Frank Foxx led the Vol's ground attack, but all they had to show for it at halftime was a 32-yard field goal by Alan Duncan. They would have needed eight more field goals to have been close to even with the 28 points the Bulldogs had.

As he had the previous year, Jimmy Streater came into the game on the second series of the third quarter and won his starting job back. It wasn't enough to win the game though. He put together an eleven yard touchdown run, a 21-yard TD pass to Anthony Hancock, and another touchdown run of fifteen yards. On each of the fourth quarter touchdowns, the Vols tried for the two-point conversion. Each failed.

One drive of 97 yards was classic Streater. He threw to Reggie Harper for 18, to Billy Arbo for 15, to Hancock for 19, and then again to Hancock for the 21-yard TD. By that time in the fourth quarter, there were very few Vol fans left in the stadium to watch the drive . . . or to care.

"It was a funny feeling on the bench," Streater said. "It was right for David to start because he got the job done last week. I was able to move us some this time. I don't know whether that will mean I am the quarterback next week or not. I guess the coaches will want to look at the film."

Actually, the coaches wanted to burn the film, but they were required to look at it. One milestone was set. UT assistant athletic director Gus Manning watched his 300th consecutive game.

For the game Jimmy was the leading rusher with 38 yards and the leading passer with 137 yards on ten completions in 20 attempts.

THE FIRST PLAY OF the game set the tone for the Tennessee-Duke game. Tennessee assistant coach Billy Cox had noticed a defensive tendency in the Duke defensive backfield that he thought he could exploit—quickly. He had Billy Arbo and Jeff Moore to change receiver slots for the first play. Moore was a step faster. He was going to streak down the field at the snap and Jimmy was to hit him in full stride.

Jimmy faked a handoff, stepped back, hesitated a moment, and then threw deep down the middle. Moore caught up with it at the Duke 25-yard-line and went in for the touchdown.

"I thought for a split second I had overthrown Jeff. That shook me." He hadn't. It was a 66-yard score, and the rout was on. The Vols won 34-0.

"Personally, I think this was our best effort so far. This was what we were talking about when we called on the team to put it all together," Coach Majors said after the game.

Indeed they had. Greg Gaines and Danny Spradlin on the defensive side had ten tackles each. Alan Duncan had field goals of 23 and 53 yards. Billy Arbo made a remarkable touchdown catch as he was falling into the end zone on a tipped pass. Frank Foxx showed up in the stats as a rusher, passer, and receiver. He was the one who threw the wingback pass to Arbo for the 34-yard TD.

Streater had his best game of the season—202 yards and a touchdown passing and 81 yards and a touchdown running. "While watching on the sideline at Memphis, I saw some things that helped me. I was better prepared for this game," Streater said.

Streater sustained a sprained thumb in the victory.

ELECTION DAY IN TENNESSEE and across the nation was the Tuesday following the Duke victory. In Tennessee, Lamar Alexander won the race for Governor over Jake Butcher while Howard Baker was re-elected to the U. S. Senate. In Arkansas, the young state attorney general, William Jefferson Clinton, was elected governor. The day after the election, Norman Rockwell, often referred to as the American Rembrandt, died at his home in Stockbridge, Massachusetts, at the age of 84.

THERE WERE A FEW schools that were renowned for their football reputation. Among those in 1978 and before were Michigan, the University of Southern California, Penn State, Alabama, and Notre Dame. Tennessee had once been among that elite group but had fallen on hard times as of late. However, on Saturday, November 11, 1978, in South Bend, Indiana, the Vols were to meet the Fighting Irish of Notre Dame on the football field for the first time. Before Tennessee's game with Duke, it was whispered about that Notre Dame could play their junior varsity and beat the Vols. Now they might have to dress their varsity.

Players and coaches aren't supposed to put any more thought or emphasis on one game than another. "We just take them one game at a time," is the old saw. But it was no secret that the Vols looked forward to the challenge of

Notre Dame. The game had been circled, along with the one to be played in Knoxville in 1979, for a long time. It could be historical. Jimmy Streater wanted to do his best. He had been recruited by Notre Dame.

John Chavis didn't get a chance to go to South Bend though. The walk-on from South Carolina, who came to Tennessee because he loved to watch the Vols on television, broke his thumb in Wednesday's practice before the game. It ended his season and his career as a player. He would later come back to Tennessee as an assistant and then defensive coordinator for the championship year of 1998.

Notre Dame had a quarterback by the name of Joe Montana. Their leading rusher was Vagas Ferguson who, along with Jimmy Streater, was a top recruit in 1976. The Irish defense centered around linebacker Bob Golic. They were defending national champions.

Tennessee was not to be intimidated though. The Vols came out fighting. "We talked all week about being reckless, about going for broke, that we had nothing to lose and everything to gain," Streater said.

After Notre Dame drove for an opening field goal, Streater led the Vols downfield 69 yards in 14 plays for a touchdown. He passed to Jeff Moore for 19. Kelsey Finch ran for ten behind a big block by Frank Foxx. Streater had keepers of six, five, and seven yards. Then Frank Foxx ran a sweep and got the touchdown. The Irish got another field goal before the half, but the Vols led, 7-6.

The avalanche came in the third quarter. Notre Dame scored 18 points when Tennessee's kicking game broke down. A Dale Schneitman punt was blocked, resulting in an eventual touchdown. Another punt was returned 45 yards by ND's Dave Waymer, leading to a field goal. When ND backed Tennessee up with a punt to the three-yard line, Streater fumbled three plays later when he was blind-sided. The Irish punched it in for another TD and led 24-7.

Streater's best was yet to come. "We had another play called," Streater explained later. "I read the blitz from

Notre Dame. I checked off to a pass to Reggie Harper. Then Notre Dame backed out to its normal defense. I knew Phil Ingram would break open when the safety broke across." The play started at Tennessee's 27-yard line and covered 73 yards in all. It brought the Vols to within ten points, 14-24.

Late in the fourth, Streater was intercepted by safety Joe Restic who had been burned on the Ingram TD. Restic returned the interception for a TD and the final score of the 31-14 decision.

"Streater is the best option quarterback I've seen," said Bob Golic after the game.

Craig Puki and Jimmy Noonan had great games on the defensive side. However, where Tennessee had been so proud—in the kicking game—they broke down.

Jimmy won the battle between him and Montana. Jimmy was 15 of 26 in passing attempts for 194 yards and a touchdown. Montana was 11 of 25 passing for 144 yards and no touchdowns. In addition, Jimmy outrushed Montana by 36 yards to 7. The touchdown pass from Streater to Ingram was the third longest in UT history to that point.

"There was progress showing," Coach Majors said. "The Tennessee team today would have soundly defeated the Tennessee team of six weeks ago."

THE VOLS WOULD HAVE to win their remaining three games to avoid another losing season. The task was formidable. Tennessee had not won three games in a row since the middle of the 1974 season. Ole Miss, their next opponent, had thrashed the Vols 43-14 in Memphis in 1977. This contest would be a highly spirited battle. By the end of the game there were a total of 222 yards in penalties on both teams.

Noonan, Puki, Simpson, James, Steve Davis, Lee Otis Burton, Danny Spradlin, Finch, and Streater weren't to be denied though. After falling behind 17-7 at halftime, the Vols exploded for 34 points in the second half to win 41-17.

"We're building and we're getting better," said Puki.

"Beating Ole Miss was important. They dog-whipped us last year. We had to get them back."

Roland James had a spectacular day. He had a punt return of 34 yards that set up a 25-yard run by Simpson for a TD. He had two pass interceptions. He picked the second one off at the Tennessee ten-yard line and ran it back 90 yards for a TD.

"When I saw Steve Davis in front, I knew I was going all the way," James said. "When you have someone like him ahead of you, you can expect to get the block."

"Those who paid $10 got their money's worth just watching Roland James," UT assistant head coach Joe Madden said.

Finch had two TDs on 80 yards rushing while Simpson led the ground attack with 137. Jimmy played his usual sound game, getting a touchdown by ground and throwing for 129 yards. Bobby Emmons also punched one across for a TD.

"This is certainly the high point of my time at Tennessee," Coach John Majors said. "I told the team, no matter how long I stay, I'll never forget this day."

Jimmy was beginning to approach records that had been set years before. For the year, he was now up to 1609 yards and into third place for single season yardage behind Dewey Warren with 1757 and Bobby Scott, the leader, at 1786. In this game he had passed Condredge Holloway's single season effort of 1582 yards.

He wasn't thinking about individual records, but was focusing on the team's season record. "We needed this one badly. We're in the stretch run and want to avoid a losing season. Winning our last three games will build momentum for next year."

AMERICANS ACROSS THE COUNTRY celebrated thanksgiving the following Thursday while the Vols awaited the next game with Kentucky who would come to town on Saturday.

However, in Jonestown, Guyana, religious cult leader Jim Jones had led over 900 followers to a caldron of cyanide, fruit-flavored drink and tranquilizers, on the same day as the Vols had defeated Mississippi. News now splashed across the front pages of newspapers and onto the screens of televisions of the mass murder and suicide that had just been discovered in the South American country. Congressman Leo Ryan of California and some staff members were gunned down by Jones' followers before they did themselves in.

KENTUCKY HAD WON TWO in a row over Tennessee. The Vols had to win to preserve their chances of a winning season.

With defensive pressure from the Vols that resulted in five turnovers by the Wildcats, and with five field goals by Alan Duncan, Tennessee waltzed by Kentucky, 29-14.

Duncan was a remarkable story in his own way. He was a walk-on whose parents were Baptist missionaries in Kenya. The five field goals were a school record and tied the SEC record. He got a chance to break the conference record in the fourth quarter but came up a bit short and to the left. Duncan credited snapper Steve Porter and holder Billy Arbo for his excellent outing. Duncan had lived at various places around the country before he ended up in north Knox County at Powell. From there it was just a short drive to UT.

Those grabbing an interception from Kentucky were Danny Spradlin, Roland James, Dennis Wolfe, and Greg Gaines.

Streater's daring runs were becoming routine now. They were more or less expected. His 21-yard TD run along the west sideline in the fourth quarter was described by Marvin West as a "magic move." He made two Wildcats miss him in a stirring dash to the flag.

Jimmy led the team in rushing yards with 92 and threw for 75. His total yardage of 167 pushed him past

Dewey Warren into second for single season yardage behind Bobby Scott by only ten yards with one game left in the season.

SHELL OIL COMPANY ANNOUNCED it would start nation-wide rationing of fuel and cut back to seventy-five per cent of what it distributed the year before.

Around the Southeastern Conference as Tennessee prepared for its season-ending game with Vanderbilt, two men would be coaching their last games. Fred Pancoast would be out after the game with the Vols, and at Florida, Doug Dickey was fired on Wednesday. He would finish the season against Miami already having lost to Florida State and Bobby Bowden.

Before the game with Tennessee, Vanderbilt Coach Pancoast said, "I'm worried about the conduct of the Tennessee game. I've cautioned our players about it. I remember Bill Battle's last game as coach. Tennessee had a player thrown out before the kickoff. There were a lot of near-fights. Tennessee's players were just turned loose. There wasn't much discipline." His words some how found their way to the Tennessee team's bulletin board.

THE PLAYERS AND COACHES were able to shout "Three in a row" after the Vols routed Vandy, 41-15. The victory brought the season record up to as even as it could be—5-5-1. The seniors felt they gave the lower classmen something to build on. They were going out on a winning note after four or five years of struggle and turmoil. Instead of finishing ninth in the ten-school league as they had in 1977, this bunch had moved the squad up to a share of fourth place.

Jimmy finished the season in style, running for two touchdowns and passing for 163 yards. He totaled 235 yards for the day and broke the single-season yardage record by jumping ahead of Bobby Scott's 1786 yards to 2011. The record would stand until 1984.

130

"This is a significant accomplishment," Jimmy said after the game. "I guess it's the best thing since being named a high school All-American." He moved ahead of Stanley Morgan into fifth place in career yardage with a year to go. Significantly, he not only led the team in passing yardage but also in rushing with 593.

Alan Duncan had also kicked two more field goals to gain the single-season record in that category with 13.

Over at the University of North Carolina, Jimmy's brother Steve had finished his sophomore season with several tackles as a defensive back and a 40.7 yard average on 44 punts. Jimmy was as proud of his brother's accomplishments as he was of his own. He just wished they could have played together in college. But there was always pro ball if they made it that far.

"COACHING IS A COMPETITIVE profession . . . . I guess you could say the championship is all it amounts to anymore. We came close, didn't get it, and finally the university president exercised his judgment," Doug Dickey said after his last game at Florida.

ALTHOUGH JIMMY ENJOYED THE individual accomplishments and records he had broken, he still hated not to be on a winning team. For two years now the team had not had a winning record. It had improved and so had he. He wanted 1979—his final year at UT—to be different.

He heard about Dickey being fired at Florida and about Pancoast at Vandy, but those didn't mean very much. He looked in the newspaper and saw what Coach Bryant had told him when he was being recruited had come true. Alabama was the SEC champion and the national champion.

"Jimmy, come to Alabama. I think we have the young men to win a couple of conference championships and a national championship during your playing time."

1979

In the spring of 1979, Jimmy played baseball again. His mother, father, Eric, Faith, and Steve would get to watch him on occasion. His high school coach, Babe Howell, would also find time to come and watch Jimmy.

Jimmy was more than just an athlete. He had other interests. In the spring, his thoughts not only turned to baseball but to a young lady from Morristown, Tennessee, who always came to watch him. As a matter of fact, Jimmy and Dana Williams had been seeing each other since he was a sophomore.

Dana was going to be a nurse. She was attending Walters State Community College in Morristown. Born in New York, Dana was a year older than Jimmy.

"She was a beautiful girl," Coach Howell remembered. "When I would go over to watch him play baseball, she would be there along with Jimmy's parents."

BUT THOUGHTS OF LOVE and marriage would have to be put on hold for another year or so. Jimmy needed a job if he was going to be married. This was his last college season, and he would have to show that he could play at "the next level."

Jimmy looked at the football schedule for the fall and circled four games in red. All games were important, but these would have special meaning for him. *AUBURN* had beaten the Vols badly in 1978. They were the first SEC game. Winning that one was crucial to a good start.

GEORGIA TECH was big. Coach John Majors had

132

mentioned how it had once been a heated rivalry. The 1956
game was still talked about in Big Orange Country. *ALA-
BAMA*—yes, Alabama—was always huge. The Tide had
owned the Vols for the decade of the '70s. Defending
national champions and a coach who had recruited him
made it especially large for Jimmy.

NOTRE DAME would visit Neyland Stadium. It was
time for revenge on another program that had beaten them
in 1978—another school that had recruited him.

That was all the motivation that Jimmy and those
who worked out through the summer on their own needed
for the fall. It would be his senior season. Individual
records could fall, but more than anything else, he wanted
to go out on a winning team—a nationally ranked team.

ALABAMA WAS RANKED NUMBER 2 and Notre
Dame was ninth when the 1979 season opened. Pollsters
were not impressed with Tennessee, so the Vols did not
appear among the pre-season Top 20. On the same day the
polls came out, Indiana basketball coach Bobby Knight's
Puerto Rican conviction of assaulting a police officer was
upheld by a Puerto Rican appeals court. If Knight ever set
foot back in Puerto Rico, he would face a six-month jail sentence and a $500 fine. He said he wasn't going back.

In a pre-season roundup of the Vols, Marvin West
wrote in the *News-Sentinel*, "Assuming these Vols get their
act together, perform most of the time at their ability level,
this is likely to be a high scoring team. . . . Tennessee
quarterbacking is another team strength. Jimmy Streater
starts the season as the man to beat for all-conference
honors. The combination of Jeff Olszewski, David Rudder,
and Tim Sharp add up to better-than-average depth. . . .
Boston College probably won't see a better offensive line
than Phil Sutton, Mike Jester, Lee North, Bill Marren, and
Tim Irwin."

"Perform most of the time at their ability level" were
very prophetic words that would come back to bite the Vols

in at least three games during the season.

BOSTON COLLEGE WAS SUPPOSED to be a twenty-point win for the Vols. It wasn't. They struggled, but finally managed to pull it out, 28-16.

Jimmy had a touchdown run of fourteen yards, a fumble, and a botched pitch-out. Smooth running back James Berry rushed for two TDs, and Hubert Simpson added another. Alan Duncan kicked a 40-yard field goal and one extra point.

On defense, Craig Puki, Kenny Jones, and Val Barksdale kept the Eagles caged.

Jimmy's favorite pass target was Anthony Hancock who caught six passes for 85 yards. Jimmy finished with 139 yards passing and 31 running. But he was still concerned with the fumble and bad pitch-out. "I still don't know what happened on that pitch," he said after the game. "It was just bad on my part, I guess."

At least the Vols had won their opener on a Saturday when there were upsets of Wake Forest over Georgia and Miami of Ohio over Kentucky. It was also the first opening game win for Coach John Majors since he returned to Tennessee.

THE POINT EXPLOSION THAT everyone was expecting came the next week against Utah in the nighttime home opener before 85,783 screaming fans.

The fans didn't have anything to scream about during the first quarter, though, as Utah jumped out to a 3-0 lead. Tennessee could not even move the ball for a first down. But with the second quarter came the point barrage.

Tennessee had a freshman from Griffin, Georgia, whose high school career in football didn't take off until he was a senior. Willie Gault didn't consider himself a college caliber football player when he was in high school.

"If I got any kind of scholarship, I thought it would have been in track," he said.

He was fast. He proved that on his first college reception in the second quarter of the Utah game. Jimmy passed, Willie caught, and the crowd cheered. The *PLAY* covered 69 yards and Utah was history.

"We hadn't been able to get anything established in the running game, and we had to do that," Streater explained after the game. The pass to Gault started as a Streater keeper with Reggie Harper ready for a drop-off pass if necessary.

Jimmy scrambled left and turned up field. But before he reached the line of scrimmage, the defense turned downfield to meet him. Gault took off.

"I ran a post pattern and was bumped inside. When they went up on Jimmy, I headed for the corner. When Jimmy saw me, I was open by ten yards," Gault recounted. Jimmy threw it to Gault for his first of many receptions.

Jimmy remembered Gault years later. "I always told 'Sweet' Willie just to run as far as he could and I would try to throw that far. Boy, it helped having someone as fast as Willie out there."

After the dam broke with the Gault catch, which was the seventh longest in Vol history, Jimmy threw other touchdown passes to Reggie Harper and Anthony Hancock. Jimmy ran for another touchdown before turning the fourth quarter over to Jeff Olszewski who ran for two TDs of his own.

The Vols won 51-18. They were gaining depth at receiver and running back. Ten receivers caught passes during the game, and, including Jimmy's and Olszewski's runs, the Vols cruised for 265 yards on the ground.

Jimmy had 188 yards and three TDs by air and 54 yards and the other TD by ground. He was named United Press International's offensive player of the week and the Associated Press' back of the week in the Southeast.

Some fans were skeptical. "I thought they looked really good, but we'll have to wait until they play somebody until we know for sure," said Jack Wilson of Greeneville.

135

The Jimmy Streater Story

THE VOLS WERE NOW on a five-game winning streak with Auburn coming to town for their first conference test. Jimmy had not been on a team that had beaten the Tigers. Auburn had seven victories against only two defeats to the Volunteers during the '70s. This was one of the games that Jimmy had circled in red. It was Tennessee's turn.

THE LARGEST CROWD IN Southeastern Conference history (85,936) welcomed the collision of the Tigers and the Vols. The teams waited at the tunnel exits to see who would go onto the field first. Coach Doug Barfield wanted his Auburn Tigers to wait and run out at the same time as the Volunteers to avoid the storm of "Boos" that would rain down on them if they came out first. Coach Johnny Majors held his players at the east entry.

"I didn't think Auburn would come out first, but I wanted to see. I knew when the kickoff was scheduled and we were going to show." Tennessee ran out in a blaze of orange—shirts and pants.

The afternoon was to be electric, and Gary Moore was the one who threw the switch. Gary had come in with the same class as Streater and struggled through the losing and barely winning. He was from Meigs County High at tiny Decatur about fifty miles from Knoxville. He was a solid runner and kickoff returner. The previous year he had a return for a touchdown called back against Auburn because of a penalty.

On the opening kickoff, Moore was not to be denied this time. He caught the ball on the two-yard line on the north end of the field and ran south by southeast 98 yards toward the double deck of Vol fans in the south end zone who had not taken their seats. He didn't stop until there were six points on the scoreboard. He was enveloped by the shouts and cheers as he was mobbed by his teammates in the valley between the fans.

"The main thing was the two upbacks, Terry Daniels

136

and James Berry," Moore explained after the game. "When I caught the ball, I went five or ten yards up the middle, then, they opened me to the sideline. Once I got to the 45, I saw one of our guys and their kicker, so I just made the kicker commit himself." And Moore was gone.

It was the only runback of an opening kickoff in John Majors' coaching career. "I hugged his neck when Gary got to the bench," Majors said.

If Jimmy needed any jump-starting, Gary's run did it for him. Jimmy was to have the best afternoon to date of his career. First, the Vols won, 35-17; secondly, they did it in style. Jimmy rushed for a total of 106 yards and threw for 158 with 12 completions in 20 attempts. He threw to Reggie Harper for a first-quarter touchdown. With four seconds left in the first half, Jimmy skirted the end for a six-yard TD run.

The defense was just as ferocious as the offense. Val Barksdale squeezed two interceptions from the air while Danny Martin got another one. Barksdale added 15 tackles to his stats, Craig Puki knocked 13 ball carriers to the turf, and Greg Gaines was just one behind with 12. Steve Davis, Kenny Jones, and Brad White also played inspired defensive ball.

"This was the best 60 minutes of football by our team since I've been at Tennessee," John Majors said after the game.

Jimmy compared this game with Auburn to the previous year's. "This time we had great blocking. I'd glance back after handing off, and there'd be holes two people could run through. This is the first time I've played a whole game without the other team getting to me while I was in the backfield. That's inspiring."

How did Coach Majors help Jimmy through the game? "I said nothing. He was doing so well, I didn't want to confuse him. He showed great poise, courage against a team that humiliated us last year." Majors also praised the play calling of Lynn Amedee.

The Jimmy Streater Story

Jimmy ended up with two touchdowns running to go with the one he threw to Harper.

"Are you the best quarterback in the Southeastern Conference?" a reporter asked Jimmy in the dressing room after the game.

"On my part, I feel I'm the best in the country. But you guys decide that. I'm just the guinea pig out there on the field. That will take care of itself."

"What about when you held the ball up before you got to the end zone on your 28-yard TD run? Were you trying to rub it in Auburn's face?" another one asked.

"No. I thought I was in the end zone. I'm not that type of player."

Looking back on the game on the following Monday, Marvin West wrote, "Jimmy Streater may have had his best day, as a combination passer, runner, and leader. The bright quarterback did some fast thinking to go with his 264 yards in offense."

The Auburn victory pushed the Vols into a six-game win streak over the last three games of 1978 and the first three of 1979. It was the longest string of victories since the 1972-73 seasons. The Vols next would face Mississippi State which had a one win and two loss record.

The Vols' win impressed many in the Southeastern Conference, including Florida's new coach Charley Pell whose Gators got beat the same Saturday by Mississippi State.

"Mississippi State got the big play when they needed it to beat us. But Tennessee must really have looked good. Tennessee will beat the daylights out of them."

Pell's quote was a bold headline in Monday's Knoxville *News-Sentinel* sports section. Matt Edwards from Knoxville Bearden High School played for Mississippi State. His father cut the story out and sent it to his son. In addition to a place on the State players' bulletin board, a copy of the headline was carried onto the field of play by State player Alan Hartlein who wore it between his hip pads and pants. State was inspired and Tennessee was not. The results were not pretty.

A SATURDAY AFTER JIMMY Streater was hailed as possibly the best quarterback in the SEC, he was bombarded with a chorus of boos and racial slurs when he left the field at the end of a 28-9 loss to Mississippi State.

While he was still struggling on the field, a white woman walked behind the bench area of the Vols and yelled, "Why don't you get that colored quarterback out of there and play somebody who can do something?" It was loud enough for the players to hear, and they were shocked. But her shout was mild compared to others.

Although Jimmy had 40 yards rushing and 150 passing, he had a poor day—as had the whole team. He threw three interceptions. He botched a pitch-out for a twelve-yard loss, was decked for an eleven-yard sack, threw too hard to a wide-open Reggie Harper, and missed James Berry along the sideline on what would have been a sure touchdown. Anthony Hancock dropped another of Jimmy's passes which very easily could have been a TD.

Tennessee was just not good enough to win in the SEC when the players were not performing up to their ability. The State wishbone attack tore the Vols up. State only had to throw six times while running over, through, and around Volunteers for 320 yards.

Jeff Olszewski came in with 7:54 to go in the game and led the Vols to their only touchdown. The game in Memphis was supposed to be a home game for the Vols, but the crowd was equally divided in numbers. Then some of the fans turned on their own team.

"I'm glad I never have to play in Memphis again," Streater said after the game. The Vols had lost three in a row in the river town.

"In no way does Streater deserve abuse. Several Vols were shocked at the abuse in Memphis. So-called Tennessee fans, perhaps just a few, had racial overtones in cutting criticism of the Vols.

"How soon fans forget that Jimmy Streater has twice been the South's offensive player of the week in the first month of the season," Marvin West wrote in his Monday column.

"I don't think there is a place for it," Coach Majors said in a Tuesday press conference. "Unfortunately we can't cure all our ills. It's a sickness in our country. I know for every person who is negative, there are hundreds of others who are positive."

One reason Jimmy didn't go to Alabama was that he feared how the first black quarterback would be treated there if things didn't go perfectly. With Condredge Holloway having paved the way at UT, he was willing to be UT's second black quarterback. Now some of those who called themselves fans were calling him names and questioning his ability because of his color and race.

But Jimmy never dwelled on the negative. There was another game to get ready for on the following Saturday—one that he had circled in red.

When he was asked twenty years later about racism in the South during his playing career, Jimmy didn't remember any. "Everybody always treated me well. They were all fair. I don't remember any racism, or taunts, or slurs, or name-calling."

THERE WAS A BIT of tension among players and coaches the following week as they searched for answers to the loss when things had been going so well. Starting strong safety Greg Gaines quit the team, saying he was tired of all the personal criticism. This left a depth-impaired secondary looking for bodies to fill the holes. Freshman Bill Bates from Farragut would get a look, according to coaches.

The World Series would open during the week with the Pittsburgh Pirates playing the Baltimore Orioles. Georgia Tech was coming to Knoxville with a losing record—1-2-1—but the losses were to Notre Dame and Alabama who just had one loss between them, and both were ranked in the top ten. Tech would be bringing a pass-oriented team just when UT was shifting their defensive secondary.

JIMMY STREATER ROSE FROM the depths of despair of the boos and taunts at the Memphis State game to lead the Vols in an offensive show. On the defensive side, Craig Puki and the revamped secondary carried the day by shutting out Pepper Rodgers' Ramblin' Wreck.

The Vols started slowly once again. At the end of the first quarter, they led 3-0. The onslaught came in the second when Tennessee struck for three touchdowns.

Puki intercepted a Mike Kelley pass at the Yellow Jacket 38, and the Vols drove it to the end zone with Gary Moore going the final two yards for six points.

Tech fumbled on the next possession at the UT 39. Moore pounded it ahead. Then Jimmy found Anthony Hancock across the middle for a 25-yard TD. Tech punted on their next possession and the Vols drove 60 yards in a little over two minutes. Jimmy threw the final thirteen yards to Reggie Harper to make it 24-0 with eleven seconds left in the half. In the locker room, the players knew they were cruising again. The coaches warned against letdowns and emphasized keeping up the intensity.

Six minutes into the third quarter, Jimmy made what was probably the prettiest run of his career—a 43 yard off-tackle keeper for a touchdown.

"A piece of poetry" one reporter wrote. "It was a thing of zig-zagging beauty, perhaps his most picturesque," wrote another.

"I wish I could have seen that in slow motion," a Georgia Tech fan said.

"Jimmy Streater has made many dazzling runs for Tennessee in his four years at quarterback," wrote Tom Siler of the *News-Sentinel*. "But the best yet came in the third period. Jimmy motored those spider legs as he swung right, carried that broomhandle torso through a slight opening, broke against the grain and scooted 43 yards to the end zone. Georgia Tech was already beaten and that counter made it 31-0.

"But there have been few more beautiful runs on Shields-Watkins Field than that piece of wizardry. That's why Jimmy is possibly the most-feared single performer in the Southeastern Conference."

"I'm so excited for him," Puki said. "I love watching him play. You never know what he's going to do next."

Jimmy didn't want to talk much about himself after what he said following the Auburn game about being the best in the country and then being booed in Memphis the following week.

"I love to be able to give my fullest ability on a run like that. It gives me a thrill to know I'm able to do that."

"We haven't seen a quarterback who could do the things Streater does," Tech linebacker Henry Johnson said. "Streater is their offense. He's the fastest option quarterback I've ever seen."

Noseguard Ivey Stokes agreed. "Streater is what killed us. He's tricky, real tricky. Their offense seems to be just a bunch of big plays and Streater is the cause of all of them."

"He's fantastic," Tech Coach Rodgers said. "Tennessee should be proud to have a quarterback like him."

The revamped secondary also did well. Roland James, Danny Martin, Wilbert Jones, and Bill Bates proved themselves a cohesive unit. Carlton Gunn had stepped into the noseguard position and played exemplarily.

Jimmy finished the game with 96 yards and two TDs passing. His 43-yard magical run lifted his rushing total to 103 yards for the day.

JIMMY WAS NOW THE ALL-TIME TOTAL YARDAGE LEADER FOR TENNESSEE. His career total was 4210, which surpassed his friend Condredge Holloway's old record of 4068. He played less than three quarters before

Coach Majors turned the offense over to Jeff Olszewski. There were six games left in the season to add to the records.

"It couldn't have happened to a nicer young man," Coach Majors said. "I'm very excited. He is very talented, a true winner."

"I'm proud of it," Jimmy said, "but I'll be a whole lot prouder after the season is over."

Near the end of the game, the public address announcer told everyone that Jimmy had broken the record previously held by Holloway. All in Neyland Stadium then rose to their feet and gave Jimmy the ovation he deserved. What a difference a week made.

"WE'RE BACK ON TRACK like after the Auburn game," Gene Eblen, a fan from Kingston, said after the Tech game. "We'll give Bama fits." And it was true. Alabama was on the minds of all fans before they arrived home from the Georgia Tech game. The Tide had rolled over the Gators of Florida 40-0 at the same time Tennessee was beating Tech. Alabama had beaten Tech 30-6 in the first game of the season. They were undefeated and ranked Number 1 in the country. In five victories the Tide had rolled up 219 points to the opponents' 9. Was this a steamroller of a team or one which had played weak teams?

ON WEDNESDAY OF ALABAMA week, the Pittsburgh Pirates won the World Series over the Baltimore Orioles. Former Knoxville Bearden High and University of Tennessee star Phil Garner played for the Pirates. He was in the running for Most Valuable Player until beaten out by teammate Willie Stargell.

Knoxville's Big John Tate was scheduled to fight Gerry Coetzee in Pretoria, South Africa, for the World Boxing Association's heavyweight title just a few hours after the Vols played the Tide on Saturday.

While Alabama was at the top of the polls, Tennessee

had sneaked into the Top Twenty—18th in the AP and 19th in the UPI. According to Florida's Charlie Pell, there was no need to play the game or for Alabama to play any more games. The Tide should just be declared the National Champion—even if half the season hadn't been played. "This (Alabama) is by far the best team. To me, they're the uncontested National Champion."

Alabama had a wealth of talent and depth. Some believed Tennessee was a one-man offensive show with Jimmy Streater. Tom Siler, trying to size up Alabama's strategy in a column during game week, wrote, "Alabama will shoot linebackers and use the safety blitz to tear up Jimmy Streater's intentions. . . . Tennessee's offensive line must provide support of Streater and the offensive plan if the Vols are to reach the end zone enough to make a game of it."

Tennessee would face the most devastating wishbone attack in the country. The Vols had fallen apart when confronted with Mississippi State's two weeks before. And State was no Alabama.

But to Jimmy this was just another challenge. No one ever accused him of not having the confidence to play quarterback. Along with his talent, he had an air of victory about him. A quarterback had to be confident in going up against teams like Alabama. If he weren't, he'd be destroyed. Sometimes, to those who didn't know him, Jimmy would come off as a little cocky, as when he held the ball up on the way to a TD against Auburn and when he said he thought he was the best quarterback in the country. "If you're going to say it, you've got to play it," Jimmy would repeat. He always intended to "play it" and only "say it" when asked.

This Alabama game was another of the ones he had circled in red before the beginning of the season. The Vols had won against Auburn and Georgia Tech. Two red circles down and two to go with the Tide and Notre Dame.

In the past two years against Alabama, Jimmy hadn't

shown what he thought he could do. In 1977, he was held out because of injury. In 1978, he had left the game in the third quarter with a bruised hip and the Vols trailing 30-3. He had passed for 45 yards and rushed for 48. He had yet to score against the Tide.

Bear Bryant was asked in a press conference call the week of the game about what problems Jimmy would present for Alabama on game day.

"He'll present a multitude of problems," Bear said. "Streater'll be a problem for our players, our coaches, our fans . . . everyone in the state of Alabama," he continued without ever really answering the question. Bryant was never accused of giving away his game plan to the press or opposing coaches. He would always butter up the opponent to where those reading his comments would think Alabama's opponent each week was the top team in the country. He would downplay his own team's ability and merely say if they played hard they might have a chance to win.

Kickoff was a little after 2:30 on a beautiful afternoon in Birmingham. For once, things went Tennessee's way at the beginning of the game. This was one of Alabama's home fields, but Tennessee was getting the breaks and bounces.

Tide quarterback Steadman Shealy fumbled twice in the first quarter. Tennessee's Carlton Gunn captured the second one at the Alabama 14. With that opportunity, Jimmy, after a running play, hit Phil Ingram for an eleven-yard TD off a newly installed play with a triple set to the left.

Tennessee started another possession in the first quarter from their 37-yard line. In a ten-play drive they chopped the Alabama defense apart with short power plays behind Hubert Simpson, a thirteen-yard Streater scramble, a Streater pass to Simpson for 15, and then with Jimmy running it in from three yards out. It seemed so easy now. Jimmy had scored by air and by land. He wanted to beat them and beat them badly. It was still the first quarter and the Vols led 14 to 0. That was the good news. They had time to score 56 at 14 per quarter.

The bad news was they were up 14 to 0 and it was still the first quarter. On the far sideline prowled the best coach in college football at the time. He was thinking. All the years of experiences were whirling through Bear Bryant's steel trap of a mind.

When asked after the game what he was thinking, Bryant said, "I was wondering what I was going to tell all you reporters about what happened to a supposed Number 1 team."

But what he was really thinking was of ways to come back. He looked at his players and saw they had more depth of talent than Tennessee. If he could get a score before halftime and slow Tennessee down, the Tide would be okay. He had to bring more pressure on that slithery quarterback Jimmy Streater.

Tennessee drove again. Simpson powered ahead. Then a pass from Jimmy was just beyond Reggie Harper's hands. The drive stalled. Alan Duncan kicked a 45-yarder. Tennessee 17, Alabama 0, with two minutes gone in the second quarter.

The Vols stopped another thrust of the Tide with Brad White recovering another fumble. But on the next series, a pass thrown by Jimmy was tipped and then intercepted. Bama drove in for a TD.

The teams exchanged punts for the remainder of the half. The Tide had stopped the flood of points by Tennessee but had not figured out yet how to hold onto the ball and counter the Tennessee scores. The Tide fumbled again near halftime with Bill Bates recovering. Streater went for the bomb to Anthony Hancock, but it was just off his fingertips.

"When you touch them, you're supposed to catch them," Hancock would say later. He thought that possible touchdown would have put Alabama too far behind to catch up. At halftime it was 17-7.

In the dressing room, the Bear and his senior leaders got things straightened out. The Tide was not ready to give up their Number 1 ranking or to end their record winning streak. They came out with a vengeance.

Tennessee muffed a chance to go up by another touchdown after Danny Martin intercepted a Bama pass and returned it 31 yards. Terry Daniels fumbled and Jimmy was intercepted again. Alabama took over on the UT 30 and drove quickly for the score behind Major Ogilvie. Tennessee 17, Alabama 14. But it was as though Tennessee knew that the Tide could not be turned back.

Alabama stuffed Tennessee without a first down in the third quarter. The Tide drove for the go ahead TD. Their clinching TD came in the fourth behind an eighty-yard drive.

The Vols didn't give up or lie down. They fought. They scratched. They tried every way to come back. It reminded Jimmy of his last game in high school against Pisgah. He went down throwing, always looking for a receiver to turn the tide.

A throw to Anthony Hancock for an apparent touchdown was called back on a penalty, and that was it. Alabama 27, Tennessee 17. Jimmy had passed for 106 yards and a touchdown. But he had two interceptions. He had run for another touchdown. But he was held to minus four yards rushing because of several sacks.

The Vols were not satisfied with coming within ten points of the eventual national champion. It was a red circle game that the Vols didn't win. "They're just Alabama," Jimmy said after the game. "They don't believe they can lose."

Now Coach Bryant was ready to say his team was good. "It was the greatest I've ever heard of anybody making this kind of comeback against Tennessee. I think Alabama is a champion now. If we can come back and beat Tennessee like that, I think we can beat anybody." They could and they did.

Despite the loss, the Vols impressed some pollsters and stayed in one of the top twenty lists.

The Jimmy Streater Story

Big John Tate beat Jerry Coetzee in Pretoria, South Africa, the same day for a share of the heavyweight championship.

"WHAT IS A RUTGERS?" was heard around Knoxville a lot before the Vols' next game. Some compared the school from up East with a vegetable—a rutabaga—and said they were going for 59 cents a pound. There was a lot of joviality in the air before the homecoming game. They always scheduled a pushover for homecoming, didn't they? Coaches went recruiting. Players had a week off to think about the Alabama defeat and the team they would play after Rutgers—Notre Dame—another red circle game.

Marvin West should have been a coach or a soothsayer in addition to his job as a writer. "This is a hazardous time for the Vols. Rutgers, in case you haven't noticed, comes after Alabama and before Notre Dame, a difficult time for peak concentration," he wrote a couple of days before the game.

Kevin Kurdyla, offensive tackle for Rutgers, stood in the middle of Shields-Watkins field after the Scarlet Knights had beaten the Vols 13 to 7 and looked at the emptying stands. "Well, I guess they know what a Rutgers is now. They know we come higher than 59 cents a pound." Indeed.

"You don't know how much this hurts," Tennessee's Bill Marren said after the game. He was from New Jersey. This was his senior year. "It's embarrassing as a team. With me, it's unbelievable."

"Their stunts with their tackles really worked," Jimmy said. "The tackles were getting through, and I had to option off against them instead of against the defensive ends. It became a quick option." And Rutgers shut down the rushing game. Tennessee had only 95 yards on the ground. It was the Vols' first loss to an Eastern school in 38 years.

Streater completed nine of 19 passes to his teammates and threw three into the hands of Scarlet Knights' defensive backs. Jimmy had seven yards rushing and no touchdowns.

IT WAS A LOW time for the team with the unexpected loss. But a more serious thing had happened to some Americans in a foreign land that riveted the attention of the nation. In Tehran, Iran, more than 60 hostages at the U.S. embassy were seized by militant followers of the country's despotic leader. It would be fourteen and a half months before most of them were freed. On the home front, interest rates soared to 15 1/2 per cent.

WHAT HOPE WAS THERE to beat a real football school, rich in tradition, as Notre Dame was, if the Vols couldn't put away Rutgers?

For the Tennessee players, this was the chance to show that the team's character was more like the one that had beaten Auburn and Georgia Tech and had given fits to Alabama than like the one that had fallen to Mississippi State and Rutgers. For seniors, like Jimmy, Roland James, Craig Puki, David Rudder, Bill Marren, Kyle Aguillard, Johnny Watts, Nate Sumpter, Alan Lynn, Gary Moore, Mike Jester, Steve Davis, and Phil Sutton, this was the one chance to make history. This was the first time that Notre Dame would come into Neyland Stadium to play on Shields-Watkins Field. A win against Notre Dame would be memorable—a game they could point back to in years to come and say that was when UT turned the corner to get back into national prominence.

Notre Dame was ranked 13th in both polls. They had what was considered a huge offensive line in 1979, averaging 257 pounds per man. Joe Montana was gone, but Notre Dame had a Heisman contender at running back in Vagas Ferguson, who had 3096 rushing yards for his career. He was the record holder for Notre Dame and had come in with the same class that Jimmy had in 1976. At the time of his recruitment, he was ranked the second best player in the nation while Jimmy was ranked ninth.

By Wednesday of game week, ticket demand was the greatest in history. Knoxville's Lindsey Nelson, who broadcast the Sunday replay of all Notre Dame games, said all of Notre Dame's 5000 supply went fast. "Our sponsors have been asking me for tickets. It's tough."

In the weekly press conference, the coaches from both schools commented on the strengths of their opponent. "Notre Dame linemen, year after year, look like they come out of the same mold," John Majors said.

"We had a lot of trouble with Jimmy Streater last year. His tremendous quickness and all-around ability is what scares you. I'd rather defense a dropback quarterback. Not only is Streater dangerous when he pitches the ball out but also when he keeps it. He can break a big play," said Notre Dame coach Dan Devine.

That was what the Vols wanted—some big plays and a whole lot of good little plays.

HUBERT SIMPSON HAD BEEN in and out of the doghouse with Coach Majors, but when the coach wanted a back who could play in a physical game, he knew where to turn. Hubert was ready.

"The coaches knew I liked contact," Simpson said after the game. "I thrive on it. The more I get, the more I give 'em. I like the toughness."

He was tough. He ran over, through, and between Notre Dame linemen and linebackers for 117 yards on 27 carries for a record-tying four touchdowns in the Vols' 40 to 18 victory.

"When Simpson is hot, he's very good," said Coach Majors. "When he cranks up and goes, he goes good."

"I was going to give them something to measure Vagas Ferguson by. My plan was to outdo Ferguson," Simpson said.

For the first time since 1958, fans rushed the field and tore the goalpost down at the north end. Police did not interfere, except to guard the south goalpost from a similar fate. The crowd was a record 86,489.

Notre Dame scored first, going 80 yards in ten plays. Some Vol fans thought they were in for a long afternoon.

But Tennessee came back on a long drive of its own behind the running of Simpson and Streater, the blocking of Tim Irwin and the other offensive linemen, and the throwing arm of Jimmy. With three and a half minutes left in the first quarter, Jimmy tied the score with a five-yard run, eluding Notre Dame linebacker Bob Crable with a magical move.

Hubert scored his first touchdown just two and a half minutes into the second quarter on a 24-yard gallop with Mike Jester and Lee North cutting off the linebackers. UT 14, ND 6.

Lemont Holt intercepted a Notre Dame pass just moments later and returned it 13 yards to the UT 46. On the next play, Jimmy read an option key perfectly and sped off tackle for his longest run of the year—51 yards—before he was knocked out of bounds at the Notre Dame three-yard line. Catching his breath, Jimmy handed the ball off to his friend Hubert on two successive thrusts for the TD. Vols 21, Irish 6.

On the Vols' kickoff, the Irish receiver stepped out at the one-yard line. On the next play, Brian Ingram smothered quarterback Rusty Lisch in the end zone for a two-point safety. Vols 23, Irish 6.

The Irish kicked from their twenty and the Vols pounded it back 66 yards for another score. Jimmy threw to Reggie Harper for eleven, to Anthony Hancock for 48, and the final yard was punched in by Hubert. UT 30, ND 6.

Notre Dame fumbled the kickoff and booted it out at the seven. Wilbert Jones intercepted Lisch. Then Tom Gibbons intercepted Streater. The Irish drove for a touchdown behind the passing of Lisch and running of Ferguson who got the TD with four minutes left in the half. The try for a two-point conversion failed. UT, 30, ND, 12.

The Jimmy Streater Story

On the next series, Tennessee fans sat in silence when Jimmy was sandwiched along the line of scrimmage by two ND defenders. "Somebody hit me as I was trying to fall. Somebody hit me from one way, and somebody else hit me from the other. One was high, one low. I wasn't able to protect myself. My foot got caught in the turf a little, and that was it," Jimmy recounted.

David Rudder came in to replace Jimmy, who was taken to the dressing room. Rudder scrambled for 15 but fumbled with ND recovering. The Irish drove down field with a fury. At the Vols' one-yard line with time running out in the half, Kenny Jones, Brad White, and Craig Puki ganged up to take Ferguson down and preserve a solid halftime lead.

When Jimmy returned to the field after halftime, he was wearing a three-piece gray suit instead of the Tennessee orange uniform, and he was limping along on crutches. Thousands of fans stood and applauded. He had sustained a partially torn ligament in his right knee and was through for the day, and perhaps for his career, according to those who looked at the knee.

The Vols weren't through. They scored ten more on another TD by Simpson and a 35-yard field goal by Alan Duncan while holding the Irish to one more touchdown by Ferguson.

In a little less than two quarters of playing time, Jimmy had 66 yards and a touchdown on the ground and had thrown for 75 yards.

"There have been times Vol fans wanted a white quarterback," Marvin West wrote the next day. "A few, in Memphis, said so. It was just a week ago many of the same paying customers booed the little man, called for a replacement, asked more leadership, greater skill. Suddenly, with everybody thinking Jimmy may be finished, with the Vols leading at the time, 30-12, Streater was a fallen hero. Remember all those dazzling plays, the arm like a cannon, the school-record total of yards running and throwing?

"Streater insists his Tennessee career is not over. He isn't ready to put it away.

" 'I got to get well and go one more game. I have some unfinished business. I still haven't played up to my potential. I want to do more,' he said.

"Pardon me, while I applaud," West finished.

JIMMY COULDN'T GO THE next week against Mississippi at Jackson. For all the good that was done, the whole team should have stayed home. The Vols found themselves at the bottom loop of their yo-yo year and lost 44-20.

The score was tied at 14 at the half, but Ole Miss beat up on the Vols in the second half with a 30-point barrage. It was a rout, a knockout. It was awful.

They missed Jimmy on offense (David Rudder and Jeff Olszewski had but 90 yards of offense between them), but he didn't play defense. The 44 points were the most scored against the Vols during the year. Two fumbles near the goal line were turned into Rebel touchdowns. John Fourcade picked apart Tennessee's secondary when he needed to. But mostly, the Rebs just ran over the Vols for 289 yards and six touchdowns.

Hubert Simpson was still hitting on all cylinders. He again carried the ball 27 times as he had against Notre Dame. This time he had only one TD to go with his 174 yards.

The Vols had an unofficial deal to take the Bluebonnet Bowl bid. Coach Majors would shake hands after the game and be all smiles. That was the plan. After the loss, Coach Majors said he wasn't accepting the bid then. The Bluebonnet people were off the hook if they wanted to look elsewhere. But it turned out they didn't because they had promised the other bowl team—Purdue—that they would provide them with an opponent with a national flavor and a vulnerable pass defense.

ONLY WINS OVER KENTUCKY and Vanderbilt would allow the Volunteer players to hold their heads high enough to accept the Bluebonnet Bowl bid and go to Houston for the New Year's Eve clash with Purdue. If they lost either of the next two, there was a feeling that the seniors would go to Coach Majors and ask him to get them out of the bowl game. If they had nothing else, they had pride, and they knew a team with five losses didn't belong in a bowl.

Jimmy's knee had not healed enough to let him play at Kentucky, but the leg of Alan Duncan was in fine shape. He kicked a 25-yard field goal with five seconds left in the game at Lexington to give the Vols a 20-17 victory.

"I said, 'Lord, I'm not praying for the win. I just want to do my job.' I know the Lord doesn't care who wins," Duncan said after the game. He also praised Jack Jolley who did the snapping and Phil Ingram who held for the field goal attempt.

Hubert Simpson continued on his bullish ways of rushing. He had started with Notre Dame with 117 yards, then continued at Ole Miss with 174 yards, and walloped Kentucky with 181 yards on 35 carries.

Jeff Olszewski performed better with six of twelve passing for 74 yards.

Although Kentucky outgained Tennessee by over a hundred yards, the Vols did what winners are supposed to do—they found a way to win. Simpson provided the ground work, and Duncan provided the foot.

Phil Fulmer was at the game. The ex-Vol was an assistant at Vanderbilt and was scouting the Vols for the next week's game.

Now the Vols didn't feel bad about accepting the Bluebonnet Bowl bid. They wanted to finish strong with Vanderbilt and then take off for New Year's Eve in Houston.

VANDERBILT DECIDED TO PLAY like Tennessee on Saturday. To start the day, Vandy players ran through the T formed by the band in a backwards direction after

Tennessee had exited to the west sideline. This antic did nothing to help their standing with fans in the south end zone area where Vandy would have to exit after the game.

They then copied the Vols by playing one good half and one poor half. Vandy's good half was the first where they jumped to a 10 to 0 lead over the Vols. They smiled when they heard Vol fans booing their own team. Vandy then collapsed in the second half and Tennessee exploded for a 31-10 victory.

Jimmy and senior linebacker Craig Puki were both recovering from injuries and were going to sit out unless they were desperately needed. They were. When the Vols fell ten behind, they both came in to lift the offensive and defensive sides of the ball.

Anthony Hancock summed up Jimmy's return to the huddle in the first quarter after Jeff Olszewski had started the game. "I tell you when Jimmy came in, you could feel the difference in your body. It was 'Bird's back. Let's go.'

"We just started shaking his hand, saying, 'Welcome back, Bird,' and he said, 'Let's go, Y'all.' We knew what we had to do."

The point explosion came in the third quarter. Jimmy found Hancock on a 41-yard break to the post for a TD.

Four plays later when Vandy punted, Roland James picked it up at the Tennessee eleven after the ball had bounced. He ran across field and then darted up the left sideline to the end zone. The 89-yard return was the fourth longest in UT history.

Jimmy and Anthony weren't going to let Roland steal all the thunder. They teamed up for a record-setting 85-yard pass and catch for the third TD of the third quarter. It broke the record set in 1969 between Bobby Scott and Lester McClain as the longest in UT history.

Jimmy went on to break two more records that had been held for nine years by Scott. He broke the number of interceptions thrown in a season by one. He hit Vandy end

Phil Swindoll right in the hands in the first quarter to give Jimmy 16 interceptions for the season compared to Scott's old record of 15. He broke Scott's career passing yardage record by scorching the Commodores for 221 yards on 13 of 23 attempts. He now held the career passing record at 3433 to Scott's 3371. He added to his career yardage mark, lofting it to 4807 compared to Condredge Holloway's old record of 4068.

"Bobby Scott called me early this week and said he wanted to wish me luck and hoped I could break the passing record," Jimmy said after the game.

Some of the outstanding seniors had a fine game. Roland James had an interception and the punt return for a touchdown. Gary Moore set a career kickoff return record with 996 yards on 41 returns. Jimmy set his records. Craig Puki came in and gave the defensive unit a lift when they needed it.

Bowl performances did not count in individual records. Jimmy was averaging 181 yards per game when he was injured in the Notre Dame game and missed two and a half games. Another 450 yards would have looked good on his stats, but Jimmy was more excited that the Vols had won their final home game.

Around the Southeastern Conference, Alabama was undefeated while Florida had not won a single game. The Gators had tied one to end up with a 0-10-1 record. At least Vanderbilt had won one to end up 1-10. The two Mississippi teams that beat the Volunteers ended up with worse overall records.

THE BLUEBONNET BOWL IN Houston was to be a reward for the hard work of the players during the year and a recruiting tool for the coaches. The seniors would go out in style, while the underclassmen would have something to build upon. Coach Majors could point to Tennessee's bowl appearance when he sat down in living rooms of recruits. He could tell them they could go to one too if they came to

Big Orange Country.

In 1965, the Vols had gone to the Bluebonnet Bowl and beaten Tulsa behind the quarterbacking of Dewey "The Swamp Rat" Warren. "Warren was as courageous as anyone I've seen," wrote Marvin West in a column before the 1979 Bluebonnet Bowl. "He would stand in the pocket, ignore the rush, and deliver the football on time and on target."

Jimmy was a different type of quarterback, but no one could question his courage. He came back from injury to finish out his career. He often sparked the Volunteers to a comeback when things looked dour, as they did after two and a half quarters of the Bluebonnet Bowl.

Tennessee decided not to play the first half and let Purdue jump out to a 14-0 halftime lead. The Boilermakers punched in another TD in the third quarter before the Vols came to life. Once they did, though, it was a wild finish.

With just under three minutes to go in the third quarter, Jimmy found Glenn Ford for a seven-yard TD strike. The touchdown had been set up by another beautiful pass and catch between Jimmy and Anthony Hancock that covered 56 yards. The Vols, desperate to catch up, tried for the two-point conversion but failed.

The defense, behind the head-knocking of Craig Puki, Brad White, and Steve Davis, stopped Purdue. The Vols drove 70 yards in 12 plays. Phil Ingram started one way, reversed fields, and finally lofted a horrible pass that was caught at shoe-top level by James Berry for a TD. Hubert Simpson blasted over for the two-point conversion, and suddenly it was Tennessee 14, Purdue 21. It looked possible.

A Wilbert Jones blitz, a poor punt, and a Roland James return of 19 yards put the ball at the Purdue 17. Jimmy swept for 13, kept again for two, and handed off to Simpson for the final two and a TD. Tennessee 20, Purdue 21. The decision was made quickly to go for the two-point conversion and the lead. Simpson slammed across again, and with 3:42 remaining in the game the Vols were up 22-21.

Purdue quarterback Mark Herrmann wasn't through either. He threw to Bart Burrell for 18 and then 13. A pass interference call against Danny Martin moved the ball another 14. Then Dave Young beat freshman Bill Bates for the final touchdown. Purdue tried a two-pointer of their own but Bates intercepted.

Jimmy came back throwing in the last desperate minute and a half. There were no timeouts left. This was not San Antonio and this was not the Alamo, but this was another bunch of Tennessee Volunteers who would go down swinging.

Five passes got the Vols to the Purdue 23-yard line. Time, the season, and Jimmy's college career ran out. He had 270 total yards to Mark Herrmann's 265.

The game was like so many—one good half and one bad. Like the season—one good game and one bad. This bunch gave fans some excitement if not enough victories.

"Wasn't that something, the way Jimmy came back," David Rudder said.

"I'm certain I never had a group come back from such depths. We could have been humiliated. This team gave a great, great, great effort," Coach Majors said.

"From the way it ended up, I am proud of our effort as a team," Jimmy said.

For the season, Tennessee ended up 7 and 5. Purdue finished at Number 10 in the polls. Alabama won the National Championship.

IT WAS THE LAST game of college football for the 1970s. Jimmy could look back on the '70s as a time of coming of age. He was a high school All-American at Sylva-Webster and then won All SEC honors for his efforts at UT.

Now it was time to prepare for the 1980s. What would life hold for him? Professional football? Marriage? Family? Money? Health? He hoped the 1980s would be as good to him as the past decade.

Part Three:

Life After Tennessee Football

1980–Present

AME Zion Church where many of Jimmy's ancestors are buried in the cemetery.

Sylva-Webster Football Field

1980-1981

Jimmy Streater came to the realization early in 1980 that his future football career might not be in the National Football League but in the Canadian. He received feelers from NFL teams. Some asked him if he would change positions to be a receiver. Some were concerned with his knee injury from the Notre Dame game. Also, he had been banged up in other games. Just how durable was he?

Jimmy went ahead and played baseball, trying to let the football cards fall where they would. He visited with his family in Sylva. He and Steve talked football and baseball. Steve had just finished his junior year at the University of North Carolina. He had done well as a defensive back and punter. He had a total of 57 tackles for the year and averaged 41.2 yards on 75 punts. Brother Eric was now playing football at Sylva-Webster and his future looked promising.

Football was where Jimmy would earn his living. He still lacked several hours of class work to get his degree from the University of Tennessee. His major was in psychology. His mother and father had wanted him to go to a university to get an education and a degree. He was on the road to that but there would be plenty of time.

Jimmy was young—just 22 in the spring of 1980—and he was counting on at least a ten-year career in pro ball. After that he could always fall back on his degree and work as a sports psychologist if he went on and obtained his master's. Better yet—he would put back enough from his pro career to live on for years to come.

"Get your degree," his mother prodded him.

"What about us?" Dana would ask. "Am I going with you where you go? Are we ever going to get married?"

"I need to know *where* I'm going first, Dana. During the season there's not much time for anything but football. I want to have a job first—some money. Then I'd feel like I could support you and you could quit your nursing job."

The NFL draft would be the last two days of April. Then he would know for sure if he would be going with one of those teams or if he would more probably have to look to Canada for his future. It was hard waiting. This time he wouldn't really be the one choosing from several bidders. It would be back like what had happened to his great grandfather George Rogers. Several rich owners would look over the stock of players available and decide which ones they wanted in this "slave market" of the draft. Only in this slave auction, the slaves got rich if they were drafted high enough.

To pass the time waiting for draft day, Jimmy spent hours with other friends and with Dana. They would go to movies, to concerts, to other sporting events, and on March 31, 1980, to one of the biggest events to come to Knoxville in the form of professional boxing.

Big John Tate who had won the bronze medal at the Montreal Olympics in 1976—the same year that Jimmy came to UT—was going to defend his heavyweight title against Mike Weaver.

Tate had won his share of the divided heavyweight title on the same day that the Vols had lost to Alabama's sterling comeback in Birmingham. Tate had gone to Pretoria, South Africa, the home of apartheid, and beaten the white home country hero Jerry Coetzee.

Jimmy shook his head and grinned. Big John wasn't scared to go to a segregated country and fight the white man's hero. Now he was going to defend the title against a "brother." Jimmy had to admire someone with the courage of Big John.

On Monday night, Tate would face Weaver in the Stokely Center just around the corner from Gibbs Hall. Why

162

not go and watch this local hero? It was going to be on national television on ABC but was going to be blacked out in Knoxville because there were a few seats that hadn't sold.

The crowd was almost like one of those that gathered for a Saturday football game. Over 12,000 fans packed the center for the main event. They had watched some preliminary bouts, but Big John was whom they had come to see. UT's pep band played "Rocky Top," and UT cheerleaders fired up the crowd. Big John Tate had the home floor advantage. Ace Miller, who had trained Tate since the beginning, was in his corner. Tate was the shiniest product of the many fighters that Ace had trained and worked with over the years. Finally there was a heavy-weight national champion in Knoxville. The football team had won the national championship in 1951, but there had been no local national champion since. There was really no hope for a basketball national championship—on the men's side. Here was Big John, and he was the champion.

And he could have probably won on that night too, except for one thing. Big John began to listen to the shouts of his fans. "Big John Tate! Big John Tate!" the crowd roared over and over as the fight wrapped up its fourteenth round and began the fifteenth. Big John was safely ahead on all the judges' scorecards. There was only one way that Mike Weaver was going to win—a knockout.

Big John listened to the cheers of his followers instead of the man in his corner who knew boxing. Big John was going for the knockout too.

A bone-shattering left hook from Weaver caught Big John on the side of his jaw and across the point of his chin. It was like a lumberjack had just cut the last inch into a towering redwood, stepped back, and yelled, "Timber!"

Big John was out before his body toppled and then thudded to the canvas. He didn't move. The crowd became as silent as if the dull sound of Big John's body falling to the canvas was the funeral peal from the bells of First Baptist Church. This just couldn't happen to Knoxville's hero. Not

Big John. Say, it wasn't so. This was an out-take of a bad movie. Run it back and play the real scene where Big John knocked out Mike Weaver.

Now Jimmy Streater sadly shook his head. How could someone like Big John lose it all with one inattentive act? Why had the cheers died out? Where was the applause?

TWO VOLUNTEERS WERE TAKEN in the NFL draft on April 29 and 30, 1980. Altogether, the affair went twelve rounds over two days in selecting 333 players. Roland James was picked in the first round by New England. The Patriots already had former UT stand-out Stanley Morgan. They also chose Vagas Ferguson of Notre Dame in the second round.

Craig Puki went to San Francisco in the third round.

Of those top ten incoming college freshmen in 1976, four were chosen in the first three rounds of the draft of 1980. Curtis Dickey was a first-round choice of the Baltimore Colts. Vagas Ferguson went to the Patriots. Scot Brantley, linebacker from Florida, was taken by Tampa Bay in the third round. Anthony Munoz was a first-round choice of Cincinnati.

The NFL teams drafted 18 quarterbacks, but Jimmy Streater was not one of them. Some of the quarterbacks taken were Gene Bradley, Paul McDonald, Gary Hogeboom, Eric Hipple, Craig Bradshaw, Scott Brunner, Mark Malone, Rusty Lisch, and Ed Luther. Jimmy had better numbers than most of those taken, but they had the bodies and styles that the professional teams in the NFL wanted.

The NFL teams were looking for quarterbacks that fit a mold of being tall, durable, bright, and ones who had a dropback passing style. The optioning, elusive, running quarterback was not a hot commodity. If NFL quarterbacks weren't passing, they were handing the ball off to big pounding fullbacks and speedy tailbacks. Jimmy's abilities and talents were not a good match for the NFL teams.

Chris Cawood

THE DENVER BRONCOS CALLED and offered
Jimmy a tryout—as a receiver. Jimmy thought it over. The
NFL paid a lot more than the Canadian league. He wanted
to be a quarterback, but he also wanted to make good money
for the time that his career would last. He would give the
Denver offer a shot.

As an undrafted free agent, he went for a week of
workouts with the Broncos but decided quickly that being on
the receiving end of the ball wasn't what he wanted to do.
The last pass he had caught was from his brother Steve in
high school. There it was fun. But defensive backs in the
NFL were just as fast as he was and had killer instincts.
There was no pocket of protection for a receiver going over
the middle, jumping high for a reception, and exposing his
rib cage to the shoulder pads and helmets of linebackers or
defensive backs.

To the north, there were several American quarter-
backs who were making a good living playing in the CFL.
Among them were his old friend Condredge Holloway, at
Ottawa, and Warren Moon.

The game was different in Canada. The field was
longer, there was more motion allowed, and each team was
limited in the number of "imports" (American players) they
could have on their squad. The season started earlier in the
year and ended earlier because of the climate. The Grey
Cup was the Canadian equivalent of the Super Bowl in the
NFL.

Any city in Canada would be too far for his parents,
brothers, and sister to come watch Jimmy play. But the
same was true of most pro cities in the U. S. He had to
make his decision based on what was best for Jimmy, Dana,
and their future plans.

Toronto was just across the border from the U. S. It
was just a short drive to Niagara Falls, the romantic
honeymoon capital. And the Toronto Argonauts wanted
Jimmy.

A Toronto fan remembered, "I recall that the signing

165

of Jimmy Streater was greeted with much enthusiasm by the Toronto media at the time as well as by the Argos' new head coach, former NFL great Willie Wood. Wood had succeeded another NFL great, Forrest Gregg. Streater was compared favorably with former Tennessee great Condredge Holloway who was starring at Ottawa at the time."

The money was nowhere near what a competent quarterback would make in the NFL, but still it looked like a lot to Jimmy. He would make in the $60,000 range, depending on several performance factors. Johnny Majors had come to UT with a salary of $42,000 in 1977. For 1980, Jimmy felt he was being paid very well.

Jimmy took part of his signing bonus and bought his folks a new car. He didn't have to. They were both working people who usually bought their own things. But Jimmy wanted to show that he remembered all the hours that his father coached him and brought him along.

Jimmy liked Coach Wood and general manager Tommy Hudspeth. Toronto was the largest city he had ever been to, but with football occupying his time, Jimmy didn't believe he would get lost or homesick.

As had been true of Jimmy's high school career and at UT, there were quarterbacks already at Toronto who were more experienced than he was. This would be another time when he would have to prove himself, wait for his opportunity, and then step in and prove he was a player.

Mark Jackson was out of Baylor and would play the most for Toronto in 1980. Tony Adams was called "747" because of his throwing ability. But Jimmy didn't mind waiting. He was getting paid. He was learning a new system. In high school he was into his junior year before he became the starter at quarterback. At UT he grabbed the position in his sophomore season by beating out more experienced players. All he needed in Toronto was a year—a good year backing up Adams or Jackson—and he would start accumulating some stats and begin breaking records of his own. That was Jimmy's plan.

Chris Cawood

THE RE WASN'T MUCH TIME between the end of baseball and classes at UT and the beginning of the Canadian football season. The first game was scheduled for July 9 against Montreal at Toronto's Canadian National Exhibition Stadium.

It would take Jimmy much longer than six weeks to learn the Argonauts' system and adjust to the Canadian style of play. What he had on his side was raw talent and ability that could be molded to the Canadian game if he were given time to develop.

Canadian teams generally dressed only two quarterbacks for each game. Jimmy was third-string behind Adams and Jackson. But in the fourth game of the season when the Argonauts played at Ottawa where Condredge Holloway was the quarterback, Adams went down with a serious knee injury. Jackson took over as the starting quarterback and Jimmy moved up to second.

It was just like high school. Jimmy moved up because the starter had a knee injury. This time, however, he only moved up to the backup instead of the starting position.

Back in Sylva, North Carolina, Jimmy's die-hard fans tried to find every opportunity to watch him. Cable television was just becoming popular, but it had not reached to many of the homes in the area. There were restaurants and other beverage establishments that had cable access to the Canadian games.

When he knew Jimmy's Argonauts were going to be on, Coach Babe Howell made his way with some other friends to watch the Sylva Streak.

"We would fight for a place to go watch," Coach Howell recalled. "Jimmy didn't get to play much, but we could see him standing along the sideline. He stayed near the head coach carrying a clip board and helped to signal the plays in. There were a lot of sea gulls flying around their stadium. When I'd see Jimmy, I'd kid him about all those

167

gulls flying around and him being the one to shoo them off the coach."

Another Canadian fan, Ravi Ramkissoonsingh, remembers that late in the 1980 season, Jimmy received substantial playing time in a game at Montreal. "It was apparent that Streater had the mobility and scrambling ability to play in the CFL. However, his talent was quite raw and he required some strong coaching, which the Argos didn't have much of back in those days."

Jimmy spent most of the season watching and learning. He dressed out for twelve games, but Mark Jackson played most of the time. It didn't bother Jimmy. He had learned to be patient before. His time would come.

The season ended in November with the Argos finishing last in the Eastern Conference with six wins and ten losses.

His stats for the season were minuscule. He had completed nine passes out of 24 attempts for 141 yards. His longest pass was 37 yards. He had two interceptions and two touchdowns. He carried nine times for a total of 38 yards. His longest run was 20 yards. His season totals for 1980 were less than average game statistics for him during his career at UT. And because of things that would soon begin occurring, these would be the total of his career stats for professional football.

WHILE JIMMY'S SEASON WOUND down with little accomplished in the way of stats, his brother Steve was having a remarkable year at the University of North Carolina. From his defensive back position, Steve had made 51 tackles. He had five interceptions. His punting improved to an average of 43.4 yards on 59 kicks. He was named All Atlantic Coast Conference as both a punter and defensive back. That had never happened before—to be named all-conference at two positions.

North Carolina was 10 and 1 for the season, having lost only to Oklahoma.

168

Steve and the rest of the Tarheels would go to Houston to play in the Bluebonnet Bowl, just as Jimmy had the year before. Steve was named Most Valuable Defensive player for the game.

Once again, the brothers, who were separated by just a year in age, were almost twins in accomplishments. Jimmy went to Tennessee. Steve enrolled at North Carolina. The two states shared a joined heritage. Tennessee was carved out of North Carolina. Eastern Tennessee and Western North Carolina shared the Smoky Mountain National Park. North Carolina stretched eastward to the ocean while Tennessee reached westward to the Mississippi River. Between them they spanned almost half the nation.

Jimmy was All-SEC and Steve All-ACC. Both would play in the Bluebonnet Bowl. But Steve could brag to his older brother that they defeated Texas to take the bowl title and finish Ninth in the AP poll and Tenth in the UPI poll. Jimmy's Volunteers had lost to Purdue in the Bluebonnet and had not finished in the top twenty.

These were good talking and arguing points when the brothers got together. They fed on each other's successes as much as their own. Jimmy still held out a hope and belief that one day they would play together in pro ball somewhere.

When the NFL draft days came in April of 1981, the brothers again shared something in common. Neither one, despite their talents, abilities, and all-conference honors, was drafted by an NFL team.

"Steve, it's just what we've been hoping and waiting for," Jimmy told his brother from Toronto. "You can come to Canada and make it like I'm doing."

"I don't know. I'd rather play for an NFL team. I've gotten some free-agent feelers. I've talked to L.T. about it."

"Steve, wait and talk to your agent. See what he thinks is best. Lawrence Taylor can demand big bucks with the New York Giants, but what will they pay you in Washington?"

169

"I don't know. I'm flying up to Washington in the morning to talk with Coach Gibbs. If they make me a decent offer, I'm signing."

"Be sure, brother, be real sure that's what you want to do before you sign."

Jimmy was living and working out in Toronto. The next season would be when he would make his move to first team. He had to be ready. The next day Steve left a message on Jimmy's telephone answering machine that he had signed a free agent contract with the Washington Redskins. He would talk with him later.

Jimmy got the message, called up a football friend, and went out to a restaurant to celebrate his little brother's signing. He didn't get home until nearly midnight on Friday night. The light on his answering machine was flashing again. Steve couldn't wait to talk with him. He wanted to tell him the details of the contract.

But when he punched the button, it wasn't Steve. It was his Aunt Margaret. She said to call. It was important. Jimmy looked at his watch. It was too late. She would be in bed. But she said it was important, so he called.

"Have you heard about Stevie?" she asked when he got through.

"Sure. He left me a message. He signed with Washington. That's great."

"No, not that."

"What then?"

"He's been in a wreck. On the way home from the airport after he got back from Washington. His car flipped. He broke his neck. I don't know if he's going to live." And then she started sobbing. Jimmy's hand that was holding the phone became cold. He sat down, still clutching the phone to his ear. No. No. No. It had to be somebody else. Steve's voice was still on the recorder.

"Aunt Margaret, you sure?"

"Yes, James and Shirley are at the hospital at Chapel Hill. Can you come?"

Steve's roommate Tryess Bratton was in the car with Steve when the accident happened. "I took Steve's car to the airport to pick him up. We were driving back, about four miles between the airport and I-40, when Steve lost control of the car in the rain.

"We hit an embankment and flipped over onto the pavement." Bratton was not hurt seriously.

The doctors told Steve's family that he had sustained two fractures at the level of the sixth cervical vertebra. He was, temporarily at least, paralyzed from the neck down. It would be at least two weeks before they would know if he would regain full use of his legs.

"Some of the nerve damage will heal in time," Dr. Joseph DeWatt told them. "Steve may be able to walk again some day." He was listed in fair condition, conscious and alert in the intensive care unit.

When Jimmy arrived and walked into the room, he wasn't prepared for what he saw. Steve lay motionless on the bed. Around his neck and head was a metal halo that stabilized him and assured no movement. There his eyes were, active as ever, darting from one family member to the other to the ceiling to the machines.

Jimmy looked at his brother. His youthful, muscular, athletic body was still there. The connection had been broken. The signals weren't getting through.

Jimmy tried to make conversation. He even asked, "Were you wearing your seat belt?"

Steve could not shake his head, so he mouthed a whispery, "No."

Jimmy looked up. The room started to spin. Grayness enveloped him like a glove. He toppled to the floor just like Big John Tate had when he took Mike Weaver's knockout punch. And now the doctors, nurses, and family members rushed to him.

171

The Four D's

J ust as surely as Steve Streater's car had flipped over on its top and broken Steve's neck, Jimmy's world was soon to be turned upside down, in an unswerving connection between the two brothers.

Steve's football teammate, Lawrence Taylor, left contract negotiations in New York and rushed back to North Carolina when he heard about Steve's injury.

Sunday, May 3, was to be Steve Streater Day in Sylva. It had already been declared by the Jackson County Board of Commissioners. University of North Carolina head coach Dick Crum was to be the main speaker. The tribute to Steve was postponed indefinitely while he lay in the intensive care unit.

Cards from well-wishers poured in until the count was beyond 10,000. Students from Sylva-Webster and Steve's junior high made a 30-foot scroll, signing their names, wishing him well, and telling him to hang in there.

Jimmy's fainting was laid to the stress of seeing his brother in the condition he was in. He quickly regained consciousness and appeared normal.

People in Sylva and Jackson County thought of

Steve's tragic accident in connection with two prior incidents that had taken star athletes' lives or careers. Tommy Love, who coach Babe Howell described as a "Greek god in a football uniform," died at age 22 from a heart attack during his football career at Michigan State. Jerry Cagle, another star athlete from Sylva-Webster, had signed to play football with the University of Kentucky. However, in July 1972, two weeks before he was to leave for Kentucky, he was almost killed in a car accident. Cagle was returning from an All-Star baseball game in Greenville, North Carolina, when the car he was a passenger in ran underneath a tractor-trailer truck. One passenger was killed. Cagle's chest and throat were collapsed. He was saved from immediate death by a Green Beret soldier who was passing the scene and performed a tracheotomy on him when he was strangling on his own blood.

Now, Steve's accident was a weird third occurrence over a period of ten years.

This was the first tragedy in the Streater family. Sister Faith was ten years old and growing into a beautiful young girl. Brother Eric had taken over where his older brothers had left off at Sylva-Webster. From the quarterback position he had led the Golden Eagles to another state championship in 1980. He was going to enter his senior season in the fall of 1981 with many colleges interested in the services of the third Streater brother.

After a week, Steve had not regained any use of his legs. The prognosis was not good. He would regain use of his arms, but he was paralyzed from the chest down. Jimmy went back to Toronto, and the rest of the Streaters went back to Sylva. Shirley and James commuted to Chapel Hill every weekend.

DANA WORRIED ABOUT JIMMY'S fainting spell. Was there something else involved? He had told her about his first college game where he became nauseated and dizzy at halftime. He had to be re-hydrated and missed almost the entire second half of his starting debut. Was this the same thing reoccurring?

Jimmy told her to put it out of her mind. He was a strong athlete. There was nothing wrong with him that a little rest wouldn't cure. It had been a long flight and drive from Toronto to the hospital in Chapel Hill. When he saw Steve, he was shocked. He fainted. No big deal.

Still, Dana wasn't satisfied. Jimmy should have some tests run—blood work and such. She searched her nurse's mind for what the symptoms would indicate.

There was no time for medical checkups. Jimmy had a football season coming up, now less than two months away. He had bided his time in 1980 during his first year with Toronto, but this would be the year he would make his move as he had in high school and college.

THEN THE NEWS CAME that the Argonauts were having a shakeup in the organization. Now, Jimmy would have to prove himself again. Toronto fans had cheered when they had read about Jimmy's signing in 1980 because he was compared to Condredge Holloway, another former Volunteer quarterback, who was then playing at Ottawa.

The next thing Jimmy learned was that the manager had signed Condredge Holloway away from Ottawa, and he would be coming to Toronto as their quarterback. Condredge was one of the people responsible for Jimmy going to UT. Now he would have to compete against him at Toronto. But the question the fans and management were asking was, "If we have the real Condredge Holloway, do we need someone who is like Condredge but with five years' less experience?"

Jimmy looked forward to the competition. He could learn a lot from Condredge. He might have to be the backup for one more year, but he would finally make it in the CFL.

Jimmy found that his concentration was lacking. His mind was divided between football and Steve. Two weeks went by and Steve still lay in the hospital. Jimmy talked to his parents and they would tell him of any slight signs of improvement. Jimmy would call Steve's room, and someone would hold the phone to Steve's ear.

Toward the end of May, Jimmy was into full practice, but Steve was still in the hospital. Jimmy would find himself calling a play in the huddle and when he would look to a receiver, he would see Steve instead.

One day he was calling a play in practice while kneeling in the huddle. When he stood, his world began spinning again. He dropped to his knees and had to be helped off the field. He wanted to believe it was the heat of early practices—that he hadn't had enough fluid.

His knee that was injured in the Notre Dame game began to swell, and he missed some practice days. The doctors advised surgery, but Jimmy wanted to wait until after the season. Then in another practice, he fainted again.

This was too much. The team doctors and Dana insisted that he undergo a battery of tests.

Diabetes. "What do they mean I have diabetes? What is that? What do I have to do to cure it? I can't have something like that. I'm too strong."

The Argonauts didn't want to take a chance on a quarterback with a bum knee and diabetes. The coach and general manager told Jimmy it was time to retire.

"Retire? I'm 23 years old. I can't retire. I want to play football," Jimmy told them. He couldn't believe his life was spiraling out of control.

"We can't use you, Jimmy. We'll try to work out a trade for you. Maybe you can overcome this."

Jimmy was traded to Montreal but didn't make the team for the season. He had a partial year's salary and a signing bonus. By the second week of June, he and Dana had gone home to Knoxville. She was licensed as a nurse in Tennessee and she could work in Knoxville. Jimmy would have knee surgery and work on control of his diabetes.

Steve was still in the hospital when Jimmy and Dana returned to Knoxville. Jimmy had never been in this

175

šituation before. He couldn't play football or baseball. He had no job. His brother was still lying flat on his back in Chapel Hill. He had lost control of his life.

"Jimmy, we've known each other for years and have been through a lot together," Dana told him one day. "Everything hasn't worked out exactly like we planned it yet. But we need to be committed to each other. Are we going to get married?"

"Married?" Jimmy asked. "Sure, we've always said we were going to get married. I wanted to get established in pro ball first though."

"Jimmy, it's time now."

With Steve in the hospital and his parents driving back and forth to Chapel Hill every weekend, Jimmy and Dana decided this was not a time for family celebration. So, they went to the City-County Building in Knoxville on June 12, 1981, and were married in a private ceremony.

DEPRESSION BEGAN TO FOLLOW Jimmy like a black cloud. Even after the marriage, Jimmy's life view did not improve. He paid little attention to his diabetes. His knee operation went okay with merely an arthroscopic invasion. But he couldn't run like he used to. The pro football season was progressing in Canada but without him.

Steve came home from the hospital after two months but there was no improvement—no movement or feeling in his legs. He would be in a wheelchair for the rest of his life doctors told him. But Steve still had faith and hope. He believed he would walk again some day.

Jimmy's dark moods began to last longer. He would try to go places where he would see old-time friends or Tennessee fans who remembered his playing days. The cheers had died out, but there was always the pat on the back and the remembrance of the Georgia Tech or Notre Dame games. But when those things began to fade, he only had left the hope of going back to Canada for 1982. Jimmy kept up with his old Toronto organization. Despite the efforts of Condredge Holloway, the Argonauts got off to a horrific 0-11 start and finished 2-14.

Later in 1981, Steve went back to the University of North Carolina and took some more course work toward his degree. Jimmy had some hours to take to finish his degree in psychology at UT, so he also began a slow process of taking a few courses. But the campus reminded him of his playing time and the fact that he wasn't playing now.

When people asked him how he was doing, he would say, "Fine."

"What about Canadian football?" they would ask.

"I'm going back to Montreal next year," he would tell them. He didn't mention his diabetes or depression. He was a big enough man to overcome those without any help.

Jimmy's attempt to go back to football in Canada in 1982 was also met with failure. Holloway was leading Toronto to a Grey Cup game, but Jimmy couldn't play with Montreal.

JIMMY HAD BECOME AN avid golfer in the off seasons between football and baseball. Now, if he were invited by someone to go for a round at one of the courses in Knoxville, he would jump at the opportunity.

"That was where I got my first cocaine," Jimmy would recount years later.

"I was playing a round of golf with somebody I thought was a friend of mine. It was a hot day. I had been talking about Steve, my knee, and my being down all the time. This guy asks whether I wanted some coke. I thought at first that he meant Coca-Cola.

"But when he took the little bag out of his golf club bag, it wasn't Coca-Cola. It was cocaine. That was my first time. I never used any drugs in high school or college. Up to that time I was clean. He offered and I used. The beginning of the end."

More than drugs, though, Jimmy had already become addicted to other things that gave a rush of adrenaline.

177

Cheers and applause were enough for him while he was playing in high school and college. When he was with Toronto for the year in 1980, he became almost—if not altogether—a gambling addict.

"I had what I thought was a lot of money then. Worse, I believed I would always have a lot of money. I loved the machines at Atlantic City or Las Vegas. I never gambled on sports teams, but I loved cards, the roulette wheel, and the slots. That was exciting.

"I know of some days where I gambled away $5000 or more. Some days I would win, but I lost more than I won. I loved the thrill of the ringing bells, and all the employees were so nice to me when I was a high-rolling gambler."

When Jimmy was offered that first free hit of cocaine, he didn't think about his mother's and father's warnings, or about Aunt Margaret and Uncle Ray, or about what his younger brothers and sister would say if they knew, or how his aged grandmother would handle it if she were told. No, those were not things he wanted to think about.

What attracted Jimmy to cocaine was the promise of relief from his present worries in a simple and easily taken form. There would be no counseling sessions for depression or doctor prescribed drugs. While he used cocaine he could forget that he had diabetes. Surely somebody with diabetes couldn't feel that good.

Cocaine had become the drug of choice for the upwardly mobile. Its use could be hidden longer. There was no tale-tale odor like in spilt alcohol. There was no smoky aroma that clung to clothes as in marijuana. You could carry enough in a little baggy for a day's use. Unless somebody knew you were using, you could deny it. Many people used it and went about their daily lives, only feeling better, he was told.

Jimmy had read about some famous people who had become addicted to cocaine. But they didn't have his will-power. If they did, they wouldn't have become hooked. He could take it or leave it. Or so he thought.

The worst that could happen would be if he became addicted and had to go to one of those clinics like the Betty Ford one in California and get off it. There would be no life-long consequences. Or so he told himself.

The only problem was its cost. Cocaine was expensive. The first hit was free, but there were no handouts after that. You might be Jimmy Streater and be famous, but you would still have to pay for your fun, for your high, for your irresponsible fight with your demons of depression.

Jimmy and Dana had put aside a lot of the money he was paid in Toronto and Montreal. He had gambled part of it away, but there was enough left to buy drugs—for a while.

IF JIMMY HAD BEEN watching for signs from God, he might have recognized one when he suffered what was described as a heart attack. He was hospitalized in Knoxville. Diabetes, depression, and drugs were not good for his heart. Later he had to have a heart catheterization in North Carolina.

But Jimmy was deluding himself. He wasn't looking for signs from God. He wanted to play football. He wouldn't have to do coke then. Football would be his drug of choice.

In 1983 he went back to Montreal and then was traded to Edmonton where Warren Moon was starring. He was released and came back to Knoxville.

JIMMY CONTINUED ON HIS rampage of drug use and self-destruction when he returned to Knoxville in 1983 with Dana. He ran through what money they had left and then began to borrow from friends or tried to buy cocaine on credit.

Dana found out and asked Jimmy to get treatment. He wouldn't. Then she did the only thing she could think to do. She called and told Jimmy's parents. "Jimmy's a coke addict; he's run through all our money; he won't go for help, and I don't know what to do."

Jimmy's mother was at a loss for what to do. She

179

and James had their hands full already with Steve's injury and care. Eric was at the University of North Carolina playing football and Faith was just ready to go into middle school.

JIMMY AND DANA SEPARATED in November, 1983, and were divorced in 1984. They agreed to the terms. There were no children, no real estate, and very little else. Dana received a 1982 Buick, a ten-speed bicycle, a bedroom suite, two end tables, and a 19-inch color television. Jimmy left with a 1978 MG, a men's ten-speed bike, a water bed, living room suite, a stereo system, and a 12-inch black and white television. Jimmy was responsible for paying debts to GMAC on his car, a Sears credit card, and a personal loan at Valley Bank.

In the divorce papers, Jimmy was listed as living on Moody Avenue. That was true in more ways than one. He was actually a resident of the street of broken dreams that was paved with the cobblestones of the four D's—diabetes, depression, drug use, and divorce.

His plans for a ten-year pro career were over. He thought his life should just as well be over. There was no place to go—except home. He packed his bags and headed back to the mountains and Sylva.

180

Christmas In Jail

J immy could act rationally and sensibly at times despite his drug use. That often made people think he wasn't using, but he was. One sensible thing that Jimmy did was to complete work on his degree from UT in 1984. He was able to take home to Sylva a BA in psychology. He had a 2.30 grade point average. There wouldn't be a lot of high paying jobs in Jackson County or Sylva for someone with just a BA in psychology. As the old saying went, with that and fifty cents he could buy a cup of coffee.

A reference book titled *Drugs and Drug Abuse*, published by the American Addiction Foundation in 1983, described cocaine and its then known use and effects. "Cocaine is a powerful central nervous system stimulant which produces heightened alertness, inhibition of appetite and need for sleep, and intense feelings of euphoria."

Those were exactly the reasons Jimmy was hooked. When he started by snorting the powder, he felt "good." The memories of his diabetes, his divorce, his dismissal from pro ball, and brother Steve's condition faded into the morning sunshine like the fog lifting from the Tuckaseegee River. He didn't eat as much and he could go long periods of time on little sleep.

"Very heavy users may sniff up to 10 pure grams (10,000 mg) per day, although most users take substantially less. A common pattern among users in social settings involves sniffing into each nostril 20-30 mg of cocaine. (These units are referred to as 'lines.') Administration may be repeated two or three times an hour over several hours."

Jimmy used in "social settings." He rarely used alone. "Yes, I would use with others. We all would be doing it. But sometimes, I just wanted to be by myself even when I was with other people."

Use of cocaine can also cause headache, pallor, cold sweat, rapid weak pulse, along with rapid, irregular, and shallow respiration. Those were some of the signs that Jimmy displayed when he had been hospitalized for what he thought was a "heart attack."

While Steve Streater was leading the Olympic Parade for the 1984 Los Angeles Olympics through the main streets of Sylva from his wheelchair, Jimmy was hooked on coke and couldn't get off.

He would live with his parents, then have an apartment of his own, and then move on to some other place. His days revolved around satisfying his habit and trying to find enough money to support it. It wasn't easy. There were drugs in Sylva, and Asheville, and Chapel Hill, but he knew more suppliers in Knoxville.

One close friend who should know remembered when Jimmy was at the height of his drug use. "One time Jimmy, when he was in the midst of his drug problems, told his dad that he needed to go to Knoxville to pick up his diploma at UT. Jimmy convinced him to drive him over there. When they got to Knoxville, he had his dad drive down to some back street and told him to stop. He told him he needed to go in that house for a little while. He made a drug purchase there and came back. That was the only time I know for sure that he actually used one of his parents to help keep his drug habit going, unbeknownst to his dad."

"Other effects may include tremors, vertigo, possibly severe agitation, increased spinal cord reflexes, muscle twitches, and paranoid symptoms," according to the text book.

So, there was a down side to the feelings that Jimmy and others who were addicted to cocaine received. "I was paranoid," Jimmy recalled. "I'd always look around, thinking somebody was going to turn me in. Some of the ones I did drugs with were real loud. I told them to keep it quiet because their noise may attract the cops."

Cocaine breeds an "intense psychological dependence." If users can't get their "hit," they can become depressed for that reason alone. This depression, added to what Jimmy already had, resulted in an uncontrollable urge. He had to have his coke, and he would do anything short of violence to get it. "The dependence liability of cocaine is among the highest for all drugs because the euphoria it produces is very powerful and it is easily administered in different forms."

Jimmy progressed from being just a sniffer to the more exotic and elaborate ways of taking cocaine. "Since cocaine is highly soluble in water, large amounts can be dissolved and administered by injection directly into the bloodstream."

He moved from sniffing, to free-basing with a water pipe and heat, to making his own "crack," to injecting it directly into his bloodstream. If there was a way to take cocaine, Jimmy learned it. The process of making crack seemed like a lot of work, to hear Jimmy explain it. But at the time, he believed the effects were worth the efforts.

During his drug use years, Jimmy moved from Knoxville to Sylva to Chapel Hill to Greensboro to Durham and back to Sylva. There were probably other places too, but they are wiped from his memory. He worked as a car salesman, as a grocery clerk, and at convenience stores. His efforts were aimed more at getting enough money to support his habit rather than any long-range career moves.

BY 1987 JIMMY WAS becoming desperate in his race to keep up with his drug needs. He would go back and forth to Knoxville to make buys and try to borrow money. His jobs were now trickling down to nothing.

Steve was back and forth between Chapel Hill and Sylva. Eric had just finished a stellar career at the University of North Carolina as a receiver. He had amassed twelve touchdowns and 1364 receiving yards in his years. He was preparing to go to Tampa Bay, and if that didn't work out, he would play in Canada. Faith entered her junior year in high school in the fall of 1987.

By this time, Jimmy skirted the periphery of the family circle. He was sullen, withdrawn, still depressed, and still feeding his immense appetite for cocaine.

On a trip to Knoxville, he came across a piece of mail that was sent out by a local window and door company. The document was actually a credit ticket for anyone who wanted to order windows or doors. But it looked just like a check. All Jimmy had to do was to snip off the bottom part that said it was a voucher for window credit, fill in a few numbers, and take it back to an unsuspecting store owner in Sylva.

On November 1, 1987, Jimmy Streater began his spree of petty crime to support his cocaine habit. He cashed the check for $250 at the Sylva Package Store.

It proved so easy to pull off that Jimmy did other small fraudulent transactions in Jackson, Buncombe, and nearby counties.

"Jimmy lived near the hospital. One day he was walking from his folks' home by the hospital toward downtown. There was a flower delivery lady who had just carried some flowers into the hospital. She left her purse in the car, and Jimmy just reached in and got it," one local officer recalled.

Jimmy was in and out of Sylva to his various haunts around North Carolina and Tennessee. Nobody could get a good handle on where he was exactly. None of his crimes ever involved any violence. And all of his thefts were of rather small amounts. At one time he had committed twelve acts of forgery or fraudulent transactions. But all twelve added up to only $500. In 1987 Jimmy's crimes were not the highest priority of law enforcement.

Any relative's money was fair game for begging,

borrowing, or stealing by Jimmy.

"I got to a point to where I was so drug dependent that I would have done anything short of hurting someone to get money," Jimmy recalled. "I was hooked and I was hooked bad."

While he was trying to look after his drug habit, Jimmy let the care of his diabetes slide. Sometimes he would almost go into shock. From 1984 through 1987, he made four trips to the emergency room of Harris Memorial Hospital in Sylva. In 1986 he stayed a week. In 1987 it was four days. His debt to the hospital grew to close to $5000. He lost weight and his athletic appearance changed so that he looked like a skinny old man.

Jim Ashe, who went through school with Jimmy just one grade behind, remembers the change in Jimmy well. Ashe went on from Sylva-Webster to Southwestern Community College and to Western Carolina University before joining the sheriff's department of Jackson County in 1981. He worked hard and steadily moved up the ladder to chief deputy.

"Jimmy was manipulative. He was never violent. He would play confidence games. He would build your confidence in him and then take advantage of it. The Jimmy Streater I knew from school was a quiet and kind person just like his mother. He was a very considerate person.

"When Jimmy got on drugs he became desperate in meeting his need at that time which was substance abuse. He tried every means that he could to obtain money or the controlled substance.

"He was incredibly skinny. He lost a tremendous amount of weight."

WHEN THINGS GOT A little hot in Jackson and the surrounding counties for Jimmy, he made a trip to the Atlantic City, New Jersey, casinos. These had been some of his favorite watering holes when he played with Toronto. He had a little money and just knew that his luck was about to turn around. He would hit it big on one of the machines or play his cards right and win a bundle.

When he had played his little nest egg down to nothing, Jimmy was angry, disgusted, and more depressed than ever. He had no money, no drugs, and no hope.

As he was walking out of the casino, an older lady carrying a big purse was just a few paces in front of him. On an impulse, Jimmy grabbed the purse from her arm and sprinted toward the door. He stumbled over his own feet after just a few steps and sprawled to the floor. The woman ran after him and stood over him wagging her finger at Jimmy as security guards closed in.

He was charged with strong-armed robbery, released on bond, and fled back to North Carolina.

"It would have been funny if it hadn't been so sad," Jimmy recalled years later. "I was once so fast and elusive, but I was run down by a little old lady when I stumbled over my own feet."

Jimmy didn't return to New Jersey, but he continued his criminal ways back in Jackson County. His parents had tried to help bail him out of scrapes for as long as they could. Finally, the police were informed that Jimmy could be found at his parents' home on Streater Drive behind the hospital in Sylva. On August 31, 1988, Jimmy was arrested on twelve counts of forgery and uttering worthless checks and taken to the Jackson County jail. The jail sat immediately behind the courthouse where Jimmy ran up the steps each day during his high school training regimen. Now he could not even see the steps through the bars on the windows.

SOME OF THE LOCAL folks were now well aware of Jimmy's problems with drugs and with the law. Carey Phillips was a classmate of Jimmy's at Sylva-Webster who wrote for the local newspaper—*The Sylva Herald and Ruralite*. Phillips had been the statistician for the football team when Jimmy was breaking all the records back in

1975. Now, he, like many of those in Sylva, didn't know what to think about what Jimmy was doing to himself. "It was a local tragedy to us who knew Jimmy. His arrest and experience through the court system was treated the same way as we would have anybody else's. We didn't run any big story. About everybody in town already knew anyway. But it was noted where we list those who are arrested, indicted, or convicted. I was there the night of that classic game with Pisgah and I really regretted what Jimmy had gotten himself into."

Jimmy's drug use and arrest were family tragedies too. Eric had just completed his first year of professional football with British Columbia in Canada. Faith was entering her senior year in the high school that had changed its name to Smoky Mountain High when the students from Cullowhee High School were absorbed. The Golden Eagles were let loose and the school adopted Mustangs as its new symbolic name. Faith was preparing to star on the basketball team. Steve was back and forth between Chapel Hill and Sylva, still paralyzed from the chest down.

To Coach Babe Howell, Jimmy's predicament was sorely regrettable. The young man he loved so much was sitting in jail. How do you talk to someone about his drug problems?

"I would have liked to have wrung his neck," Coach Howell said. "But, you know, it's hard to talk to anybody when their mind is not with you. I would try to talk to him. I just couldn't get through."

To this day, Jimmy's sister Faith says, "It's really hard to talk about. It was hard to handle."

BEFORE JIMMY HAD BEEN in jail ten days an unusual incident occurred. This was the first time he had been without cocaine for more than a week. His cravings were so strong that he was wondering how he could get his "fixes" while in jail.

Jackson County's jail was old, didn't have adequate

space, and evidence lockers were a thought that had not occurred to those who gave the sheriff's office money. Evidence from some cases was stored in a cabinet in the kitchen area where some inmates ate or had access to. It was a locked wooden cabinet.

One day shortly after Jimmy's arrest, officers made an arrest for cocaine possession and brought the "rock" cocaine to the storage cabinet in the kitchen. Jimmy was present when the deputy brought it in. "Jimmy, look what we just got off of somebody over in town," the deputy said and waved the package around before locking it away in the cabinet.

It wasn't long until the deputy left and Jimmy was at the cabinet. He pried the door out where the hasp met the lock just enough to get his skinny hand inside and snatch the bag of cocaine.

"I looked at that cabinet later on," Chief Deputy Jim Ashe recalled, "and that space was so small when you pried it out that I bet I couldn't have stuck a banana in that opening."

If Jimmy was anything, he was a sharing person. He gave some of the cocaine around to other inmates and injected himself with some more. For a while the sheriff's office didn't know the cocaine was missing. But when they looked in the cabinet for the evidence, it was gone and there was no sign of forcible entry.

It had to be an inside job. They did a shakedown of the cells and found what was left of the cocaine. Other inmates pointed to Jimmy as the thief.

All of Jimmy's other charges had been minor compared to this. He had never been charged with any law violation related to his drug use except for the forgery that went to support it. Now, though, the sheriff's office was upset. Not only had Jimmy stolen and used the cocaine, he had ruined their case against the one from whom they had confiscated the cocaine by tampering with the evidence.

On October 24, 1988, the grand jury of Jackson

County added to Jimmy's problems by indicting him on two counts involving the cocaine. The jury found there was sufficient evidence to believe that Jimmy "did break and enter the evidence locker of Detective David Hall and removed a quantity of cocaine contained therein that was in Detective Hall's custody as evidence in pending criminal cases" and that he further did "give a controlled substance, cocaine, which is included in Schedule II of the North Carolina Controlled Substances act to Ronald Ward, Jr., who was at the time an inmate of the Jackson County Jail, which is a local confinement facility."

Once again another schoolmate of Jimmy's had to do her job and not let sentiment get in the way. Christy Buchanan was two years behind Jimmy at Sylva-Webster. She later married Kole Clapsaddle who had been a year ahead of Jimmy in school and who had been on the 1974 football team with Jimmy. Chris Clapsaddle was now a rising star in the district attorney general's office. She had presented both cocaine charges to the grand jury and received the indictments.

Jimmy's bond was set at $50,000. He languished in jail over Thanksgiving. Even with a bondsman securing the bond, he would have to raise ten percent of the bond amount or $5000 to get out. His thirty-first birthday arrived on December 17. There was no celebration in his jail cell.

Jimmy called Coach Boyce Deitz to see if he would help make his bond.

"I was outside. My wife told me Jim Streater was on the phone. I told her to tell him I'd call back later. In about twenty minutes, she told me Jim's on the phone again. That happened about three times. Then she told me he had said what he wanted was to get out of jail. Could I come and see him?

"I didn't want to fool with him. I didn't call him back. But I thought about it all day until four or five in the afternoon. I thought that it wasn't very big of me not to talk to Jimmy. If he was needing help, I needed to call him.

"So, I called. He was real upset and crying. He said he was in jail and that he wanted someone to get him bond and get him out. I drove down to the Jackson County Courthouse and went to the jail.

"I hadn't seen Jimmy in months, maybe a year. They took me into a holding area and brought him in. When he walked in I was shocked. He looked like an old man. His hair had turned gray. He sat down and crossed his legs. Although he had always been real skinny, it was just like crossing two broom handles.

"It was a pitiful sight and we had a long conversation. He told me his bond amount. I wanted to get him out but I didn't. I talked to the prosecutor and learned that there was a hold on Jimmy from New Jersey. I was told I would be doing him a disfavor to get Jimmy out on bond. Because once they released him, he would be shipped up north to New Jersey. It was better for him to be in jail in Jackson County where everybody knew him than to have to go to a New Jersey jail."

Coach Deitz walked away bothered and perplexed. He couldn't help Jimmy in the way that Jimmy wanted.

JIMMY KEPT TRYING TO get out on bond. On his brother Steve's thirtieth birthday, December 22, 1988, the judge allowed Jimmy to appear for a bond reduction hearing. He thought if he could get his bond reduced from $50,000 to $35,000 he could get out in time for Christmas with his family.

Judge James Downs listened to Jimmy's petition to lower the bond and the prosecuting attorney's objection. He then made the following findings of fact:

"1.   The Defendant has immediate family in the Jackson County area including his mother, Shirley Streater, his father, James Streater, his aunt, who lives nearby to his mother and father, and his brother, Eric Streater, who will be residing in this area until March, 1989.

"2. The Defendant is not presently employed and his

last employment was at the 'Pantry' which is an overnight, 24-hour, Seven-Eleven type store in Greensboro. Before that the Defendant was a car salesman for University Ford in Durham, North Carolina, where he worked for 2 1/2 years.

"3. The Defendant has no assets and no liabilities.

"4. The mental condition of the Defendant is relatively good although the Defendant suffers from sugar diabetes which requires regular insulin injections. The Defendant has suffered from short term insulin deprivation while he has been in the Jackson County jail.

"5. The Defendant, if released, would not be a danger to himself nor would he be dangerous to the community.

"6. Since March, 1988, the Defendant has resided in Sylva, North Carolina, and he lived in Sylva, North Carolina, from the time of his birth until 1976 when he left for college.

"7. The Defendant has a history of flight to avoid prosecution under a warrant in New Jersey alleging that the Defendant committed strong arm robbery.

"8. The Defendant has charges pending in Buncombe County, where he is under a $2,000 bond, but the specifics of that bond have not been addressed because of the pending charges in Jackson County.

"9. The Defendant has been indicted for twelve counts of forgery and uttering or six combined indictments which equal twelve separate felonious counts and the total amount of the checks involved in these indictments is $500.

"10. The Defendant has been indicted for tampering with state's evidence, to-wit: cocaine.

"11. The Defendant has been indicted for two counts of providing drugs to an inmate, arising out of the same cocaine stated above.

"12. The Defendant has been indicted for three counts of possession with intent to sell or deliver and sale or delivery of cocaine, also arising out of the same cocaine as stated before.

"13. The Defendant has been indicted for one count

of conspiracy to traffic in cocaine, arising out of the same cocaine as stated above.

"14. The Defendant has been indicted for two counts of providing drugs to an inmate, arising out of the same cocaine as stated before.

"15. The Defendant could be convicted of some or all of the foregoing charges, but some of the charges are duplicitous and the state will have to elect to prosecute under not all of the foregoing charges.

"16. The Defendant could receive, if found guilty on all of the foregoing charges, a presumptive sentence of up to 40 years.

"17. The state would not object to a transfer of venue upon a guilty plea in this case, and Defendant could, if he so elected, proceed in this manner and have his charges disposed of prior to the scheduled court date of January 30, 1989.

"18. The Defendant will be ready for trial on January 30, 1989, although the state may not be ready at that time.

"Based Upon The Foregoing Findings of Fact and Conclusions of Law, It Is Therefore Ordered, Adjudged, and Decreed that the Defendant's bond will not be reduced at this time from its present level of $50,000 secured, and the Defendant's motion to reduce said bond is DENIED."

JIMMY WAS TAKEN BACK to the Jackson County jail where three days later he had Christmas dinner of turkey and dressing, cranberry sauce, and green beans with the other inmates around the table in the kitchen, an arm's length away from where he had stolen the cocaine.

The Spider
and
The Arm

J immy had spent 153 days in the Jackson County jail
when he went to court to plead guilty to all the charges
against him on January 30, 1989. There was a plea
deal which was worked out between his appointed attorney,
Jay Coward, and the prosecuting attorney, Chris Clapsaddle.
All twelve counts against Jimmy would be disposed of on his
guilty plea. The sentence was ten years for the cocaine
related charges and five years for the forgery charge.

Jimmy received as good a deal as could have been
expected. The sentence on the forgery charge was a five
year maximum term with a "presumptive" or minimum term
of two years. Jimmy would receive credit for the time served
of 153 days. He would be sent to a minimum security prison
at Salisbury, North Carolina. The charges related to the
drugs were combined and suspended for five years, subject
to five main terms of probation.

"I don't think Jimmy received any special treatment,"
Chief Deputy Jim Ashe recounted years later. "But, of
course, with him being local and without at that time a
criminal history, I think all that was taken into consider-

193

ation. They also knew he was diabetic. None of his crimes involved any violence."

Jimmy had to agree not to use, possess, or sell any controlled substance. There would be periodic urinalysis upon request of his probation officer. He would have to take drug counseling at the Smoky Mountain Counseling Center. Jimmy had to become gainfully employed or submit to his probation officer statements from 15 employers that he was seeking employment each month. Lastly, he had to make restitution to those he had taken money from through forgery and bad checks.

Otherwise, he would be free. Jimmy readily agreed. But the task ahead of him was impossible in his mind. He didn't believe the counseling would end his mad craving for cocaine.

He was sent away to prison on February 3, 1989, and served three and a half months before he was released on parole. He didn't meet the terms of his probation and parole and was returned to prison again on October 11, 1989, but he was paroled again on November 28. He said he now understood the terms of his parole and probation and would abide by them. But the task again looked overwhelming.

He stopped seeing his probation officer. He was unable to get regular employment. He went to counseling for a bit but dropped out. He liked the drugs better than the talking. And he continued using.

He moved around and hid from the law. His probation revocation lingered. Officials knew he would show back up some day. He didn't really pose a threat to the community in a violent manner. And sooner or later someone would report that he had bilked them out of some money and he would be arrested.

Jimmy spent time in Chapel Hill where Steve was and would come back to Sylva on occasion. Again, he paid little attention to his diabetes, and spent more time tracking down drugs.

Toward the end of 1989, he was carrying an arm-load

of wood into the house for heat when he felt a sting on his left arm. He swatted at his arm but thought little of it, except that it was late in the season for wasps to be active.

The bite, he later learned, was from a brown recluse spider. The sting was so bad that the pain traveled down to his fingertips and up to his shoulder. He rubbed it and put a salve on it, but the burning continued day after day.

His arm began to swell, but Jimmy left it unattended by medical doctors. The only relief he could get came from cocaine. He injected some into the same arm. There was temporary relief, but the burning ran like tongues of fire from his fingertips to his shoulder.

He lanced the infected site with a razor blade and squeezed his arm until a flow of yellowish-white puss ran out. For a bit he had some relief. But the infection roared back even stronger and with greater swelling. The fingers of his hand, usually skinny, swelled up like a stalk of bananas. He couldn't remove his UT letterman's ring—the one possession that reminded him of his glory days. His arm was so hot and tender to the touch that he returned to snorting cocaine instead of injecting.

After a month's time when the swelling and roaring pain had not subsided, the pain and a dizziness traveled to his head. He walked into the emergency room.

The doctor palpated the arm until Jimmy screamed, took his temperature, and ran some quick blood tests. Jimmy's mind was a fog. The doctor looked at the site of the original bite and saw the unmistakable imprint of the spider.

"We've got to get you into surgery, Jimmy," he counseled.

"Why? What is it?"

"Probably a brown recluse spider bite. It has a tale-tale signature. You're diabetic. The infection has just eaten up your hand."

"What are you going to do?"

"Take off your hand, Jimmy. It's the only way to save your life. If the infection gets any nearer to your vital organs, there won't be anything we can do for you."

There was no choice. Jimmy nodded his approval and he was rushed into a preparation room for the operation at the University of North Carolina Hospital at Chapel Hill.

IN THE OPERATING ROOM, with Jimmy already under anesthesia, the surgeon found that Jimmy's infection was more severe than he originally thought. They couldn't stop with the amputation of the left hand, nor with the arm to the elbow. They had to take Jimmy's entire left arm and into the shoulder before they could find flesh that had not been ravaged by the gangrene type decay. He would have been dead within twenty-four hours without the amputation.

When he awoke and realized his arm was gone, he screamed as loud as he ever had. Five days later, when he learned that his letterman's ring had been lost, he cried out again.

The Bottom
Of The Well

Recovery from the arm amputation took a full four months. Jimmy's shoulder was a horrible sight. Skin had to be taken from his leg to graft onto the wound. There were whirlpools, rehabilitation, and more skin grafts. The site was so large that the skin grafts had to be monitored closely. The skin is the first line of defense against infection. It keeps bad microbes out. Any infection of Jimmy's wound could have gone directly to his heart or lungs. The doctors were covering a gaping hole with the new skin where his arm and shoulder had been.

Jimmy was too weak to steal to support his cocaine habit. Now, he not only would be an unarmed bandit but also a one-armed thief. The doctors monitored him so closely that he went off coke temporarily. His insulin and blood sugar were watched with regularity by nurses. His mental depression remained, but his physical health improved.

Over in Jackson County, word got around that Jimmy was in Chapel Hill in the hospital and that he had lost his arm to a spider bite. There were doubters and skeptics about the spider bite. "More likely an infected needle," some said.

The good side of the problem for Jimmy, if there could

197

be any good gleaned from the loss of his arm, was that those watching over his probation and suspended sentence also were aware that he was in a hospital and had lost his arm. It wouldn't be very sporting to try to revoke his probation while he was in such dire straits or to require all those conditions that had been set down. They could wait and see what happened in a few months.

Jimmy came back to Sylva after his recovery from the amputation. It was like he was being killed one piece at a time, and he knew he was his own executioner. He applied for Social Security disability or Supplemental Security Income if he didn't have enough work credits. With his severe diabetes, which was termed "brittle" by the doctors, and now having lost his left arm, it was apparent he was disabled from all jobs that he had ever worked at.

While he was waiting for the application to be approved, Jimmy moved back in for a while with his parents. Coach Deitz still lived nearby.

"I remember the first time that I ever saw him walking down the road near my dad's house from his house after they had taken his arm off. It was the first time I had seen him like that, and it was just like a big slap in the face."

THE YEARNING FOR COKE soon returned. Until his disability was approved, Jimmy had no income and no way to earn enough money to support his uncontrollable craving. His parents weren't about to give him money without knowing exactly where it was going.

Jimmy returned to crime. Brother Eric had completed two years as a receiver with British Columbia and had moved over to Winnipeg by the time Jimmy stole a credit card on June 18, 1990. The charge was financial transaction card forgery with a Visa card. With Jimmy being back and forth between Sylva and Chapel Hill still receiving treatment for his arm, the arrest was delayed, but it was inevitable.

On August 17, 1990, Jimmy was arrested again and this time by former schoolmate and now deputy sheriff Jim Ashe on a charge of possession of stolen goods and financial transaction card forgery.

Jimmy filled out an affidavit of indigency and was appointed an attorney. In the affidavit, Jimmy indicated that he had not filed an income tax return since 1987.

For some strange reason, he was allowed to make bond. He never showed up for the scheduled hearing date, and a *capias*, a court order for his immediate arrest, was issued by the sitting judge on October 22, 1990. Jimmy knew his time was up. He was on the run, and when he came home for his birthday, Steve's birthday, Christmas and New Year's, his parents had to make a call that they didn't want to make. Jimmy was out of control and beyond their help. They called the sheriff's office and reported that Jimmy was at their home. He was taken to jail on January 9, 1991.

He faced the judge a little over a month later on February 21, 1991. As he had always done, Jimmy did not dispute that he was guilty of the charge involving the credit card. Former schoolmate Chris Clappsaddle was the state's prosecutor. Jimmy was sentenced to one year on the credit card charge to run concurrently with the ten years that would be imposed on the prior drug related charges.

His probation was revoked based upon the credit card charge. This time he was sent to a prison where they meant business—the maximum security prison at Raleigh that Jimmy and other inmates called The Wall. He arrived there on February 26, 1991.

Jimmy's ten-year plan of a professional football career had gone terribly awry. While Steve was marking the tenth anniversary of the wreck that broke his neck and ended his career, Jimmy was in fear for his life when he was thrown in with the most violent criminals in the state.

"You could buy protection for a carton of cigarettes a week or so," Jimmy recounted. "But I was small and really unable to protect myself, considering my condition. I had to protect myself from sexual attack by letting the word get around that I had AIDS. I looked frail and sickly anyway, so it wasn't much of a stretch for the others to believe that."

For the first time in his life, Jimmy was separated from the view and even the thought of the mountains of his home county. "The wall was twenty or thirty feet high. I couldn't see out. I couldn't look toward Sylva and see even a hint of a mountain. We were totally isolated from the outside world. For the first time, I finally came to a realization of what a life of crime would lead me to. I wanted out. I obeyed the rules. I did everything possible to shorten my time."

One incident made Jimmy even more aware of how tenuous the thread of life was in prison. "I played cards for recreation. Several of us would play. A pack of cigarettes might be the limit of the pot. There was one guy who everybody called Psycho. I didn't know why at the time, but I soon learned.

"We were playing cards—four of us including Psycho. Well he lost and got real mad at one of the others. He pulled this homemade knife—a shank—out of his clothes and stabbed this other card player. The guy died, and I knew for sure how Psycho got his nickname."

AFTER FOURTEEN MONTHS IN the maximum security prison at Raleigh, Jimmy went before the parole commission for consideration of early release. The prisons were crowded. Jimmy again was assessed as non-violent. Perhaps after the hard time he had served, he would be okay to release.

On May 6, 1992, J. W. Reed, a parole case analyst, notified the clerk of court: "This is to advise that the North Carolina Parole Commission has granted Community Service Parole to the above referenced person. He will be required to pay into your office a Community Service Parole fee of $100. In addition, this person will also be required to pay a

200

$20 per month supervision fee for each month he is under parole supervision.

"Release from prison should occur in the next few days."

And indeed Jimmy Streater put behind him the prison at Raleigh on May 21, 1992. He headed back to Sylva. From the time his legal troubles began in 1988 to his release from prison in 1992, Jimmy had missed out on some important happenings in his family.

Faith graduated from Smoky Mountain High in May 1989. She was a star in track and basketball. She had gone on to play basketball at Anderson College in South Carolina.

Eric finished five years in the Canadian Football League in 1992. He had starred with Winnipeg and had been a receiver on a team that won the Grey Cup. He had career totals of 27 touchdowns along with 3192 receiving yards.

When Jimmy arrived back at Sylva as an ex-con with one arm and diabetes, there were very few job opportunities. However, he was approved for a disability income. He moved to a small apartment within a mile of the Jarrett House hotel and restaurant in Dillsboro.

JIMMY'S DIABETES WAS STILL not under his control. He knew he was supposed to check his blood sugar level and take his insulin. He did it on a hit and miss basis. "One time I became so depressed and discouraged that I threw my insulin away," Jimmy said.

What kind of diabetes did Jimmy have and how severe was the problem?

"Jimmy's diabetes has afflicted him terribly. I would venture that his is more 'serious' for a given blood sugar level than others. I have no proof," said Dr. Paul Strumph, Jimmy's endocrinologist, of Asheville Endocrinology Consultants.

Diabetes can go undetected for a dozen years or more. Was Jimmy's nausea, dehydration, and dizziness during the halftime break of his first college football game against California a symptom of diabetes? Nobody can say.

The longer diabetes goes undetected and untreated the greater the chances of complications such as vision loss, kidney and heart disease, nerve damage, and foot and lower-leg amputations. It is estimated that as many as eight million Americans are now walking around with undetected and untreated diabetes.

Symptoms include constant urination, abnormal thirst, rapid loss of weight, irritability, weakness and fatigue, nausea and vomiting, drowsiness, itching, blurred vision, slow healing of skin infections, and tingling or numbness in the feet.

Diabetes awareness and education was a project of recent Miss America Nicole Johnson who developed the disease when she was nineteen. "My platform was diabetes awareness and saving lives," she told an interviewer from *Parade* magazine.

Diabetes is divided into two main classifications—type 1 and type 2. Although type 1 was 20 to 30 per cent less prevalent in persons who had an American background that included an African heritage, that was the type that Jimmy had. While type 2 can be treated with oral agents in most cases, type 1 is always treated with insulin.

Jimmy's diabetes was a strong factor in the infection that led to his arm amputation.

"Diabetics are more prone to poor circulation. Poor circulation can make one more prone to infection. Also, high blood sugar levels interfere with healing. So, a diabetic under excellent control might not be expected to be more prone to infection, but one under poor control would be," Dr. Strumph said.

In the later stages of severe diabetes, if the patient is not on a proper diet, checking his blood sugar level, and taking insulin, there is always the possibility of blindness, nerve deterioration, and the loss of toes, feet, and legs because the tissue actually dies due to poor circulation. So, with the best of care, diabetes is difficult to control, and it is hard to predict a particular patient's outcome. With poor control and a lackadaisical attitude, diabetes is a time bomb that is set to explode at any minute in the form of a coma, death, or stroke.

JIMMY BECAME VERY WITHDRAWN after his parole from prison. He stayed in the small apartment and had little to do with his family. Very few people from his association as a youth knew he was in town.

"I felt such shame that I didn't even want to leave my apartment. I didn't want to be seen by anybody. I knew people around were asking, 'Whatever happened to Jimmy Streater?' and I imagined that the answer would be, 'Well, you know, he's on drugs.' "

For almost two years, Jimmy hung in the shadows of Sylva and Jackson County. His appearance had changed from the exuberant, charismatic youth of Sylva-Webster days to a hardened, old-looking man who wobbled by with just one arm. At 34 years of age when he was released in 1992, Jimmy couldn't imagine anything good happening to him the rest of his life.

He did enough to keep his parole from being revoked—paid his fees, went for the monthly check-ins—but never gave up completely his drug use.

"I should have thrown away my cocaine instead of my insulin. But cocaine had become my life."

It was in March, 1994, when Jimmy was only 36 that he once again was given a harsh reminder of how serious his diabetes was.

Alone in his apartment, he thought it was time to take his insulin. He stood to go get the vials and fell to the floor. The room seemed to be whirling. He stood again and again fell.

"It was a funny feeling at first. It was like a child falling when he gets off of one of those merry-go-rounds in a park after spinning at a high speed. But then it wasn't funny. I couldn't stand up at all. It became real scary. I was able to crawl to the phone and call 911."

That was the last thing Jimmy remembered until he woke up in Harris Regional Hospital in Sylva. The hospital property adjoined the property of his parents. He knew the place well and had visited the emergency room there on many occasions.

"I was in this room and the doctor comes in and looks me in the eye," Jimmy remembered.

"Mr. Streater, you've had a stroke."

"I'm sorry to admit that despite my college degree and having been married to a nurse, I was unaware of exactly what a stroke was. I had heard of old people having a stroke, but I didn't know the full implications. I expected to recover and get out at the most in a week or two. But the doctor told me differently."

The stroke had hit more on the left side than the right of Jimmy's body, but the damage was such that both legs were paralyzed. All he had left that he could use was his right arm.

"I was just devastated. I couldn't believe it. Diabetes knocked me out of football. I didn't pay attention to the infection from the spider bite and I lost my arm. Then it hit me again by taking my legs out from under me. I couldn't sit up without help. I couldn't go to the bathroom. I couldn't stand. My flashy moves on the football field at Sylva-Webster and at UT were just a distant memory."

When it came time for Jimmy to be released from the hospital in April, 1994, his parents had little choice. The combination of Jimmy's diabetes, his drug dependency, and his paralysis was more than they could deal with at their house. Steve was there most of the time himself in a wheelchair.

The decision was hard, but one that they had to make. Jimmy would have to recover in a nursing home. The first one that could take a case of his kind and that had an available room was the Canton Health Care Center at

Chris Cawood

Canton, North Carolina, about 30 miles away.

When they drove Jimmy to the nursing home, he sat strapped into his wheelchair in the ambulance. It passed by the football field in Canton where the classic high school game was played out in 1975 between the Pisgah Black Bears and the Sylva-Webster Golden Eagles. Jimmy had fought to the end in that game, throwing the ball downfield as time ran out.

Now the ambulance moved slowly by the football field and then passed the Champion Papermill. Just a couple of blocks past the papermill on Main Street, the ambulance eased into the parking lot of the nursing home.

Jimmy was wheeled out and inside for admission. He held onto the side of his rolling chair with his one hand and looked around. These were old people. He couldn't see anyone as young as he. Some waved at him, but they didn't know him. Some sat in their wheelchairs with their heads leaning over, drooling onto themselves. There was an old lady holding a doll. She was talking to it as though she thought it was her child. There was a smell about the place that he would have to get used to. Despite the efforts of the efficient staff and nurses, there was the occasional stringent odor of bleach and urine.

There were smiling faces of the nurses and they wanted to be helpful. Jimmy sat quietly. It was as though he was going back to prison. They wheeled him into the small elevator that took him to the third floor. Then he was pushed down the hallway to the room that would be his new home.

"We're going to leave you alone for a bit. Will you be okay?" the nurse asked.

Jimmy nodded his head. When the door closed, Jimmy let his head fall over until his chin rested on his chest and hot tears began to fall onto his shirt.

Recovery
And
Redemption

S lavery and imprisonment are sometimes more states of mind than physical realities. The chains that bind us are formed link by link by our own hands, and the cell bars that hold us in are forged on the anvils of our lives. Great-grandfather George had been a physical slave but appeared never to have felt that he was. When the Emancipation Proclamation and the end of the Civil War gave him his freedom, he stayed on where he had been for years, bought property, and thrived, fathering sixteen children.

Jimmy had tasted actual prison and remained under the mind numbing slavery of addiction. He wasn't much different in age—36 in 1994 when he entered the nursing home at Canton—than his great-grandfather George was when he was set free. George bought his first hundred acres of land in Jackson County when he was 39. George overcame slavery and became a free man. Jimmy overcame freedom and enslaved himself.

The first hurdle that Jimmy had to overcome if he were to be free again was the decision as to whether he wanted to live or let himself die. It was in his hands.

His trip from Sylva to Canton had been somewhat of a surprise. Jimmy thought when he was ready to be released from the hospital that he would go home to his parents' home in Sylva and they would take care of him.

Now he sat forlornly on the third floor of the Canton Health Care Center in the town of his fiercest high school rival.

From the front porch of the nursing home, a visitor could look to his right and see the Champion Papermill just two blocks away. The low gray buildings supported piping that vented steamy water vapor, resembling a pod of beached whales puffing out their last breaths. There is a distinctive aroma that emanates from any papermill. They say that when you live there long enough you don't notice the acrid odor. The same can be said of nursing homes. But to visitors and those just entered, the smell lingers in the memory long after thoughts of escape have fled.

From his wheelchair, Jimmy looked around him at those who were his companions in the place that was like a warehouse of dying carcasses for some and a haven of hope of recovery for others. Jimmy saw many more of the former than the latter.

He could do nothing on his own. Although the paralysis was more on the left side than the right, there was no way he could walk. His right arm was his best remaining limb. He was dressed by a nurse. His bed pan was emptied by someone else. He was fed like a child. He could barely chew because of the paralysis on the left side of his mouth that let food dribble from his mouth like a baby.

He had been a handsome youth who many said could have been a movie star. He had taken pride in his appearance, his clothes, his hair, and his grooming. His disability now was embarrassing because of what it had done to his ability to care for himself.

When he was alone one day, discouraged, depressed, and angry, there suddenly came to his memory a Bible verse from his years in church as a youth. He couldn't remember the exact location in the Bible, but he believed they were the words of Jesus to one of his apostles.

"When you were younger, you girded yourself, and walked where you wished: but when you are old, you will stretch out your hands, and another will gird you and carry you where you do not wish."

Jimmy wasn't old in years, but he felt every day of a hundred in spirit. Did the Lord have a plan for him—for the rest of his life? *"Feed my sheep."* Yes, those were the words of Jesus that went with the other part, Jimmy remembered. *"Feed my sheep."* But what did that mean to him in the nursing home? He continued to be pulled between blaming God for his being in the nursing home and taking responsibility himself. There was a tug of war between trying to take control and turning control over to God. He had to learn patience and self-control.

PREACHERS AND MEMBERS OF nearby churches would sometimes visit on Sunday afternoons. They would go from room to room to anybody who wanted a visitor and talk or sit for a few minutes. For a while, Jimmy ignored them, wanting to stay in his little cocoon of despair. But one day a preacher came in and sat down.
"How're you doing?"
"Fine," Jimmy said.
"You're new here."
"Yes, came over in April."
"Can I do anything for you?"
"No, I'm fine."
"Okay, see you next week," the preacher said and began to head for the door.
"Wait a minute, preacher," Jimmy said. "I do want to ask you one thing."
"What's that?"
"Do you remember a verse from the Bible that says

something about when you were younger you dressed yourself and went where you wanted but when you are older someone else will dress you and take you where you don't want to go?"

The preacher smiled. "It was Jesus speaking to Peter in the gospel of John."

"Peter? He was one of the main apostles, wasn't he?"

"Yes. Jesus was making a point to Peter that if he followed Jesus he would lose control of his life. He would turn it over to Jesus."

"Was Peter a good man?"

"Headstrong. He bragged that he would never deny Christ, but on the night of Christ's betrayal, Peter denied him three times before the cock crew."

"Three times?" Jimmy asked. "Denied him?"

"Yes, but Peter turned into a strong Christian."

"Is that the same verse where Jesus tells him to feed his sheep?"

"Right at the same place."

"What does that mean? Who are the sheep?"

"I'd say they were the other followers of Jesus. 'Take care of your brothers and sisters,' is what Jesus is telling Peter."

"Did Jesus forgive Peter for denying him?"

"Yes, I believe so," said the preacher.

"Thanks. That's all I wanted to know," Jimmy said.

When the preacher left, Jimmy thought about all the times he had "denied" Christ in his living. He thought back to the time when he had mouthed off to the reporter and told him that he thought he was the best quarterback in the country. That was a long time ago. *Feed my sheep.*

THE DOCTORS TOLD JIMMY that it could be up to two years before he would recover any use of his left leg.

"Will I be able to walk again?" Jimmy asked.

"Maybe. In time."

"In a year?"

209

"Maybe. Try for taking a step in January. That'll give you something to shoot for."

"December," Jimmy responded.

JIMMY'S ATTITUDE DID NOT change overnight. His staying in the nursing home assured him that he would not be using drugs, but his depression concerning his condition was still wearing on him.

"Jimmy had to decide if he wanted to live or not," recalled one of the nurses who was there at the beginning of his stay.

Jimmy gradually took an interest in those around him. He looked around and noticed he was the youngest. He still had a chance to get out while most of those at the Canton home didn't. He would sit and listen to the older men talk about their experiences in World War II or Korea. One was missing both legs. Most were in wheelchairs that they never would escape.

Over a period of months in 1994, Jimmy became the upbeat resident of the nursing home. He would talk to anybody who could or would listen. He went to the recreation room and watched television or played cards. He welcomed visitors who came from the churches.

Mike Dayton, who played against Jimmy in high school football, lived just a mile from the nursing home. He went to visit.

"When I first saw Jimmy, it was like he had almost given up," Mike remembered. "But then he started to take an interest in things."

Another young man who had been in a car accident was brought to the nursing home. He was paralyzed from the neck down. A friend who was dying of cancer also called on Jimmy.

Jimmy thought about how he had once treated his brother Steve. "I'd sit in the car and wait for Steve. I'd get impatient and blow the horn. He'd say, 'Jimmy, you just don't know. I'm paralyzed. It takes time for me to get dressed and put my pants on.'

"After I had my stroke, I realized what he had been through. I called Steve and said, 'Man, I'm sorry. I can see what you mean about it taking time.'"

Now Jimmy could think about Steve and how they were both in wheelchairs. Twenty years before, they had competed against each other in everything. They pushed each other to be the best each could be. If they got together now, all they could do would be to have a wheelchair race. No, they couldn't do that, Jimmy thought, Steve would have the advantage—he had two arms.

Mike Dayton began to drive Jimmy to services at Beulah Baptist Church in Canton where Virgil Holloway was the preacher.

"When I first met Jimmy at church, I decided I would go and visit him at the nursing home and try to cheer him up. When I came out from visiting him, it was me who had been uplifted by Jimmy. He had a great attitude. He had the greatest attitude of anybody I've ever seen. He didn't look at his infirmities and complain. He was grateful for all the blessings from the Lord."

It took a while before Jimmy got to that stage. As he was recovering, he still became angry and frustrated. As soon as he got to know someone, that person would die. It happened over and over. One time two of his old friends died on the same day. It was the turning point for Jimmy because of what happened after his friend Claude Roberts died.

"I was sitting near my friend Claude Roberts. He was an old man, around 80 I'd say. I had become very close to him. He had cancer. But he always liked to smoke a cigar. He asked me for a glass of water that day. I went and got him some. We were both in wheelchairs. After he drank some, I wiped his face off where he had dribbled some water out of his mouth.

"Then the next thing I know, he was dead. I had never seen death face to face, eyeball to eyeball. He was breathing, and then all of a sudden he was gone. It astonished me. The same day another friend, Mr. Israel, died.

"When I knew that Claude was dead, I started to my room in my wheelchair. People die. They don't come back. I was wondering why. I was asking God, 'What's happening? Why am I doing this? Why am I here?'

"Then, all of a sudden, someone touched me on my shoulder. I looked around and there was this man standing there."

"Are you Jimmy?" he asked.

"I said, 'Excuse me?'

"He asked, 'Are you Jimmy Streater?'

"I told him I was. He asked how I was doing. Then he asked if I had given that man some water and wiped his face. I told him that I had. Then he said the strangest thing.

"He said, 'You shall be blessed, my son.' Then he turned and walked away. I had never seen him before. I didn't get his name. I've never seen him since. He was about five feet-ten inches, and 170 pounds. He was a white man with sandy hair. He wore a white shirt and a tie with a sweater. He had glasses but his eyes were sparkling blue.

"After he left, I went down the hall and asked the nurses and anybody I could find who he was. Nobody had seen him. I believe he was an angel."

From that day forward, Jimmy believed that God still had plans for him. He would turn his life over to Jesus and see what happened. He would *"feed my sheep"* where and when he could. For the foreseeable future, that would be with the residents at the Canton Health Care Center.

IF GOD HAD PLANS for him, Jimmy figured he was going to have to do his part about getting around. His promise of walking again would have to be renewed. There was very little physical therapy available, but there was at least one nurse—Linda Kirkpatrick—who pushed him to get better. She wouldn't let Jimmy feel sorry for himself when he had bad days. She would kid with him and, in her own way, spur him to get out of his wheelchair.

He had to be helped out of his wheelchair. Then he'd lean against a wall or hold on to a railing. With his left arm gone, he tilted to his right anyway. Now, with his left leg and foot paralyzed, he was even more a one-sided person. There was no way he could walk. He could lean and tilt, but his left leg would not support him to let his right leg take a step.

To explain it to someone who was not paralyzed, Jimmy likened it to times when he was younger and his leg would "go to sleep." There was no feeling in it. It might as well have been a pants leg filled with cotton stuffing for all the good it was doing.

"More exercise," Linda would tell him. "Stand against the wall, press it to the floor. You'll get it going."

Jimmy held on to the rail and stood for as long as he could on his right leg while waving the left one about. He had no control of the foot or ankle. If only he had two arms and a pair of crutches, he could do it. He could use a walker if he had two arms.

He would lie in his bed and try to lift his left leg. At first, he could only get a quiver of movement at about the thigh.

"What are you doing?" people would ask when they saw him leaning against the wall or holding on to a rail. "Do you need help?"

"No. I'm going to take a step without falling before New Year's."

He marked time by the major holidays—the Fourth of July, Labor Day, Halloween, and then Thanksgiving. They all passed without Jimmy taking his first step.

He could stand longer against walls and hold on to the railing, but the coordination of left foot and right just weren't there. There was some feeling returning to his left leg, but the foot and ankle seemed to have minds of their own.

The Jimmy Streater Story

One day he was lying in his bed, trying to lift his leg. "Patience, Jimmy," he told himself. He thought about how funny it would be if it weren't so sad to him. Here he was a shell of the great athlete he had been. He remembered walking over his grandmother's farm and into the woods. Sometimes there would be the translucent shells of locusts or cicadas hooked to the bark of the tree. The insect had flown away with just the husk remaining.

Twenty years before, he had jumped farther than anyone in that part of North Carolina—23 feet and four inches. His legs had let him fly over the ground in track. In basketball, he had jumped to the hoop. In football, he had given a defender a leg and taken it away.

His athletic abilities were gone, but was the spirit still there? "Patience, Jimmy. Self-control. Turn it over to Jesus."

ON THE DAY BEFORE his 37th birthday, he wheeled himself to the recreation room. Nurse Linda Kirkpatrick followed him. There were two older women in the room staring toward the television on the wall.

Jimmy lowered the footrest of his wheelchair, put his feet on the floor next to the wall, and pushed himself into a standing position. Linda handed him a metal cane and moved the wheelchair out of the way while Jimmy leaned against the wall.

Jimmy looked around the blank walls of the room and remembered the walls of fans in Neyland Stadium on that Saturday of his first college game when he ran eighty yards for a touchdown against the University of California. He was then lost in a sea of cheers.

Now he looked at Linda, leaned away from the wall, and took his first step. She nodded her approval.

Homecoming
1995

J immy slowly recovered the use of his legs. His first steps in December of 1994 were quickly followed by more struggles to get back at least to some semblance of the person he used to be. He thought he could do it. He had faith. If the angel had asked him about the glass of water, there must be a purpose in it.

Progress was painfully slow. He was learning to take his own blood sugar count and to give himself insulin shots into his abdomen with just the one arm. He could look into the mirror and know there was nothing else bad that he could bring on himself or could be cast upon him that he hadn't already faced.

There were a couple of things he wanted to do. He had contacted the jewelry company that made the Tennessee lettermen's rings and started to pay for a replacement. And when he was asked, he said he would like to go back to see the University of Tennessee play football in the fall of 1995—maybe the homecoming game would be good. He had not been to a UT game since he played in 1979.

(Here the author must enter a personal note: This chapter is written from my viewpoint. I arranged for Jimmy to come to homecoming and I was with him for the time he was in the Knoxville area. Some of the words here are my opinions based on my observations.)

The homecoming game was scheduled for September 30, against Oklahoma State. I started preparations early in July. With Jimmy's diabetic condition and his partial

paralysis in his legs, there would have to be special accommodations.

In talking with Jimmy, I learned that he wanted the
trip to be about more than his going to the game. He was
beginning to turn his life around. He was drug-free for the
past year since he had been living in the nursing home. He
wanted to speak to young people and tell them his story. "If
I can touch just one young person's life, it will all be worthwhile," he kept telling me.

Jimmy had to be accompanied by a nurse to monitor
his insulin use and blood-sugar level. I wasn't a season
ticket holder for UT football, so I would have to arrange to
buy tickets—but not just any tickets. They had to be some
that he could walk to easily.

Parking. Parking on game days was always a
disaster in the vicinity of Neyland Stadium. I had to be able
to get Jimmy near enough the stadium to allow him to walk
with his metal cane. He wanted to speak to young people—but where? He also wanted fans to know he was
there—that he was coming back.

I was still promoting my book of the previous
year—*Legacy of the Swamp Rat*—so it would be no problem
to set up a couple of autographings at bookstores in the
Knoxville area. Those were arranged for Davis-Kidd
Booksellers in west Knoxville on Friday night before the ball
game and at Campus Bookstore at the corner of Cumberland
and 17th for Saturday before the game.

Jimmy wanted people to know he was coming, so I
began to write a story for the newspaper about Jimmy and
his homecoming. I had it ready to send to newspapers by
the middle of August. Near the first of September, I sent
the story to several daily papers in Tennessee and North
Carolina and waited to hear from their sports editors as to
whether they were interested in using it. As a former
reporter, I knew that newspapers generally looked down on
submitted articles and wanted to protect job security and
quality by having their own reporters write the feature

articles they used. My story about Jimmy also was rather long.

While I waited for responses from the newspapers, I was attempting to make the other arrangements necessary. I went by the UT sports information office to see about seating and left a letter there and with others in sports administration. This is what the letter said:

"I will be bringing Jimmy Streater to Tennessee's Homecoming Game on September 30.

"As you may be aware, Jimmy has been in a North Carolina nursing home for the past year and a half after suffering a stroke. He lost his left arm several years ago. And now he can only walk with the aid of a cane because of paralysis in his legs resulting from the stroke.

"I need a seating location for Jimmy and a couple of his family members or friends either in the press box, one of the 'sky box' areas, or someplace else that he could enter without walking a long way. Also, could he have a car parking pass for a nearby place?

"This is Jimmy's first homecoming in 16 years, and he is looking forward to a good time.

"Thank you for your assistance."

When I dropped copies of the letter off at the offices in Stokely, I made it plain that I would still pay for Jimmy and his guests even if they were in the pressbox. I knew there would be elevator transportation to the press box area or to the sky boxes.

"The press box area is definitely out," someone in sports information told me.

"You mean even for the homecoming game? This is supposed to be a pushover. The press area is going to be so crowded that you can't find room in a corner for Jimmy?"

"It's against policy. We can't do it."

"Well, I thought I had heard of other people besides the working press being up there sometimes," I said.

"Bowl scouts and such. But that's a special thing."

"And you can't do that for Jimmy Streater who has

had a stroke and can barely walk?"

"No. But I'll send you around to talk to the associate athletic director who handles the sky boxes. He might have someone who could have Jimmy as a guest."

So, I walked around and waited for the associate athletic director in charge of sky boxes. We had a cordial talk. He said he would check around and let me know.

I left and went on with making the other arrangements. The Boys and Girls Club in Knoxville said they would be honored to have Jimmy speak to their group on Friday afternoon before the Saturday ball game. Ernie Brooks would help make the arrangements.

Two weeks later, I began to hear from the newspapers about the story I had written. I had a call from the sports editor of the Chattanooga *Free Press*. When I called back I got his secretary.

"You're the one who wrote that story about Jimmy Streater?" she asked.

"Yes."

"Well, I open the mail. I read it and just cried."

No kinder words could ever hit a writer's ears. I had touched an emotion. But were they going to use the story or just use it for a tissue to wipe her tears away?

"Oh, yes. We're going to use it. He'll call you back with the details."

Joe Biddle, sports editor of the Nashville *Banner*, called. They too would run the story.

Doug Mead, sports editor of the Asheville *Citizen-Times*, said they would run it as a three-part series the week of the game.

A week and a half before the game, I again called the sports information office at UT to check on the status of getting tickets or sky box access for the game. I had never heard a word from the associate athletic director in charge of sky boxes. The person I needed to talk to wasn't in, but he would call me back.

Later that day, one of the main men in sports

218

information did call me back. "Let me get this straight, Chris," he said. "You're bringing Jimmy Streater over to do some book signings with you and you want us to give him tickets to the game?"

My blood began to simmer. "No, I don't want you to *give* me or Jimmy anything. I want to buy a place for him to see the game. Is that too much to ask?"

"We're having a special thing for the lettermen at the Vanderbilt game. Why can't he come to that?"

"Because we have planned for two months to come to the homecoming."

"I don't know that we can help you."

"Oh, you don't? After all that Jimmy gave to the University of Tennessee? He's had a stroke and lost an arm. Do you know that?"

"I know *all* about Jimmy Streater," he said.

"Well, just forget it then," I said. "I've written a story that's going to be in three daily papers in Knoxville, Chattanooga, and Nashville in Tennessee, and in the Asheville paper. I'll just add a sentence to that story and say that Jimmy's coming to the homecoming but UT can't and won't sell him a ticket."

"Now wait. Don't get upset. Let me check and see what we can do. I or Billy Henry will get back to you."

A day later I got a fax transmission from Billy Henry saying that I could buy three tickets for face-value and they would provide a parking pass for a nearby garage. I wrote a letter thanking them for their kindness.

The UT Football Media Guide said this about the press box: "The Tom Elam Press Box opened in 1987 at Neyland Stadium. Two elevators serve the media area, which accommodates approximately **108** writers as well as movie and television cameras, bowl scouts and visiting officials." Yet there was no room for Jimmy Streater in that box. The slight was by those in sports administration and not by the coaches or the president of the university.

The Chattanooga *Free Press* ran the story as a full

page feature on the Sunday before the game. The Asheville *Citizens Times* made it into a three-part series the week of the game. The Nashville *Banner* did the story as a two-part series. The Knoxville *News-Sentinel* ran the story on Friday before homecoming in a shortened version.

As soon as the story began to appear across the state, I began to get calls from Nashville, upper East Tennessee, and Chattanooga. Where could these fans see Jimmy? And was there anything they could do for him? A fan from Chattanooga, about Jimmy's age, wanted to know which company Jimmy was paying on the letterman's ring and how much was still owed.

JIMMY RODE OVER FROM Canton, with his nurse driving, and met me at the Shoney's on Rutledge Pike. This was his first visit back to Knoxville in years and he was wide-eyed with excitement.

Don Ferguson was the nurse who accompanied him. Don was a combination practical nurse and body piercer. He carried a catalogue in the trunk of his car of examples of his body piercing expertise. I hadn't realized that there were so many body parts that were suitable for wearing "jewelry" of different sizes.

We ate and headed to the Boys and Girls Club in Knoxville for Jimmy to speak. Jimmy was met there by some fans who knew he would be speaking. They followed us over to a gym in East Knoxville where an after school session was ending.

To about 60 elementary and middle school age children, Jimmy told his story of being a great athlete and then falling to the temptation of drugs. He spoke of his lack of care for his health and how he lost his arm. The youngsters who had been noisy when we came into the gym became deathly quiet when Jimmy peeled back his shirt and showed them what was left of his left shoulder. They gathered around him, reaching out their hands, but drawing them back before they touched his scarred shoulder. Each child received a free book in which they could read about Tennessee's great quarterbacks, but they had heard and seen a story from Jimmy that meant much more.

From there it was on to Davis-Kidd where fans greeted Jimmy and had him autograph books.

At that time, Channel 10 in Knoxville was starting an all-sports channel on cable and invited Jimmy over for a 10 o'clock segment. They had arranged for many of Jimmy's former teammates to be there to surprise him during the show. They showed clips of his glory years and then brought in the other players. Jimmy was surprised and delighted. "Chicken legs," some of his teammates called out. There was almost an aura of light emanating from Jimmy's face as he visited with those he hadn't seen in years.

He spent the night in Kingston. The next morning before heading out to Knoxville, we had breakfast at a nearby Hardee's. There, other fans on their way to the ball game recognized Jimmy and came up and said hello. He always smiled and greeted them like they were old friends. They hadn't forgotten.

SOME OF HIS FORMER teammates had invited him to a pre-game get together they were putting on at the Cal Johnson Recreation Center near downtown Knoxville. For another couple of hours, these players of the 1970s' era talked, ate, and watched some videos of earlier games. Jimmy was in his element. I could almost see him being transformed back into the player he was in 1979. It was as though he wanted to throw away his cane and run across the parking lot.

LATER AT CAMPUS BOOKSTORE in Knoxville while we were autographing books, the Chattanooga fan showed up. He presented Jimmy with Tennessee jersey No. 6 for Jimmy to wear and then gave him a small box. The letterman's ring was inside. The reflection sparkled in Jimmy's eyes when he opened the box and pulled the ring out. The fan helped him to slip it onto the right hand ring finger. Jimmy now had regained one of the symbols of who he was.

IT WAS JUST A short drive past the stadium to the parking garage. Jimmy, dragging the partially paralyzed leg each step of the way, was stopped by fans who recognized him and his Number 6 jersey. Each interruption was welcomed by Jimmy as though it was another present to be opened on Christmas morning.

We walked in on the west side and found our seats in the southwest corner of the stadium. The seats were located on an aisle but about sixteen rows down. Jimmy's eyes were filled with the spectacle on the field of players ready for the game, the band along the sideline, and the beauty of the afternoon. The steps down were just a slight inconvenience.

"Shawn Bryson and I are cousins," Jimmy told me when he saw the freshman from North Carolina on the sideline.

"Is he going to be any good?" I asked.

"He's my cousin. He has to be good," Jimmy said and smiled.

AT HALFTIME JIMMY WAS scheduled for a sideline interview with Missy Kane who was one of the reporters for the pay-per-view telecast that was showing the game. With just a minute or so left in the half, Jimmy and I left our seats and started down the aisle toward the corner of the field. Fans all along yelled for him. Finally when he reached the turf and started to walk along the sideline toward the north end zone, a wave of fans in that area on the west stood and cheered when they saw him hobbling along on his cane.

"What are they saying?" Jimmy asked me.

"They're yelling for you, Jimmy," I said.

"For me?"

"Yes, wave at them."

He stopped, turned slightly toward the west, and waved. Then he walked on for his interview.

Some fans asked on a call-in radio show after the game why Jimmy was not introduced at halftime. The answer given by those on the show who were compensated by UT was that it was policy not to recognize individual players who returned for games as there were usually many former players who were there for each game.

Of course, that response did not answer the real question of why UT could not have given a five-second introduction to a player who had given so much to the university, to one who had been through so much, to one who had broken all the records when he was a player, and to one who was coming back for his first game in sixteen years.

The answer did not ring true either when fans found out that recognition was for sale by the university. If a fan gave a million dollars to the university, he could run through the T formed by the band and have his name resound all around the stadium. Jimmy had not had a million dollars to give. He only gave what he did have.

But when Jimmy was walking toward Missy Kane for the interview, a wonderful moment of recognition did occur. University of Tennessee President Joe Johnson, who was on the field for another presentation, saw Jimmy and made a special effort to come over, shake Jimmy's hand, and congratulate him on coming home.

That was all Jimmy really wanted—to come home, speak to some children, see a few friends, and let the fans know that he was coming back.

A Typical Day

After his homecoming in 1995, Jimmy returned to the Canton Health Care Center where he continues to live. His recovery has continued but very slowly. He still can only walk with the aid of a metal cane. His left foot drags along as he attempts to walk. His outlook is good even after five years in the nursing home.

He says the staff and administration are great to him. He is even allowed to keep a cat, Midnight, in his room. His simply furnished room also has an aquarium, family photos, a print of all Vol quarterbacks who ever started for UT given to him by Dewey Warren, a half bed, and a chair.

He went to Heath Shuler's wedding, has spoken to church and youth groups, and has made several trips back to Tennessee since 1995. One of his goals for 1999 is to attend the UT versus Notre Dame game in Knoxville, the twentieth anniversary of UT's 1979, 40-18 victory.

Jimmy's days are ones of routine. He has breakfast around 7 a.m. The nursing home schedules bingo one day a week and he joins in. He can usually find a man or two to play some cards. He has cable television and a phone in his room that are paid for by his aunt and a friend. He receives thirty dollars a month to spend anyway he wants.

There are setbacks for Jimmy as well. His friends at the nursing home keep on dying. He has been rushed to the emergency room several times when his blood sugar got too low, throwing him almost into a coma. He has had eye problems related to his diabetes.

On May 26, 1999, his grandmother Ada Streater died. She was 97 and was Jimmy's direct connection to his great-grandfather George Rogers.

He enjoys going to church and has attended several local ones in addition to Beulah Baptist. He has gone to High Street Baptist, Mount Olive in Waynesville, and Pleasant Grove.

The nursing home plans outings, including trips to Cherokee to the casino on occasion, and Jimmy rides along.

Frieda Smith from Asheville is now one of Jimmy's best friends. She takes him out for meals, to play miniature golf with her children, and on other outings.

"I do like to eat outside the nursing home," Jimmy said. "They try hard, but it's still nursing home food."

The nearby Pisgah View Ranch Restaurant where they serve home-style food in bowls is one of his favorites.

In the evening Jimmy can be found in front of his television and talking on the phone at the same time. Every day when it's time for *Jeopardy*, he either calls Frieda or she calls him, and they play along with the game over the phone. "She beats me most of the time, and I'm a college graduate," Jimmy said.

He keeps up with all sports and was among the happiest of Volunteer fans when Tennessee won the National Championship. "Remember, Shawn Bryson is a cousin of mine," Jimmy said.

There are other brief visits outside the nursing home with family and friends where he may spend a night or two at the most. Then it's back to the Canton Health Care Center and on with the rest of his life.

225

Part Four:

Jimmy Streater

Jackson County Sports Wall of Fame

Jimmy with best friend Frieda Smith

Jimmy Streater
In His Own Words

I want to thank my good friend, Chris Cawood, for taking the time to do the research to write the story of my life up until this time. He found out things about my distant ancestors that I didn't know. It's good to know where you came from but it's better to know where you're going.

When Chris and I talked about doing this book, he told me that if he did it he would have to tell the whole story—not just the good. It would be in actuality—the good, the bad, and the ugly. I believe he's done just that.

When young people read this, I don't ever want them to think that they want to be like Jimmy Streater. My life has not been the perfect life; of course, no one's is. It's okay if a young man or woman wants to be like I was in athletics in high school and college. They can try to emulate my success, and I wish them well at it.

But what I want to accomplish in telling my story is perhaps to make young men or women think twice before they make decisions.

When I was young, when I could outrun the opponents, when I could throw the ball over their heads, when I could out jump them in the long jump, when I could hit the baseball out of the park and field like an All-Star, I thought that I could do anything—that I was invincible.

So many colleges wanted me to play football for them. And I made a good living at professional football in Canada.

I had a good family—mother and father, uncles and aunts, and a grandmother—who taught me right from

229

wrong. I sang in the choir at church. I was a good student in high school and won many superlatives. So, I don't have anybody to blame for my bad decisions except myself.

One thing is that when you're young and healthy, you think that you can do drugs and then quit when you want to. You think that you can gamble and not become addicted. You think that disease cannot affect you. I didn't see that my decisions would have lifelong consequences.

I had a good life and I lost it. I had money that I gambled away and spent on drugs. When I ran out of money to buy drugs, I stole money by forging checks. I even tried to steal a lady's purse but was caught.

I had an athletic body but I lost it. I had a left arm but I lost it. I had a wife but I lost her. I had the ability to run faster than most and jump farther than most but I lost it. I had good health but I lost it.

When I was depressed, I didn't seek help. Instead, I turned to drugs. A "friend" said it would be okay to do coke. I should have remembered my mother's words. A doctor said I had diabetes, but I wouldn't accept it.

Instead of the freedom of the mountains and streams of Western North Carolina that I loved so much, I was sent off to a prison where a wall always blocked my view of where I was from. I live now with the record that I'm an ex-con.

When they cut off my arm, I lost my University of Tennessee letterman's ring. I was nobody. Still, I wouldn't learn.

Not until I was knocked flat by a stroke and thought that I was going to die did I realize I had to make a choice—to live, and to live the rest of my life the best that I could.

I have been living in a little room in the nursing home at Canton since I was thirty-six. I look around and everybody is older than I am. Many of them don't know they're here. Many of the ones who were here when I came are dead now.

In my room I have pictures of my family. I have a

small aquarium, a chair, and a half bed. On the wall above my bed is a Tennessee print of the quarterbacks who started for UT and on the other wall is a photo of the Tennessee versus Notre Dame game of 1979. I have a cat that I've named Midnight.

I don't want you to feel sorry for me though. I still have my life, one good arm, and legs that I can walk on with the aid of a cane. Feeling sorry for myself was what got me into this. I should have done what the doctors told me to do to take care of my diabetes. I shouldn't have turned to cocaine to treat my depression. I shouldn't have stolen people's money to support my habit. I was feeling sorry for me.

I had such extraordinary gifts as an athlete. I worked hard at it. When they were taken, I couldn't handle it.

I know that young people don't like to hear sermons. They want to do their own thing. They don't have to hear a sermon from me. Instead they can see me. I'm a walking sermon. I'm what happens when you don't make the right decisions.

But now I'm making the right decisions. I believe in angels and I believe in God. I believe I saw an angel here at the nursing home when I was at my lowest. And I believe that God still has a purpose for my life.

Little by little, I'm getting better. I still smoked cigarettes when Chris first saw me back in 1994. I've given that up. I used to chew. I've given that up. Those are little steps that I'm taking to make my body and mind clean. I'm off cocaine. I can tell you the number of years, months, and days that I've been clean.

I watch out about my diabetic condition. I take my insulin. I watch my diet. I check my blood-sugar.

When bad things happen, we always have the temptation to look back and ask, "What if?" Well, it's too late for that now. I have to look forward and ask, "What now?"

Don't feel sorry for me. And don't feel sorry for yourself when things happen that you have no control over. Remember that decisions can have lifelong consequences. There are times that you can't just go to a clinic and come out like you were before you were on alcohol or other drugs. There are times when you can't get back the money that you've gambled away. There are times that you can't get back the family that you've driven away. Consequences.

I believe God still loves me. I don't know how many years I have left. But I'm going to try to be a benefit to someone as long as I'm here.

My philosophy now is not that Jimmy Streater can do anything, but the words from Philippians 4:13—"I can do all things through Christ which strengtheneth me."

I want to speak to youth groups. I do have a story, and if young people can see me, there might be one or two I can get through to. I want to get better to where I can move out of here and have a job. I want to feel worthwhile.

All of that is in God's hands now. I'll do my part and accept His will.

Remember two things: Don't dwell on "What if?" Just ask, "What now?" And remember the words of Philippians 4:13. That is what I live by now. Pray for me.

Sincerely,

Jimmy Streater
Phil: 4:13

Author's Note

Jimmy Streater is a complex individual. After having visited with him over five years, I feel that I know a lot about him, his life, his athletic history, and other aspects of his background. I spoke to many people and researched many documents in writing this book. However, I don't pretend to have covered everything in this book, or that I know Jimmy completely.

Jimmy's problems with drug addiction and his crimes are difficult even today for his closest family to talk about.

I don't know what the future holds for Jimmy. One of his doctors has told me it is doubtful that Jimmy could live outside the nursing home environment. He needs constant monitoring of his diabetes.

There are those in Sylva and elsewhere who believe Jimmy would return to a world of drugs if he left the constant supervision of a nursing home. There are others who say Jimmy is a con-artist.

However, I believe that Jimmy only wants two things—to get well enough to leave the nursing home and a job. That's what he's told me. He says he has returned to his Christian values. I take him at his word. Is it really too much for a person to want to live on his own and to work at a job that makes him feel worthwhile?

If Jimmy could resist the allure of drugs, he would still need some home health care to live outside the nursing home. The way the government health programs are today, they would rather pay a lot more to keep someone in a nursing home than to pay a nurse to stop by a person's apartment or home once a day to check on him.

Around Sylva, Coach Babe Howell probably knew Jimmy as well as anyone outside his family. Coach Howell said this about Jimmy: "I believe he could have been a movie star, a major league baseball player, a great golfer, or pro footballer.

"Jimmy never really meant to hurt anyone other than himself. He was and is a great person."

There are some who are finished with giving Jimmy anymore chances just as there are others willing to accept him. He came off parole in 1996. But the scars of drug use, a criminal record, and his total lack of concern for his diabetes early on will live with him forever.

Many of Jimmy's disabilities could have been prevented. But it's too late, as Jimmy says, to ask, "What if?" He is living with the promise of "What now?"

For all of those with a Christian faith, there is the hope of redemption—to be rescued or ransomed.

Jimmy fully admits the errors, mistakes, and sins of his past. He wakes with the daily reminders of what those lifestyles can bring to a person. But he awakes each day with a hope and faith that the day will be good and that he will get better.

Jimmy believes in redemption—

The Redemption of the Sylva Streak.

FOOTBALL STATS FOR JIMMY STREATER

HIGH SCHOOL AT SYLVA-WEBSTER 1973-1975

TOUCHDOWNS—38 rushing; 13 passing; 5 receiving; 6 on punt returns; 4 on kickoff returns; 4 on pass interceptions.

TOTAL POINTS FROM TOUCHDOWNS—420

TWO-POINT CONVERSIONS—18

THE UNIVERSITY OF TENNESSEE 1976-1979

PASSING	ATT.	COMP.	PCT.	YDS.
1976	3	1	33.3	17
1977	105	59	56.2	742
1978	198	101	51.0	1418
1979	161	80	49.7	1256
CAREER	467	240	51.6	3433

TOUCHDOWNS PASSING: 17

RUSHING	YARDAGE
1976	7
1977	397
1978	593
1979	377
TOTAL	**1374**

TOTAL CAREER YARDAGE: 4807

HIGH SCHOOL AND COLLEGE RECORDS

HIGH SCHOOL AT SYLVA-WEBSTER

Football All-Conference

All-State

All-Southern

All-Western North Carolina

All-American (Parade)

Asheville Citizen-Times Back of the Year

1975 Outstanding Athlete of the Year

All-Conference baseball

School Records in:

Long jump, 100 yard dash, 220 yard dash, and 440 yard relay.

AFTER HIS FINAL SEASON AT
THE UNIVERSITY OF TENNESSEE
JIMMY STREATER HELD THE FOLLOWING RECORDS:

Single Season Total Offense: 2011 yards (1978); Career Total Offense: 4807 yards; Career Passing Yardage: 3433; Career Rushing Yardage for a Quarterback: 1373; Single Season Rushing Leader in 1978: 593 yards; Longest Passing Play (85 yards to Anthony Hancock against Vanderbilt); and most interceptions thrown in a season (16).

Jimmy is still Number 4 in Total Offense with 4807 yards.

Acknowledgments

Gaynell Seale has been my editor from the beginning. She has once again done a superb job in fine-tuning and manicuring the manuscript into a readable book.

There was much research, interviewing, and talking that went on between me and others to get a good grasp on this subject, and I want to thank and acknowledge those here. They are listed in no particular order.

Frieda Smith, Boyce Deitz, Charles (Babe) Howell, John Chavis, John Majors, Bill Battle, Mike Dayton, Mary Webb, Virgil Holloway, Don Ferguson, Jim Ashe, Carey Phillips, *The Sylva Herald and Ruralite*, Wanda Jones, Sara Cawood, Condredge Holloway, Gary Lundy, Ron Sutton, Marvin West, Tom Siler (and all the writers who covered UT football during Jimmy's career), Bill Dyer's *DyerGrams*, the Knoxville *News-Sentinel*, Frank Cagle, Margaret Miller, Ray Miller, Hallie Lackey, Cobey Hitchcock, Thomas O'Toole, Jean Hartbarger and the Jarrett House, the Addiction Research Foundation, all the Streaters, Dale Kennedy, Ravi Ramkissoonsingh, Ron Philip, John Ward, Western Carolina University Library staff, UT Hodges Library microfilm department, University of North Carolina and Tennessee Sports Information Departments, Dr. Paul Strumph, the unnamed Vol fan from Chattanooga who made Jimmy's homecoming in 1995 memorable, Smoky Mountain High School Librarian, George Frizzell of Western Carolina's Special Collections Department, Billy Henry, *Parade* magazine, and . . .

ALL VOL FANS EVERYWHERE WHO CHEERED, AND STILL DO, FOR JIMMY STREATER.

PHOTO CREDITS

Errors and Omissions

In a work such as this, where there are used many names, dates, statistics, and other information, there crops up from time to time a wrong spelling of a name, a wrong date, or a wrong stat.

While my editor and I have endeavored to keep these to a minimum, they will undoubtedly sneak into the text of the book. If you find one or more and are the first person to report it or them to me, I will correct the errors in the next printing or edition and also add your name to the page of acknowledgments.

You may write or contact me at the following addresses and numbers:

Chris Cawood
P.O. Box 124
Kingston, Tn. 37763

Telephone: 1-800-946-1967

E-mail: booktalk@icx.net

About the Author

This is the seventh book by **Chris Cawood.** He is a native Tennessean, a graduate of the University of Tennessee College of Law, and a former member of the state legislature.

He is married with two grown children. Chris resides in Kingston, Tennessee, where he practices law when he is not writing. His hobby is to explore the Clinch, Tennessee, Ohio, and Mississippi Rivers on his pontoon boat with his best friend Jerry Seale.

Jimmy Streater is available for personal appearances and talks to youth and adult groups. Because of his health concerns, some special arrangements have to be made. You may write to Jimmy at:

Jimmy Streater
Canton Health Care Center
27 North Main Street
Canton, North Carolina 28716
Tel: 828-235-1638

Arrangements can also be made through the author of this book:

Chris Cawood
P.O. Box 124
Kingston, Tn. 37763
Tel: 1-800-946-1967
e-mail: booktalk@icx.net

For those who might want to visit Jimmy, Canton Health Care Center is just two miles from I-40. Going east on I-40, take Exit 31, go right and stay on the main road for two miles. At about 1 1/2 miles, Champion Papermill will be on the right. Canton Health Care Center will be on the left just past the papermill.

Order other books by Chris Cawood

This or any other book by Chris Cawood may be ordered directly from Magnolia Hill Press at 1-800-946-1967 by Mastercard or Visa for $12 which includes postage and author autograph. Or you may mail your order with a check or money order to:

Magnolia Hill Press
P. O. Box 124
Kingston, Tn. 37763

Legacy of the Swamp Rat—is a hardback book about the UT quarterbacks who beat or tied Alabama in games from 1965 to 1994.

The Spring of '68—is a hardback book of love and adventure in the mountains of Tennessee.

Carp—is a mystery adventure set on the river from Tennessee to New Orleans.

1998: The Year of the Beast—is a murder mystery mainly set in Louisiana.

Tennessee's Coal Creek War—is a historical novel about a coal miners' rebellion in the 1890s in East Tennessee.

How to live to 100 (and enjoy it!)—is the story of twenty Tennesseans who lived to 100.